08

WITHDRAWN

THE
IMPERIAL
CAPITALS
OF
CHINA

❋ ❋ ❋ ❋

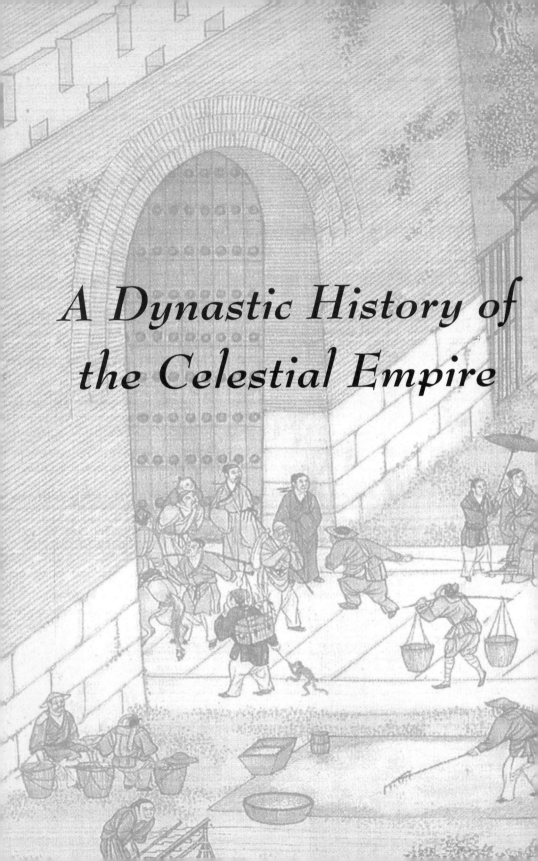

A Dynastic History of
the Celestial Empire

THE
IMPERIAL
CAPITALS
OF
CHINA

ARTHUR COTTERELL

THE OVERLOOK PRESS
Woodstock & New York

This edition first published in the United States in 2008 by
The Overlook Press, Peter Mayer Publishers, Inc.
Woodstock & New York

WOODSTOCK:
One Overlook Drive
Woodstock, NY 12498
www.overlookpress.com
[for individual orders, bulk and special sales, contact our Woodstock office]

NEW YORK:
141 Wooster Street
New York, NY 10012

Cataloging-in-Publication Data is available from the Library of Congress

Book design and type formatting by Bernard Schleifer
Manufactured in the United States of America
ISBN 978-1-59020-007-0
2 4 6 8 10 9 7 5 3 1

In memory of my brother-in law Yong Soo

CONTENTS

INTRODUCTION

I N 210 BC A STRANGE PROCESSION MADE ITS WAY ACROSS NORTH China.
Immediately in front of the imperial conveyance went a cartload of rotten fish, whose smell in the summer heat enveloped everything—horses, people, and carriages. What it also disguised was the stench from Qin
Shi Huang Di's corpse.

The chief eunuch, Zhao Gao, and imperial counselor Li Si had hit upon
this device in order to conceal the death of China's first emperor. For reasons
of their own, they wished to delay the announcement until their arrival in the
imperial capital, the northwestern city of Xianyang. There the two conspirators saw that their preferred candidate ascended the dragon throne—and Qin
Shi Huang Di was summarily entombed next to his terracotta army in a tomb
complex that is an archeological wonder of the modern world.

All that Qin Shi Huang Di built was on the grand scale: his tomb, the
Great Wall, a national network of roads, and the first imperial capital with
its elaborate buildings, covered roads, and enormous palace. During his
eleven-year reign he set the pattern for the Chinese empire. Later rulers
may not have shared every concern of Qin Shi Huang Di about the spirit
world, but they acknowledged the correctness of his cosmological arrangements at the very center of a united China. Imperial capitals were always laid
out according to cosmic principles. Chapter 1 looks at the cosmology of the
Chinese capital and explores the spiritual implications of its planning.

Chapter 2 surveys China's first imperial capitals, Qin Xianyang and
Former Han Chang'an. The labor involved in constructing Xianyang was
staggering. Hundreds of thousands toiled on Qin Shi Huang Di's palaces,
one of which was almost as large in area as the Former Han capital itself;
on his tomb complex at nearby Mount Li; on the houses he built for the
120,000 aristocratic families brought to the imperial capital from all parts

of China; and, not least, on the roads and walkways that were specially designed to obscure his whereabouts. Such intensive use of conscripted labor here, and elsewhere in the newly unified empire, was bound to provoke a popular reaction, which it did in the first nationwide peasant rebellion in China's history.

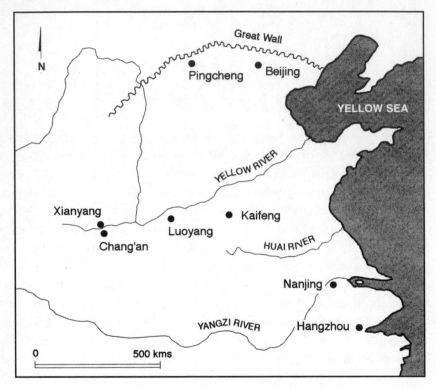

Map of the imperial capitals

The accession of rebel leader Liu Bang four years later as the first Han emperor Gaozu, or "High Ancestor," was something of a relief to a war-weary China. People expected him to rule with their welfare in mind, as the autocratic Qin dynasty had not. And they were not disappointed, for Confucian advisors helped Liu Bang set up a bureaucracy which would guide the empire through a variety of crises right down to the early twentieth century, and so make China the sole state of any magnitude to endure over such a length of time. Once examinations became the chief method of recruiting officials, the imperial capital was the destination for the learned and the talented, with the result that it was always the focus of Chinese cultural achievement. With a degree of reluctance, Liu Bang had permitted the building of Chang'an, whose name means "Forever Safe," as a capital worthy of a great empire. His successors embellished the city, which stood near the ruins of Xianyang, until the breaking of the Former Han dynasty with the rule of the usurper Wang Mang.

The capital of the Later Han dynasty, Luoyang, is the subject of Chapter 3. The removal to Luoyang, lower down the course of the Yellow River valley, was a consequence of the complicated civil war that followed the overthrow of Wang Mang. Compared with Chang'an, Luoyang was frugal, although its plan following the same cosmic principles. Despite the weak position of the imperial court during the Luoyang period, significant technical breakthroughs strengthened China, such as the perfection of papermaking, the production of steel, the stern-post rudder, and the invention of a seismograph.

Later Han emperors had turned to the eunuchs as a means of balancing the power of entrenched official families, but this tended to make the eunuchs into yet another court faction in a system already rife with corruption. Despite the supposed meritocracy, certain families were able to dominate the bureaucracy by marrying their daughters to emperors. Underworld bosses in the imperial capital had contacts amongst the higher officials and benefited from frequent amnesties as well. The periodic release of prisoners, an imperial policy believed to please Heaven, obviously created serious difficulties for the police. But it was not criminals who ruined Luoyang. Overconfident eunuchs took the drastic action of assassinating a general in 189, and enraged soldiers brought destruction on the city and ushered in a period of military rule. Large parts of Luoyang were burned down by the general's incensed men.

In 220 a military strong man by the name of Cao Pi decided to dispense with the fiction of the Han dynasty altogether. He deposed the last Later Han emperor and ruled in his own name as the first Wei emperor. Rivals quickly set themselves up elsewhere and, although the empire was briefly reunited, the final collapse of Liu Bang's imperial house inaugurated nearly four centuries of division for the Chinese empire. By 317 all of north China was in barbarian hands, first those of the Hunnish Xiongnu, later the Tuoba Turks. Chapter 4 surveys China's long period of partition by considering three capitals: in the south, Nanjing, the seat of several Chinese dynasties; Pingcheng, near present-day Datong, the first capital of the Tuoba Wei dynasty; and then rebuilt Luoyang, to which the Tuoba Wei emperor Xiaowen Di transferred his court in 494. In taking up residence at Luoyang he signaled the sinicization of his administration: Turkish speech, manners, and clothes were no longer acceptable at the imperial court.

In all three capitals, Nanjing, Pingcheng, and Luoyang, the salient event was the rise of Buddhism, which had arrived from India during the Later Han dynasty. At the beginning of the fifth century Xiao Yan, the first Liang emperor, twice became a monk in Nanjing. In Pingcheng and Luoyang, impressive cave sculptures survive as testimony of the equally fervent belief of the Tuoba Turks.

In Chapter 5 we see how the reunification of China under the Sui dynasty, which ruled from 589 to 618, led to the refoundation of Chang'an as the most splendid of all imperial capitals. In a repeat of the original Qin unification, the Sui emperors so overburdened the population with public works and foreign wars that their dynasty was swept away in another nationwide uprising. The beneficiary of the rebellion was the Li family, which produced in the legendary Tang emperor Li Shimin. The incredible openness of the emperor to different opinions was instrumental in setting an intellectual climate suited to cultural experimentation, for Chang'an thrived on a heady mixture of foreign and local influences. Though personally inclined toward Daoism, Li Shimin patronized Confucianism for the sake of the imperial bureaucracy and welcomed Buddhism as well as Christianity.

The latter religion was brought to China by Nestorian monks who traveled overland from Central Asia. Along this same route, the Silk Road, the Chinese pilgrim Xuanzang made his way to India in order to collect Buddhist scriptures. After his return to Chang'an, Xuanzang persuaded Li Zhi, Li Shimin's ninth son and successor, to build the Great Wild Goose Pagoda in order to house this collection: its majestic brick-built form still rises above the skyline of modern Xi'an.

China has always regarded the earlier period of strength and unity under the Han emperors as the assertive period of Chinese culture, when China differentiated themselves from its neighbors. But even to this day the Tang is remembered for its striking creativity and innovation. So if they refer to themselves today as *hanren*, the Han people, as opposed to *tangren*, the Tang people, they are pointing out their Chineseness. *Tangren* still carries in it the notion of cultural openness, of a willingness to adopt non-Chinese ways.

But Li Zhi lacked the strength of character of his father and soon fell under the domination of Wu Zhao, his empress. She virtually ran the imperial administration during the final years of his reign and, pushing aside two of her sons, Empress Wu declared herself emperor in 690. The only woman to sit upon the dragon throne, she ruled for fifteen years, mostly from Luoyang, a city inhabited by fewer adherents of the Li family. Her use of the examination system to recruit officials marked the triumph of ability over pedigree. A significant contribution that Empress Wu made to the Tang cultural renaissance was the advancement of poetry, since she allowed would-be officials to write poems in the final examination.

In spite of a short period of instability after Empress Wu's deposition, the Tang flourished under Xuanzong, Li Shimin's great-great grandson. Known as Ming Huang, "the Bright Emperor," Xuanzong ruled from a capital city renowned for its artistic exuberance. Poets, painters, calligraphers, musicians, and entertainers crowded its streets, many of them receiving the patronage of the emperor himself. Yet Tang self-confidence did not last. In 745 a border general by the name of An Lushan started a rebellion that devastated north China for nearly a decade. Though An Lushan died before its end, the Tang dynasty had to call upon friendly Turkish tribesmen to recover the dragon throne. The days of glory were gone.

Despite the inhabitants' suffering at the hands of both rebels and foreign invaders, Chang'an was still largely intact, and the imperial palaces remained the grandest buildings in all China. Chapter 6 traces the experience of the great city down to its dismantlement and reassembly in 907 at Luoyang. Perhaps the most important event in late Tang Chang'an took place in 845, when Emperor Wuzong suppressed Buddhism. A no less catastrophic event was the rebel occupation of 880, when the looting and destruction surpassed the earlier confiscation of Buddhist assets. But the culture products of the late Tang—the architecture, the gardens, and the poetry of the Willow Quarter women—still stand as testament to this golden age.

It remains a paradox that Northern Song imperial city, Kaifeng, which is so carefully preserved through visual as well as written records, should have almost nothing to show a modern visitor. Chapter 7 looks at this beloved city so celebrated in poetry and painting (including in the memoirs of Marco Polo). Of all imperial capitals, Kaifeng has always been rated the favorite. It acted as the capital of several of the Five Dynasties, the brief military dictatorships that brought down Tang Chang'an. In Kaifeng the imperial bureaucracy came into its own.

Although the Northern Song emperors in Kaifeng presided over an industrial revolution and reached the edge of modern science, they are remembered today for their patronage of the visual arts. So interested was the imperial court in landscape painting that Emperor Huizong added painting as a subject in the civil service examinations. In doing so, he completed "the Three Perfections," the bringing together of calligraphy, poetry, and painting, the triumph of the brush in Chinese civilization. Huizong was a talented painter and calligrapher in his own right, but he made a grave error with an alliance with the Jin, who lulled the empire into a false sense of security before falling upon Kaifeng. North China was once again taken over by barbarians.

The peace treaty of 1142 between the Jin conquerors of north China and the Southern Song was in effect a tacit admission of the inability of either side to overcome the other. For a second time the Chinese empire was restricted to the southern provinces—now, however, the richest and most populous parts of China. Marco Polo enthused about Hangzhou, which he visited shortly after the Mongol conquest, calling it "without doubt the finest and most splendid city in the world." What he missed in his delight at its elegance and energy was the reluctance of the Southern Song emperors to regard Hangzhou as an imperial capital at all. Kinsai, the name Marco Polo translates as "the celestial city," was in fact a corruption of "temporary residence," the only title these emperors could bring themselves to confer on the city, despite the charm and attractiveness of its environs. Chapter 8 discusses these considerable charms—on West Lake, an expanse of water immediately beyond the city walls, floating restaurants catered to private parties, the pinnacle of urban luxury. Some of the greatest Chan Buddhist artists lived and worked in the monasteries and temples dotted around West Lake, secluded and beautiful enough to create the ideal atmosphere for meditative self-cultivation.

Marco Polo was able to admire Hangzhou because its unconditional surrender to the Mongols in 1276. As a gesture of goodwill, the occupying Mongol troops were ordered not to molest its inhabitants or plunder their property. Kublai Khan, the grandson of Genghis Khan, had already announced his intention of becoming a Chinese-style emperor. Chapter 9 reveals how at the present-day site of Beijing he built Dadu, "the Great Capital," for his new dynasty, the Yuan. Marco Polo's description communicates something of the utter amazement that he felt on first seeing Kublai Khan's palace, "the biggest building that has ever been." Its hall alone was "so wide and so vast that a meal could be served there to more than 6,000 people." Another 40,000 were regularly entertained outside. Though excess was not typical of Kublai Khan's court, the Mongol habit of drunken feasts became normal under his successors, several of whose lives were cut short by violence as well as drink.

The hunting instincts of the steppe died hard, even with a Mongol emperor whose capital was destined to become the model for the late Chinese empire. How the Mongols changed from nomadic warriors into the settled rulers of China is the incredible story behind the foundation of Beijing, to use its present name. After the overthrow of the Mongols in

1368, the first Ming emperor Zhu Yuanzhang altered the name of Dadu to Beiping, "Northern Peace," which was renamed Beijing, "Northern Capital," by his son in 1402. Without a fight the last Mongol emperor fled first to Shangdu, then to Mongolia. Kublai Khan's grand experiment in ruling a Chinese empire ended in ignominious failure.

Zhu Yuanzhang was a commoner like Liu Bang, the first Han emperor, but Zhu Yuanzhang was quite different in his intolerance of ministerial opposition and in his readiness to kill those who persistently thwarted his plans. In Chapter 10 this move towards despotism is evident at both Nanjing and Beijing. It was the third Ming emperor, the equally forceful Yongle, who transferred the imperial capital northwards from Nanjing, Zhu Yuanzhang's stronghold. Based on the great foundation of Kublai Khan, Ming Beijing gave the Chinese imperial capital its final form.

For twenty years Yongle was engrossed with the construction of Beijing, the costs of which were said to have been incredible. Even today visitors to the Purple Forbidden City, as the imperial palace there is called, are amazed at its magnificence. Though slightly smaller than Mongol Beijing, Yong Le's imperial capital represents the culmination of traditional Chinese architecture within the context of imperial cosmology. In the middle of the Purple Forbidden City still stand the great ceremonial buildings of state: the Hall of Supreme Harmony, which contains the dragon throne itself; the Middle Harmony Hall, the emperor's tiring room; and the Protecting Harmony Hall, the place where top graduates in the palace examinations were received by the emperor in person. Behind this final ceremonial building is the Gate of Heavenly Purity, the main entrance to the inner court, the area restricted to members of the imperial family and their eunuchs.

To secure a satisfactory afterlife, the Ming emperors built themselves impressive tombs some forty-five kilometers northwest of Beijing, not far from the Great Wall. The mausoleums and the wall are the other amazing legacy of the Ming, the last native dynasty to rule the Chinese empire. Keeping the Great Wall in a state of repair became an imperial preoccupation as the steppe peoples once again grew in strength. Even though work was still proceeding when in 1644 the Ming dynasty fell, this incredibly expensive line of defense, like the Maginot Line, turned out to be of little use when the real threat appeared. Let through the gate at Shanhaiguan as allies in a civil war, the Manchus took advantage of a power vacuum in north China to establish the final imperial dynasty, the Qing.

After the end of the civil conflict that ushered in Manchu rule, the Chinese empire did enjoy an unexpected century of peace during which the population reached 400 million. Chapter 11 looks at Qing China, whose emperors became enthusiasts for the culture of China. They were, however, always careful to preserve Manchu supremacy, ruling through a governing class which combined Manchu-controlled military power with Chinese administrative methods. Though he barely altered Ming Beijing, the fourth Qing emperor Qianlong undertook a major building program in and around the capital. Within a vast walled area to the northwest of the imperial city, an array of pavilions and temples were erected around specially dug lakes. With the assistance of the Jesuits an unusual group of Western-style buildings was also constructed there and filled with contemporary European furniture. Inspired by his tours of south China, Qianlong set about recreating its lakes and hills at his enclosed garden, the Summer Palace.

Most of these extraordinary buildings suffered damage, some destruction, at the hands of British and French troops in 1860. This Second Opium War was driven, like the previous one of 1839-42, by British drug traffickers, Hong Kong-based merchants whose only concern was personal profit. The shock capitulation to a tiny expeditionary force revealed the fragility of the late empire, signaling that China was now besieged and an easy target for any industrial power bent on aggression. The siege can be said to have more than a century, since only through the foundation of the People's Republic has the country recovered sufficient strength to deter modern predators. Empress Cixi's domination of the imperial court is to blame in part for the stagnation. She actively deterred modernization and in 1898 she even imprisoned Emperor Guangxu in order to block his Hundred Days of Reform. Her greatest error was the support she gave to the Boxers in their attack on the Legation Quarter, because it brought in 1900 a punitive expedition of soldiers drawn from all the countries with diplomatic staff to the imperial capital. After this humiliation there was no chance of the last Qing emperor sitting for long on the dragon throne, and in 1912 the six-year-old Puyi abdicated in a favor of a republican president. He had lost an empire, two of them if one counts the puppet state that the Japanese established for him in Manchuria, yet he was very pleased to see that his old home had survived intact. Now restored to its former glory, the Purple Forbidden City ensures that Beijing is the ultimate destination for the modern visitor to China. The great Ming-Qing palace still reveals to the tutored eye the quintessence of the Chinese empire.

PART ONE

ANCIENT ORIGINS, C. 1650 BC ONWARDS

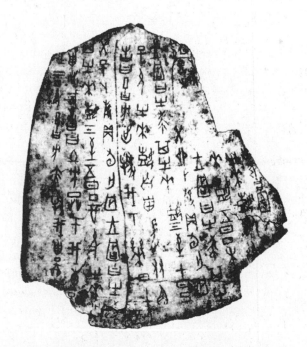

Inscribed Shang oracle bone dating from the eleventh century BC

CHAPTER 1

The Cosmology of the Chinese Capital

The capital of Shang was a city of cosmic order,
The pivot of the four quarters.
Glorious was its fame,
Purifying its divine power,
Manifested in longevity and peace
And the sure protection of descendants.

THIS ANCIENT POEM IN ALL PROBABILITY PRAISES ANYANG, THE LAST capital of the Shang kings who ruled north China from around 1650 to 1027 BC. Prior to the foundation of Anyang, or Great Shang as it was called in oracle inscriptions, the Shang dynasty had moved its capital on several occasions. The first requirement of a Chinese kingdom was a permanent capital, but these frequent moves were a necessity until the perfect location—the location that most pleased the Shang kings' divine ancestors—was discovered.

Even before the birth of Confucius in 551 BC, the pivotal importance of the ruler as the Son of Heaven formed the basis of Chinese thinking about politics. From Shang times, the earliest period in which written records were kept, we know how all earthly power was believed to emanate from the One Man, the king who was the Son of Heaven: only he possessed the authority to ask for the ancestral blessings, or counter the ancestral curses, which affected society. It was Shang Di, the high god of Heaven and the ultimate Shang ancestor, who conferred benefits upon his descendants in the way of good harvests and victories on the battlefield. Through divination the advice of the Shang king's immediate ancestors could be sought as to the actions most pleasing to this supreme deity.

Hence King Pan Geng's anxiety lest his people dally in an unlucky capital. In the *Book of History*, a collection of documents edited during the fourth century BC, are recorded the difficulties faced by Pan Geng when he wished to move the capital. Speaking firstly to the most senior members of his court, he countered their resistance with these words:

> Our king Zu Yi came and fixed on this location for his capital. He did so from a deep concern for our people, because he would not have them all die where they could not help one another to preserve their lives. I consulted the tortoise shell and obtained the reply: "This is no place to live." When former kings had any important business they paid reverent attention to the commands of Heaven. In a case like this they were not slow to act: they did not linger in the same city. If we do not follow the examples of old, we shall be refusing to acknowledge that Heaven is making an end to our dynasty. How small is our respect for the ways of former kings! As a felled tree puts forth new shoots, so Heaven will decree us renewed strength in a new city. The great inheritance of the past will be continued and peace will fill the four quarters of our realm.

Separately Pan Geng charged his nobles with stirring up trouble amongst "the multitudes through alarming and shallow speeches," a grievous crime, he pointed, out considering how their own ancestors shared in the sacrifices offered to former kings. Unless they treated the ruler, the One Man, with sufficient honor and loyalty, Heaven would inflict inevitable punishments. In order to ram home his point, Pan Geng then addressed the multitudes, who were "charged to take no liberties in the royal courtyard and obey the royal commands." He told the people of the reasons for the removal, stressing the calamity the founder ancestor of the dynasty would surely inflict on the existing capital, and let it be understood that nothing would affect his "unchangeable purpose."

Having won the day by direct speech, Pan Geng transferred everyone across the Yellow River to Anyang, where he instructed his officers to "care for the lives of the people so that the new city would be a lasting settlement." The episode is interesting for a number of reasons. Implicit are the cosmological threats of the priest-king to invoke the royal ancestors in order to punish dissidents, yet Pan Geng's conviction of impending disaster if there were no change of site was sincere: he genuinely believed that only his "great concern" stood between the Shang and their ruin.

Again it was Heaven that had given the crucial sign via the cracks on the tortoise shell. Always closely related to ancestor worship in ancient

China was divination from the cracks that develop in scorched tortoise shells or animal bones. By 1300 BC divination had become elaborately standardized; Shang kings used only such oracle materials after they were expertly prepared. On them were inscribed the questions to be asked of the ancestral spirits, and sometimes even the answers received.

How then could Pan Geng afford to ignore a warning that his divination had so clearly revealed? "When great disasters come down from Heaven," he commented, "the former rulers did not fondly remain in one place. What they did was with a view to the people's welfare, and so each moved their capital to another place." Only the conspicuous absence of a surrounding wall has caused doubt about Anyang as a capital. Was it rather a Chinese Delphi, whose purpose was principally oracle-taking? We still cannot be sure, as excavation is still patchy outside the royal cemetery and palace. It is possible that the last royal seat of government was so large and its garrison forces so concentrated that a rampart was thought to be unnecessary. On the other hand, the destruction of Great Shang in 1027 BC could have been made easier by Anyang's apparently sprawling layout. That year the city was razed to the ground.

Notwithstanding its undiscovered defenses, Anyang was the last known residence of the Shang kings and the place where the cosmology of the Chinese capital assumed its distinctive form. Employing the rammed earth method of construction, "the multitudes set their plum-lines, lashed together the boards to hold the earth and raised the Temple of the Ancestors on the cosmic pattern." In this building, according to the *Book of History*, "the king used the tortoise shell to consult the ancestral spirits, after which the court and the common people agreed about a course of action. It is called the Great Accord."

This passage captures the patrimonial nature of Chinese rule, royal or imperial. The authority of the Shang king over his people was simply an extension of his patriarchal control over his own family, an idea later developed by Confucius into a political justification for the state. Since this influential philosopher viewed the state as a large family, or rather a collection of families under the care of a leading family, the virtue of obedience was the key characteristic defining the relationship between a ruler and his subjects. When asked about government, Confucius replied: "Let the prince be a prince, the minister a minister, the father a father, and the son a son." So China could be described, indeed as it often is today, as "the Hundred Families." While he regarded correct familial relations as the cornerstone of society, Confucius possessed a profound sense of personal responsibility for the welfare of mankind. After his philosophy became dominant under the Former Han emperors in the first century BC, the Chinese empire's administrators came to see themselves as protectors of the people, inheritors of Pan Geng's fatherly concern for their wellbeing.

The special sanctity of the ancestral temple derived from its closeness to Heaven. It was the point at which two worlds met in the sacrifices conducted by the *wang*, "the king." This Chinese character is actually written in such a way as to reflect this cosmic relationship. The three horizontal strokes represent heaven, earth, and humanity, with a vertical stroke joining them together. The later character for emperor, *di*, retained this etymology but added the notion of divinity, or at least divine favor.

The first emperor of China, Qin Shi Huang Di, was pleased to adopt the title in 221 BC, the year in which he became sole ruler, because it allowed him to associate his dynasty with the semi-divine rulers of legendary times. In Qin Shi Huang Di's title, however, there was more than an element of political calculation; his superstitious nature already inclined towards the supernatural elements of Daoism (Daoist thinkers, the perpetual opponents of Confucius and his followers, particularly revered those early divine kings). Qin Shi Huang Di was fully aware of the manner of the Yellow Emperor's departure: after giving his kingdom an orderliness previously unknown on earth, this legendary ruler was carried heavenwards on the back of a dragon, along with his wives and his ministers. Endeavoring to attain a similar immortality, Qin Shi Huang Di in 219 BC began his attempts to communicate with the Immortals so as to acquire the elixir of life.

Underpinning the layout of the ancient Chinese capital, with its ceremonial center for royal ancestor worship, was a conscious attempt to mirror the cosmic order itself. Like major cities in Indian Asia, it was designed as a parallel, a miniature version, of the patterns observed on earth and in the sky: the succession of the seasons, the annual cycle of plant growth, the movements of the sun, moon, and stars. This acceptance of mankind's place in the great sweep of the natural world was sustained by a conviction that, although everything which existed was the handiwork of the gods, there were a few places on earth where sanctity was at its greatest. One of these was the ancestral temple of the ruler, the organizing feature of every Chinese capital. Around it the walls and streets were built to maximize the political power and religious authority of the ruler, the One Man who sat upon the dragon throne, facing south.

From the reign of Tang, the first Shang ruler, we can observe how close the relationship was understood to be between the ruler and the natural powers. Having seized power from the semi-legendary Xia kings, whose tyranny and corruption it is said invited their overthrow, Tang informed his subjects about the doubts he had over his worthiness to rule. He said:

> "It is given to me, the One Man, to secure harmony and peace. But I know not whether I offend the powers above and below. I am fearful and trembling, as if falling into a deep pit. Throughout my realm I command, therefore, that all abandon lawless ways and fulfil their proper duties so that we receive the favor of Heaven. The good in you I will not ignore and the evil in me I will never excuse. I will examine everything with Heaven in mind. When guilt is found in my subjects, let it fall upon me, the One Man. When guilt is found in me, I will not let it fall upon anyone else. Only through sincerity will we be able to find peace."

Little did Tang expect these words to come back and haunt him so quickly, but it was not long before north China was struck with a prolonged drought and, believing himself responsible for the calamity, he offered his own life in appeasement. We are told how Tang prepared himself spiritually for the sacrifice. He cut his hair, clipped his nails, and donned a robe of white rushes before riding to a mulberry grove in a simple carriage drawn by a team of white horses. There, as the king was about to die as a sacrificial victim, the drought ended in a heavy downpour.

So impressed was Tang by the rain-making dragons Heaven had sent that he composed a poem of thanksgiving called "The Great Salvation." Now demonstrably blessed, Tang had no hesitation in demoting the untrustworthy deity he blamed for the drought, an action that shows how in ancient China the spiritual and human worlds always complemented each other. Both were imagined as feudal in structure, with the spirits of mountains and rivers styled "duke" or "count." That Tang could remove the offending god from his fief seemed perfectly reasonable. As the Son of Heaven, the Shang king was only acting as Heaven's deputy on earth, where the dire effects of the drought were felt. Just as he delegated a portion of royal authority to own trusted relations, aristocrats, and frontier defenders, so Tang took advantage of the trust Heaven obviously placed in him to make this change in delegated divine duties.

Thus the Chinese conceived the natural features of the world essentially as an extension of themselves. Divine and human were intimately connected through kingship, an institution that elevated the current occupant of the throne into a truly charismatic figure. The king's subjects were persuaded of an invaluable link between the sacred and the secular by means of rites that dramatized the king's direct relationship with the heavenly powers. As the *Book of Rites* puts it, "Rites banish disorder just as dikes prevent floods." In the ancestral temple and other sites of royal and imperial worship, ritual specialists ensured that ceremonies were conducted appropriately.

The focus of creative energy was, of course, the palace. It was here that communication was effected most readily between cosmic planes, between earth and Heaven on one hand, and between earth and the underworld on the other. This central axis of the Chinese universe was never fixed. As we saw, the Shang king Pan Geng realized his capital was in the wrong place and, on advice from his ancestors, shifted the capital to Anyang. Changes in the sites of royal and imperial capitals were accepted as a necessity, even when a move was due to dynastic weakness.

For example, the Zhou, the dynasty that followed the Shang, was obliged to take refuge at Luoyang in 770 BC. That year King Ping hurried to Luoyang from Hao, just west of the modern city of Xi'an in Shaanxi province. Hao had been destroyed through an alliance of barbarian tribesmen and relations of the queen, who had been set aside because of the preference of Ping's father for a certain concubine. The ruler was slain, but with the aid of the great vassals, the shaken dynasty survived. A new royal residence had to be built at Luoyang, a safe distance down the Yellow River valley. As a result of the unrest, Zhou prestige declined and real power shifted to the nobles who held the largest fiefs. Despite this fundamental shift in political authority, the removal from Hao to Luoyang came to be regarded as the curtailment of Zhou spiritual power in the face of superior earthly influences, rather than the military catastrophe it actually was. Like previous Chinese capitals, Luoyang acquired a symbolic significance of its own as soon as the Son of Heaven stayed there.

The last Zhou king was dethroned in 256 BC by the forces of Qin, the feudal state from which Qin Shi Huang Di made himself the master of China. This first emperor was much influenced by two ancient schools of thought, the Five Elements and Daoism.

Water was the element Qin Shi Huang Di and his subjects believed to be supportive of his imperial (and even immortal) aspirations because Water had overcome Fire, the element associated with the previous royal dynasty, the Zhou. Prior to the overthrow of the last Zhou king in 256 BC there was already a view that the era of Fire approached its end. The so-called school of the Five Elements maintained that each period of history lay under the domination of one of the five elements—Earth, Wood, Metal, Fire, and

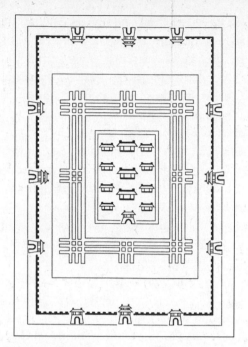

Idealized plan of Luoyang, the Zhou king's capital

Water—and that these elements succeeded each other in an apparently end-less cycle. So in turn each element overcame its predecessor, flourished for a fixed period, and then was in its turn overcome by the next element in the series. For the half millennium down to the triumph of Qin, the Zhou king had been reduced to a ceremonial role within a small domain surrounding the royal capital of Luoyang. Supposedly loyal to his commands as the Son of Heaven, the feudal rulers of the rest of China gradually turned their lands into independent states, and then competed for supremacy over their peers. During this intense struggle, the final stage of which was known as the Warring States period, feudal rulers eager to replace the Zhou dynasty sought the protection of Water, the next element in the series. Just as water quenches fire, so Water would extinguish the Fire protecting the Zhou king and hand the heavenly mandate to rule to another.

Exponents of the Five Elements school traveled from feudal court to feudal court, receiving the highest honors, as they assured one ruler after another that they were in line for Water's patronage. Coming from the comparatively unsophisticated state of Qin in the northwest of China, Qin Shi Huang Di found the theory of the Fire Elements utterly irresistible.

Qin Shi Huang Di's determination to introduce orderliness in his king-dom arose from his belief in the Five Elements. In order to inaugurate the power of Water, the element of the Qin imperial house, Qin Shi Huang Di believed that there must be firm repression with everything determined by law. Only ruthless, implacable severity could make the Five Elements accord. So the law was harsh and there were no amnesties. Black became the chief color for dress, banners, and pennants, and six the chief number. Tallies and official headgear were six measures long, carriages six measures wide, and imperial carriages had six horses.

It was Qin Shi Huang Di who introduced a new dimension into the rituals at Mount Tai, the dominant peak on the northeastern China plain. Possibly his other irresistible obsession—that of the Daoist theory of the elixir of life—led to the association of this peak with the island of Penglai, the dwelling place of the Immortals. The earliest reference to human immortality occurs in *The Book of Zhuangzi*, a Daoist text dating from the fourth century BC. It provides the standard description of "an immortal hermit with skin like ice, and gentle and shy like a young girl. He does not eat the five grains, but sucks on wind, drinks dew, climbs up on clouds and mist, rides a dragon, and wanders beyond the four seas." Most important for Qin Shi Huang Di was the ability of an immortal through a concentration of spirit "to protect creatures from sickness and disease as well as ensure a good harvest." Daoists distinguished three kinds of Immortals. First, there were the celestial immortals, who were able "to raise their bodies and souls high into the sky." The second kind were the terrestrial immortals, the inhabitants of the mountains and the forests. The last were the corpse-free immortals, who simply sloughed off the body after death. Where this third kind of immortal resided is unclear, although Qin Shi Huang Di may well have been aiming to become one himself at Mount Li, the site of his incredible mausoleum.

When in 110 BC Wu Di became the first Han emperor to sacrifice at Mount Tai, the rituals had to be improvised for the good reason that Qin Shi Huang Di's sacrificial rituals remained secret, a circumstance which almost certainly related to advice he had received about keeping his own movements and activities out of the public eye. In 212 BC a Daoist adept had warned him

> that a sinister influence was working against the search of immortality. It is my sincere opinion that Your Majesty would be well advised to change your quarters secretly from time to time, in order to avoid evil spirits; for in their absence an Immortal will surely come. An Immortal is one who cannot be wet by water or burned by fire, who endures as long as Heaven and Earth.

On hearing of this impediment to his greatest wish, the elixir of life, Qin Shi Huang Di ordered that all his palaces and pavilions were to be connected by causeways and covered walks, so that he could move unobserved between them. Disclosure of his whereabouts was also made punishable by death. How set Qin Shi Huang Di was on achieving his goal became obvious straightaway. From one of his many residences, he noticed the approach of Li Si and commented adversely on the size of that minister's retinue. A palace eunuch informed Li Si of the emperor's displeasure, and Li Si prudently reduced the number of his retainers. Qin Shi Huang Di, far from being pleased by this turn of events, was enraged to realize one of his attendants had provided information that revealed his whereabouts, if only by implication. He was so enraged, in fact, that he had all the eunuchs in his company executed, as none would admit to telling tales. "After this," we learn, "his movements were treated as a state secret, but it was always in the main palace at Xianyang, the imperial capital, that he conducted official business."

The less private sacrifices that Wu Di made at Mount Tai involved the transmission to Heaven of imperial desires, sealed in a ritual jar, and the worship of the earthly powers. In essence, these rites were the same as any emperor performed in the imperial capital. Like Qin Shi Huang Di, though, Wu Di was involved in other rituals of his own aimed at finding the elixir of life. On his climb to the summit Wu Di was accompanied by a single servant, who died shortly afterwards.

Shrouded as they are in mystery, the visits Qin Shi Huang Di and Wu Di both made to the summit of Mount Tai reflect a real worry about the length of their personal reigns, an uncertainty neither of them felt they could resolve in their own imperial capitals. By then the Shang option of moving capitals to more auspicious sites was really out of the question. Imperial houses now had to propitiate the divine largely by cosmic practices inside their permanent places of residence.

That the Daoist-inclined emperors like Qin Shi Huang Di and Wu Di felt it necessary to travel to a sacred mountain in order to make a personal sacrifice reveals how the ancient Chinese were never really happy with a symbolic replica. This was not the case in Indian-inspired cosmology, the other great Asian tradition. In the kingdoms of Southeast Asia, for instance, the planning of capital cities often depended upon the delimitation of sacred space, the area immediately surrounding a structure designated as Mount Meru, the Indian world mountain. Unlike the Khmer kings of Cambodia, who build temple-mountain tombs deifying themselves in accordance with Indian tradition, China never designed a capital around the sanctity of a king or an emperor, and never gave precedence in its layout to mausoleums for reigning or deceased rulers. Except in the ancestral temple, the realms of the sacred and secular were at all times kept firmly apart. Whereas Khmer temple-mountains faced east, again in accordance with Indian religious ideas, important Chinese buildings, especially the palace, always faced south. "To face south" became synonymous with "to rule."

The form of a Chinese capital, when terrain permitted, was rectangular, surrounded by wide water-filled moats. Regularly spaced gates were placed in its four walls, with main streets leading to the palace and other prestigious buildings. In the very center there was invariably a drum tower, whose function was the maintenance of civil order and not the worship of a divine ruler like the centrally placed temple-mountains of Cambodian capital cities.

Although some emperors were more drawn than others to the spirit world, the this-worldly tenor of Confucian philosophy set the prevailing tone for dealings with the supernatural. While the Cambodians might incarnate Indian deities in their living kings, the Chinese came to populate the spiritual realm with bureaucrats. This extension of the ways of the imperial civil service into celestial affairs, not unlike the Shang king Tang's earlier transfer there of feudal obligations, derived from the level-headedness of Confucius's outlook. Not even divination escaped his censure, since Confucius felt that Heaven was far above human comprehension—something not plumbed by scrutinizing the cracks made by heat on animal bones and tortoise shells. Nor could natural phenomena, like shooting stars, earthquakes and floods, be so readily interpreted as signs of heavenly disapproval.

The reluctance of Confucius to pronounce on religion helped in introducing a sense of balance in the supernatural world as well as the earthly one. "I stand in awe of the spirits," he said, "but keep them at a distance." Ethical concepts rather than supernatural concerns lay at the heart of his thinking. What China needed, Confucius believed, were compassionate rulers who would instruct their people by their own example in following traditional usage. He went so far as to warn progressive rulers that the setting down of laws was a dangerous innovation for aristocratic rule. Pointing out that a written law-code represents a break with custom, he astutely predicted that the code of punishments inscribed on a tripod by the ruler of Qin would be learned and honored by people above all else. Never again would those in authority be able to call upon tradition in order to declare their judgments correct. Not for a moment was Confucius suggesting that arbitrary decisions were ever justified. As he said,

If you lead people by regulation and regulate them by punishments, they will seek to evade the law and have no sense of shame. If you lead them by virtue and regulate them through rites, they will correct themselves.

Here the character *li*, which is usually translated as rites, etiquette, ritual, really means propriety. The way this Chinese word is written tells us what Confucius had in mind, for the strokes represent a vessel containing precious objects as a sacrifice to the ancestral spirits. He saw, therefore, the rite of ancestor worship as the focus of a moral code in which proper social relations were defined: the loyalty of a minister to a prince was the same as that owed to a father by a son.

Under the empire, which lasted from 221 BC till 1912, administrative requirements allowed the service rendered by the scholar-bureaucrat to be a reality as well as an ideal. Confucian scholars connected with the landowning class were one of the twin pillars of imperial society; the other was the great multitude of peasant-farmers, no longer tied to a feudal lord but liable to taxation, labor on public works, and military service. The low social position of merchants—a prevailing feature of Chinese history—was the natural outcome of economic development down to the establishment of the Chinese empire, as feudal princes had assumed most of the responsibility for industry and water-control works. But it was the blocking of all avenues of social advancement to merchants that was the effective curb, because it prevented the sons of successful traders from becoming officials. A poor scholar without an official position would prefer farming to trade as a means of livelihood, lest he spoil any future opportunity of a civil service career. Dedicated civil servants were always expected by Confucius to exhibit good manners, which he believed to be a sign of moral character. For him *li* encompassed not just the rules of politeness, but rather the correct way of approaching every thought and deed.

Confucianism so deeply instilled an appreciation of the enormous role played by education in civilized society that subsequent Chinese thought can be said to have been an interpretation of this underlying principle. Referring to the Daoists, Confucius said: "They dislike me because I want to reform society, but if we are not to live with our fellow men with whom can we live? We cannot live with animals. If society was as it ought to be, I should not be seeking to change it." It is a point constantly made down the ages by Confucian scholars whose outlook rested on a sense of personal responsibility for the welfare of mankind. This stress on service, and indeed loyalty to principle, was one of the chief reasons for the adoption of Confucianism as the imperial ideology.

It is somewhat ironic that this began in earnest during the reign of Wu Di, the Han emperor most interested in Daoism. Emphasize though Confucian ethics might the overriding importance of justice, consideration, and good behavior in the administration of the empire, scholar-bureaucrats who adhered to its precepts recognized how they needed to accommodate the spiritual anxieties of the emperors they served. A determined ruler like Wu Di was only willing to worship Heaven on Mount Tai, and hereby acknowledge his moral duties as the Son of Heaven, provided he could conduct on its summit private Daoist sacrifices of his own as well. Even though the imperial pursuit of immortality on Mount Tai ceased with Wu Di, its summit was still held to be one of the routes to longevity and contentment for centuries afterwards. An inscription on the back of a third-century AD bronze mirror tells how on Mount Tai "you will meet the Immortals, feed on the purest jade, drink from sacred springs, and receive a life that lasts ten thousand years, a high official position, and protection for your children and grandchildren." These remarkable gifts from the Immortals interestingly succeed in combining together the Daoist achievement of the elixir of life with a Confucian respect for public service and family lineage.

The immense cosmic forces believed to be concentrated on sacred peaks such as Mount Tai had to be taken into due account when selecting sites of capital cities and their associated buildings. We know how in 220 BC,

> the twenty-seventh year of his reign, Qin Shi Huang Di built a palace on the south bank of the Wei River, which was named the Paramount Temple, representing the Apex of Heaven. From the Paramount Temple a path led to Mount Li where another palace was built. The Paramount Temple was connected with the capital by a walled road.

These buildings, like others he had constructed in and around Qin's first imperial capital of Xianyang, including his tomb complex at Mount Li, were elements in a grand cosmological arrangement whose focus was actually Qin Shi Huang Di himself, as the Son of Heaven. Just how seriously Qin Shi Huang Di took the spiritual advice that he received is evident in the description of his own burial chamber. In it were placed

> models of palaces, towers and official buildings, as well as fine utensils, precious stones and rarities... All the Empire's waterways, including the Yellow and the Yangzi Rivers, were reproduced and made to flow mechanically. Above, the heavenly constellations were depicted, while below lay a representation of the earth.

Little short of the world itself, this was to be the intended home of an Immortal, once Qin Shi Huang Di's corpse had been placed inside its copper-clad coffin there.

Qin Shi Huang Di's architects and planners appreciated how the good fortune of the newly founded imperial dynasty could only be assured if all the sites chosen, and not least that of his tomb, were properly adapted to local cosmic currents, which were calculated by reference to the terrain and the movements of the stars. This ancient geomancy, ancestral to present-day feng shui, always informed the construction of major Chinese cities, and especially royal and imperial capitals. Nothing built for the living or the dead in China was ever planned without the advice of a geomancer. A desirable site was set among land forms generating auspicious, or at least benign, influences, but such locations were sometimes unavailable, so that often geomancers were obliged to concern themselves with defense against evil influences seeping into residences and tombs. The reshaping of hills, the removal of boulders and the excavation of ground considered to be unlucky could help redeem otherwise inauspicious locations, just as the planting of trees and shrubs could assist in restoring a necessary balance of the yin-yang elements. Attuning to the rhythm of nature was a vital consideration for the ancient Chinese, who explained its perfection in the yin-yang theory: it envisaged two interacting forces, not in conflict but existing together in a precarious balance that if disturbed would bring swift disaster. This perception of natural forces could have arisen nowhere else than in the loess country of northern China, where a sudden downpour or a burst embankment might dramatically alter the landscape.

Ever dear to Daoism, this theory also found its way into Confucian ethics. Dong Zhongshu, who persuaded a reluctant Emperor Wu Di to proclaim the state cult of Confucius, argued that the heavenly mandate of an emperor to rule might be upset by an imbalance of the yin and the yang. He said that since human nature possesses little more than the beginnings of goodness, society could only be saved from barbarism through the institutions of kinship and education. He stressed three relationships—ruler and subject, father and son, husband and wife—and insisted that the ruler, the father, and the husband correspond to the yang element and were therefore dominant, whereas the subject, the son, and the wife tended towards the submissive yin element.

Although Dong Zhongshu's revised form of Confucianism obviously drew on Daoist ideas, we should note how its use of a yin-yang analogy contained no supernatural dimension at all. A ruler's position of authority was granted and taken away by Heaven, but the agents for affecting change could be humble men like Liu Bang, the first Han emperor, who was welcomed by a people oppressed by the harshness of Qin rule. Liu Bang eventually won, in 202 BC, the complicated struggle between insurgent leaders that followed the overthrow of Qin Shi Huang Di's dynasty by the first nationwide rebellion in Chinese history.

This dramatic imperial failure was largely blamed by proponents of Daoism and the Five Elements on the shortcomings of geomancy, as the sites of Qin ceremonial buildings were considered to be inadequate for ruling an empire. Had Qin Shi Huang Di still been alive, he would have set about rectifying the deficiency, probably moving around large parts of the first imperial capital in the process. The uncertainties of the feng shui interpretation of landscape were legion: cosmic alignment was a perennial concern, with geomancers endlessly checking that capital cities remained well adapted to the local cosmic currents. These influences, which could suddenly manifest themselves in benign or unsatisfactory ways, needed to be kept under control. Divination might help in the selection of the general location of a capital, but the actual layout of the urban area, the positioning of the palace and administrative center, was something that could not be decided until the geomancers had completed all their calculations. Then the city was laid out as a square, or a rectangle, the surrounding walls usually having three gateways on each of the four sides.

Within these rammed-earth defenses there were nine streets running east-west and nine streets running north-south. The former had to be "nine chariot-tracks wide." Of Luoyang, the seat of the later Zhou kings, an ideal plan survives: it is not very instructive in showing where the chief buildings were situated as the royal palace is simply placed at the city's center. If there was one capital that came closest to the sought-after cosmic alignment, it was Sui and Tang Chang'an. This imperial capital was inaugurated by the first Sui emperor, Wen Di, a hard-bitten soldier of Turkish ancestry who was noted for his sternness. In AD 589 he was appalled at the human cost of building his palace there, until his wife expressed her unqualified admiration for their new home. The most henpecked of all rulers in the history of the Chinese empire, Wen Di had no choice in the face of his wife's approval but accept the danger to his dynasty of placing such a heavy burden of labor on the Chinese people.

Emperor Wen Di was right in being concerned, notwithstanding the perfectly symmetrical plan of his new capital, which stood not far from Former Han Chang'an. He called it Greatly Exulted Walled City. Unequivocal though this statement of imperial will was, the first Sui emperor was not without compassion for the sufferings of common folk, in

contrast to his successor, the emperor Yang Di. This younger son assassinated him in 604 and, brushing aside the financial restraint of his father, he
commissioned a second imperial capital at Luoyang, which was built by
hundreds of thousands of conscripted laborers in the following year. His
next project was the digging of the Grand Canal in order to link the northern and the southern provinces permanently together. Added to this were
the repairs Yang Di ordered to the Great Wall, as the northern defenses
were later called, and the war he started with Koguryo, a Korean kingdom
which stretched across southern Manchuria and the northern part of the
Korean peninsula. Defeat abroad and insurrection at home ended Sui rule
in 618, when Chang'an was captured by Li Shimin, the second son of the
first Tang emperor Gao Zu.

Considered as one of the greatest in Chinese imperial history, the Tang
dynasty retained Wen Di's Chang'an as their capital and used Yang Di's
Luoyang as a secondary capital. During the reign of the sixth Tang emper-
or Xuanzong, who came to the dragon throne in 712, Chang'an was at its
greatest with a population of nearly two millions. It was by far the largest
city in China, and for that matter in the world. There, good government
combined with a surge of creativity to produce what is now termed the
Tang renaissance, its most obvious achievement appearing in the *Complete
Tang Poems*, a collection of 48,000 poems by no fewer than 2200 authors.

Although the Tang emperors continued to occupy the halls and gardens
built by their Sui predecessors at Chang'an, they made many innovations,
the most significant of which, the construction of the Great Luminous
Palace to the northeast of the walled city, destroyed the perfect symmetry
of the Sui foundation. The Sui palace, stood next to the north wall of the
capital, while to its immediate south were situated the headquarters of the
imperial bureaucracy. These distinct quarters, the palace and administrative
cities with their own walls and gateways, still remained the place where
most official business was conducted after the construction of the Great
Luminous Palace. Here the Son of Heaven continued to sit upon the dragon throne, facing south and radiating his heaven-granted authority down
the great avenue in the very center of Chang'an, and out into the Chinese
empire at large. The dragon throne had to be placed close to this avenue's
north-south axis, since it corresponded to the Pole Star, "the very spot
where earth and sky met, where the four seasons merged, where wind and
rain were gathered in, and where the yin and the yang were in harmony."

This cosmic consideration was still apparent during the twelfth century at
Hangzhou, the southernmost imperial capital. The loss of the northern
provinces for a second time then had compelled the Song dynasty to move

south, and with reluctance agree that Hangzhou's irregular and unplanned features could serve as an imperial residence. Marco Polo knew the city by the name of Kinsai, a corruption of "temporary residence," the only title the Southern Song emperors could bring themselves to confer upon Hangzhou. The basic problem facing geomancers here was the restricted city site, squeezed onto a narrow neck of land, approximately a kilometer in width, between a lake and a river. Yet they did their best to maintain a cosmic layout, despite the placement of the imperial palace towards the south of Hangzhou, and to the west of the central street marking the north-south axis.

The name Kinsai was prophetic. Hard pressed though the Song emperors were by the Jin, the ancestors of the Manchus, there was behind these invaders from the steppes an even more terrifying enemy, the Mongol horde under Genghis Khan. In 1126 the Jin had captured Kaifeng, the first Song capital, and driven the dynasty to Hangzhou, where it became known as the Southern Song. The emperors who had ruled from the northern city of Kaifeng were then styled the Northern Song in order to distinguish them from this southern survival of a shaken imperial house. Only forays against other enemy peoples gave a respite to what was left of the Chinese empire—once the Mongols conquered the Jin in 1234, the full force of their strength was directed southwards. The last member of the Southern Song dynasty perished in a sea battle off modern Hong Kong in 1279; that the Song held out those forty-five years is testimony of the stubborn resistance put up by Chinese armies, exploiting terrain unfavorable to Mongol cavalry tactics.

Another factor in lengthening the struggle was military technology. Explosive grenades and bombs were launched from catapults; rocket-aided arrows with poisonous smoke, shrapnel, and flamethrowers were deployed alongside a primitive armored car as well as armored gunboats; and in close combat a prototype gun, named the "flying-fire spear," discharged both flame and projectiles. The Mongols, like invaders before them, became irresistible only when they adopted Chinese equipment. Yet they outdid all previous invaders in becoming the first nomadic people to conquer the whole of China. In 1263 the grandson of Genghis Khan and the first Yuan emperor, Kublai Khan, founded Beijing as his capital.

Dadu, as Mongol Beijing was called, seems to have been constructed on the site of a Jin country palace. That it conformed in its plan to a traditional Chinese capital, with a rectangular defensive wall and an inner palace city, tells us much about the motives for the transfer of the Mongol capital from Karakorum to Beijing. Close though Beijing was to the Mongol homeland, it is transparent how Kublai Khan intended to rule as a Chinese emperor as well as a great khan. Yet the Mongol approach to China was quite different from that of the earlier Turks and the later Manchus. Whereas these two invaders became patrons of Chinese culture and in so doing forfeited their own languages and traditions, Mongol emperors preferred to exclude Chinese scholars from office and rely on an administration chiefly staffed with officials of non-Chinese origin.

As a Mongol civil servant, Marco Polo could express admiration of Kublai Khan's great empire, its cities, commerce and canals, for the good reason that he was unaware of the high level to which Chinese civilization had attained prior to the fall of the Southern Song dynasty. Although the narrative of *The Travels* opened the eyes of medieval Europe to the magnificence of East Asia, Marco Polo never penetrated deeply into conditions in China, which, during his stay from 1260 to 1269, had scarcely begun to recover from the destructiveness and disruption of the Mongol conquest. The full recovery of China had to await the establishment of the Ming dynasty by the patriot Zhu Yuanzhang, a former monk, beggar, and bandit.

The last Yuan emperor abandoned Beijing in 1368 and fled to Mongolia. Hong Wu, the title Zhu Yuanzhang chose as the first Ming emperor, built his capital at the southern city of Nanjing. It was the third Ming emperor, the usurper Yongle, who moved the seat of restored Chinese imperial power northwards to Beijing. Overruling opposition to the move in a more imperious manner than the Shang king Pan Geng would have ever thought feasible, Yongle ordered his new capital to be laid out within a wall measuring some 23 kilometers in length. This wall followed the outline of the former Mongol city, except that it was about two kilometers shorter at the northern end and about a kilometer farther extended to the south. What Yongle accomplished in moving the capital northwards was a return to the rectangular grid plan of the classical Chinese city, which had reached its perfection in Sui and Tang Chang'an. It was a definite reaction from the irregular cities of south China, and notably Hangzhou.

Despite considerable rebuilding during the late twentieth century, the chessboard pattern of Beijing is still apparent, with the division of the city into distinct quarters. At the center is the Purple Forbidden City, a literary allusion to the Pole Star. Arranged in accordance with this star and adjoining constellations, the Purple Forbidden City has a north-south orientation, all its principal terraces and entrances facing south. Two sacrificial altars attended by the Son of Heaven are still situated to its south on either side of the central avenue describing the capital's north-south axis, and next to what was once the southern gateway of the outer Ming city. Emperor Yongle performed the sacred rites as the One Man on a single site in the vicinity, but about 1530 it was determined, after a thorough historical investigation by a commission of scholars, that separate altars should be built not only for Heaven and the earthly powers but also the sun and moon as well as other spiritual forces. Within one spacious enclosure today stands the Altar of Heaven, a circular three-tier terrace nearly five meters in height, and the well-known Temple of Heaven, a circular building with a triple roof of blue tiles. In this majestic building the emperor offered prayers during major festivals each year. Nearby is the Altar of Agriculture, whose sacrifices were connected with spring plowing and directed at securing good harvests. It is a direct descendant of the terrace-altars of ancient Shang times.

The last imperial dynasty, the Qing, was initially restricted to north China, since the rest of the empire was embroiled in civil war. Had the Chinese united behind one pretender for the dragon throne, the invading Manchus might have been driven out altogether. As it was, they occupied Beijing and awaited developments. By the time the people of the southern provinces were disposed to unite, there was an energetic Manchu ruler to face, the second Qing emperor, Kangxi. With the assistance of Chinese commanders who accepted that the heavenly mandate to rule had passed already to the Qing dynasty, Kangxi asserted his authority over south China, the last Ming center of resistance on the island of Taiwan falling in 1683.

It was the northern location of Beijing, an imperial capital far removed from where the majority of the Chinese population lived in the southern provinces, that really gave the Manchus their chance to seize power. By quietly occupying the city, and embracing the cosmic implications of ascending the dragon throne, Manchu rulers were able to appear as the legitimate successors of the last Ming emperor, whom they criticized as unfit to rule. One of the important planks of Qing dynastic ideology was the argument that not only had their incompetent predecessors lost heavenly approval, but more the factionalism and strife so evident amongst the imperial civil service was a clear indication that China urgently required a new and energetic dynasty. And the Manchus and the Chinese were both surprised to discover in Kangxi a model ruler. In 1684 we learn that

> the emperor visited Mount Tai. He rode on a horse through the Red Gate
> for a kilometer or so. Then he dismounted and walked up stone stairways
> for nearly twenty kilometers. After he reached the top of the mountain, he
> performed the prescribed rituals.

In these imperial duties Kangxi "led the accompanying officials" and "personally prayed" for the well-being of the empire, demonstrating his willingness to be everything expected of the One Man. Afterwards, the Manchu emperor succeeded in putting a distance between himself and any Daoist associations that may have lingered in the Mount Tai rituals by visiting the shrine of Confucius at Qufu, also in Shandong province. There he offered sacrifices to the philosopher as the one "who had given good laws to the people." He heard the ritual music and listened to lectures; he was shown the famous collection of precious objects and had pointed out to him was the place where a descendent of the philosopher had hidden Confucius's writings when Qin Shi Huang Di ordered the burning of the books.

Chinese scholars now knew that they need have no fear of Kangxi's intentions, because his admiration of Chinese culture was genuine and deep. Lacking an advanced tradition of their own, the Manchus were obliged to identify with the Confucian orthodoxy which underpinned the authority of the Son of Heaven. This antiquarian impulse soon generated an encyclopedic movement second to none, and in the fourth Qing emperor Qianlong created a collector without parallel anywhere in the world. It was near the close of his long reign, in 1793, that a British trade mission led by Lord Macartney was politely rebuffed. As Qianlong intimated, China was an empire so vast that it had no reason to engage in international trade.

The nineteenth century was to prove him wrong, as European powers and a modernized Japan lay siege to China: Beijing fell to an Anglo-French force in 1860, when on Lord Elgin's orders the Summer Palace was fired, and again in 1900 to an international expedition sent to relieve the Legation Quarter, then under attack from the Boxers. Yet Qianlong's cool response to Lord Macartney does explain why Qing Beijing remained essentially Ming Beijing. Such was the esteem in which the Manchus held Chinese ways, and such was their fear of changing age-old customs, that they were quite incapable of redesigning China's last imperial capital, lest the whole edifice of the emperor's authority came tumbling down. They understood how unwise it would be to alter the cosmic arrangements first established by the Shang kings. Nothing was to be gained in disturbing the cosmic layout of an imperial capital which, like all those founded before Beijing, had been "built in the center of the earth in order to govern the whole world."

PART TWO

THE EARLY EMPIRE
221 BC – AD 589

Bas-relief of Jing Ke's attempt on the life of Qin Shi Huang Di

CHAPTER 2

The First Imperial Capitals: Qin Xianyang and Former Han Chang'an

Why is Chang'an in so much disorder?
Because of the imperial decree
To lay the great Huo Quling to rest.
Over a hundred embroidered silk quilts
Will cover his body. Everything
Needed for this soldier's interment
Is now being readied, coffin and clothes.

CHINA'S FIRST TWO IMPERIAL CAPITALS WERE IMPROVISED CITIES. The Qin capital of Xianyang was still under construction when, in 206 BC, rebels burned it to the ground, while the makeshift appearance of Former Han Chang'an, "Forever Safe," resulted from incorporating a former Qin palace built to the south of Xianyang. Even though Chang'an was basically square in plan and oriented to the cardinal points, the northern and southern walls zig-zagged in order to accommodate the palace and the irregular terrain. Its city wall was not constructed until the reign of the second Former Han emperor Hui Di in the late 190s BC. On a number of occasions conscript laborers were assembled, local peasants as well as prisoners: one section of the wall alone required a month's work by 145,000 men. Completion of the city wall, which measured 16 meters at its base, probably took five years. Outside there was a moat, 8 meters wide and 3 meters deep. Only after the construction of Chang'an's defenses came the suggestion of a deliberate design related to two constellations, Ursa Minor and Ursa Major. The uneven line of the city wall was believed to have followed their shapes, an alternative name for Chang'an being Dipper City. In this way the Former Han capital could be linked to the enduring pattern of the heavens.

The Qin capital of Xianyang was quite different from Chang'an because it was built in a hurry, the unforeseen consequence of Qin Shi Huang Di's conquest of China in 221 BC. The rise of the northwestern state of Qin to supreme power was no means a foregone conclusion, although chroniclers always seemed to think it was. "As a silkworm devours a mulberry leaf," one wrote, "Qin destroyed rival states in turn." Isolated from the mainstream of ideas in ancient China, Qin was more open to a new spirit of government consisting of the quest for efficiency without regard to traditional morality. "The simple and unsophisticated inhabitants," we are told, "can only gain benefits from their superiors by achieving distinction in battle. And rewards increase to keep pace with achievement; thus a man who returns from battle with five enemy heads is made master of five families in the neighborhood."

Instrumental in this transformation was Shang Yang, who arrived at the Qin court in 356 BC, five years before its transfer to Xianyang. So effective was Shang Yang in persuading the Qin ruler to adopt the harsh tenets of the school of Law that society was completely recast. A new legal code strengthened the state's military power by weakening the influence of the aristocracy, breaking up powerful clans, and freeing the peasantry from bondage. In place of customary ties Shang Yang substituted collective responsibility as a method of securing order. He said that it had to be made worse to face the Qin police than fight on a battlefield. Though Shang Yang's single-mindedness made him unpopular and he did not long survive his master's death, his Legalist reforms remained in place and achieved ultimate victory for Qin. The beneficiary was King Zheng, whose name means "correct." It was to prove apposite, for he sought the correct way of furthering the Legalist aims of Qin. In this pursuit of absolute power, which Zheng achieved as China's first emperor (with the new imperial title Qin Shi Huang Di), he was ably assisted by his Grand Councillor Li Si.

In the drive for imperial unity these two men relied on force. Feudal holdings were abolished and noble families were compelled to take up residence in Xianyang. Great quantities of captured weapons were also taken to the capital, where they were melted down and cast into twelve colossal statues. Throughout the empire peasants were given greater rights over their land but became liable for taxes, war service, and labor on government works. New administrative districts were introduced with garrisons stationed at strategic points, and a body of inspectors was estab-

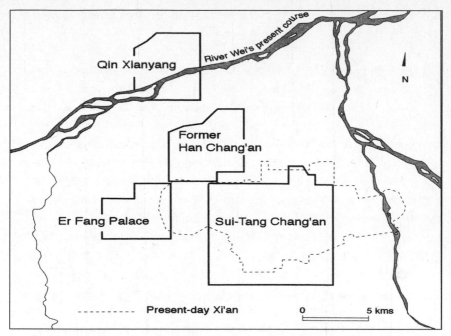

Map of the sites of of four former imperial capitals near modern-day Xi'an

lished to audit accounts as well as check on the administration of justice. There was standardization of weights, measures, currency, written script, and axle wheels. A national road network was constructed and canals improved for the supply of the army and, as a counter to the nomad threat along the northern frontier, previous defenses were incorporated into the Great Wall.

The speed at which Xianyang had to be built meant that it was never finished. The construction work for the dwellings for the 120,000 displaced aristocratic families alone was enormous. This policy of concentration, called "strengthening the trunk and weakening the branches," was used by later dynasties as a method of controlling separatism, but no emperor ever equaled Qin Shi Huang Di's assault on feudalism. His resoluteness encompassed even the imperial family.

Another major project was the great palace that Qin Shi Huang Di commissioned south of the Wei River. Still known by its popular name as Er Fang, "Nearby" Palace, it was the largest imperial residence ever built in China: its area was virtually the same as that of the Former Han capital, Chang'an. Though the surviving portions of the palace's immense earthen platform are now cultivated or covered in wild grasses and trees, it is possible to appreciate how Er Fang became the symbol of untold luxury and waste. In 212 BC we are informed that

> Qin Shi Huang Di said, "Xianyang is overcrowded and the palaces of former Qin kings too small. I have heard that King Wen of Zhou had his capital at Feng, King Wu at Hao. Between these two ancient places there is a suitable site for an imperial residence." This new palace measured 500 paces from east to west, and 500 paces from north to south. Its terraces could seat over 10,000 people, and there was room inside for raising banners twenty meters in height. One elevated road led from the palace to the South Hill at the top of which a gateway was erected. A second roadway led across to the Wei River at Xianyang, just as the Heavenly Corridor in the sky leads from the Apex of Heaven across the Milky Way to the Royal Chamber. Before the completion of this palace, Qin Shi Huang Di wanted to choose an auspicious name for it, but because of its closeness to the old capitals, it was commonly called Er Fang. More than 700,000 prisoners labored on the Er Fang palace and the emperor's tomb at Mount Li. Stone was quarried from the northern hills, timber brought from the southern forests in Shu and Chu. Three hundred palaces were built within the passes of Qin, and outside more than four hundred others.

Work on Er Fang, as indeed the elaborate funerary arrangements at Mount Li, was still in progress on Qin Shi Huang Di's death in 210 BC.

The size of the Er Fang palace was extraordinary, but then so was everything else Qin Shi Huang Di commissioned: the Great Wall, the national road system, the seven hundred palaces mentioned above, and of course the terracotta army at Mount Li. Just how big his new palace was can be grasped by a comparison with later imperial buildings. It is calculated that its chief building measured 675 by 112 meters. This dwarfs the Later Han throne room at Luoyang, which was built between AD 60 and 65. Its dimensions were merely 86 by 16 meters. The great throne room still standing in Beijing, the Hall of the Supreme Harmony, measures somewhat over 60 by 30 meters.

Such an extensive program of construction and engineering works as Qin Shi Huang Di demanded not only required huge amounts of manpower but also necessitated the collection and transport of very large quantities of building materials, thus imposing a tremendous burden on the ordinary people. This continued use of conscript labor strained the allegiance of the

Qin Shi Huang Di's famous
terracotta army at his Mount Li tomb

peasantry, especially when it was maintained by the naked force of cruel punishments. As a result of the progressive expansion of state demand for manpower there was a drop in agricultural output, with all the miseries that a shortage of food entails. It was indeed the dislocation of the rural economy that formed the background for the popular risings against the Qin dynasty. The impoverished peasants who in 209 BC staged the first large-scale rebellion in Chinese history were unconsciously responding to the unique circumstance of a unified empire: they were marking the limits of future power for a centralized government.

The atmosphere in the Qin court was always rarefied. It is difficult to see how Qin Shi Huang Di could have been looked upon without a powerful sense of awe. There had never been anyone like him. He was the undisputed ruler of the world, for then China remained isolated from ancient India, West Asia, Egypt, and Europe, totally cut off by formidable mountains and deserts. It wasn't until 126 BC, a millennium after the fall of the Shang kings, that the Chinese learned from an envoy of the existence of other civilizations. The envoy reported finding in what is now Afghanistan "cities, mansions, and houses as in China." The Han court was amazed: it had never suspected that civilization could flourish beyond China's borders. During the reign of Qin Shi Huang Di, however, there was no such awareness to balance the claim to universal authority. And Qin Shi Huang Di's obsession with immortality ensured that the dynasty tried to get a foothold in the next world as well. Embassies were dispatched to the abodes of the Immortals on the tops of mountains in order to acquire the elixir of life.

Three assassination attempts on Qin Shi Huang Di's life served to stimulate this pursuit of personal protection. In 227 BC he had narrowly escaped death in his own audience chamber at the hands of Jing Ke, an agent sent by a rival ruler. Equipped with the head of a fugitive Qin general, a map showing a gift of territory, and a poisoned dagger, Jing Ke traveled to Xianyang with the intention of taking the future emperor prisoner or killing him. Apparently

> Jing Ke took out the map, unrolled it, and exposed the dagger. Seizing the sleeve of the Qin ruler with his left hand, Jing Ke grasped the dagger with the right and struck at him. In alarm the intended victim leapt backwards so that his sleeve tore off. Though he tried hard, Zheng was unable to draw his sword, which was very long. So Jing Ke chased him round a pillar, while the astounded courtiers looked on, rooted to the ground. In Qin law a courtier was forbidden to carry weapons and the royal guard was not permitted to enter the audience chamber unless summoned. At this critical

point there was no time to call for the soldiers anyway. Thus Jing Ke chased Zheng who tried to ward off the dagger blows with his two joined hands. At this juncture the court physician, one Xia Wuzu, struck Jing Ke with his medicine bag. Zheng, however, continued to dash round and round the pillar, so distraught was he. Then a courtier shouted: "Put your sword behind you, Your Majesty!" By doing so, he found he could unsheathe the weapon and wound Jing Ke in the thigh. Disabled, Jing Ke threw his dagger but missed. Thus it was that the assassin died, not the ruler of Qin.

The brush with death marked Zheng, who "was not at ease for a long time." Except for Xia Wuzu, whom he rewarded with gold, his courtiers had not rallied to the defense. The psychological impact of Jing Ke's attack was reinforced by two other violent assaults. In 219 BC a blind musician tried to strike Qin Shi Huang Di's head with a lead-filled harp, and in the ensuing year a third would-be assassin ambushed the wrong carriage. Besides increasing his dread of dying and spurring on fruitless searches for a drug of deathlessness, these encounters led to his final aloofness from all but a small circle of advisors and indirectly abetted the intrigues so disastrous to the dynasty on his death in 210 BC.

Although the Qin dynasty was of short duration, such was the energy of its founder that this period represents a turning point in Chinese history, for the bureaucratic form of government developed under the Qin emperors became the model for future Chinese political organization, lasting until the beginning of the twentieth century. The significance of the sweeping change that Qin Shi Huang Di began must not be underestimated, as Chinese civilization flowered within the framework of a unified empire, its greatest cultural achievements almost invariably the work of educated officials and scholars who spent time in the various imperial capitals. If Qin Shi Huang Di did nothing else, he demonstrated to the Chinese people the value of unity. Since his accession the country has been united for a longer period than it has been divided, thus making China an exception to the rule that in the pre-modern era large states do not endure.

Yet Qin Shi Huang Di was not unopposed in Xianyang. When, in 213 BC, he discovered that his edicts drew criticism from the scholar-gentry, he listened to the advice of Li Si, who in reply to the Confucian contention that nothing would last which was not modeled on antiquity, said:

In the past the Empire was divided. Because there was no emperor, the feudal lords were active and in order to confuse the people they harped on antiquity. Now Your Majesty rules a united empire in which distinctions of right and wrong are as clear as your own unapproachable authority. But there are those who unofficially propagate teachings directed against imperial decrees and orders. When they hear of new instructions, they criticize them in the light of their own teachings. At court they only dare to disagree in their minds, but in the streets they openly criticize your commands. To cast disrepute on their ruler they look upon as a duty; to adhere to contrary views they consider a virtue. The people are thus encouraged to be disrespectful. If this slander is not stopped, the imperial authority will decline and factionalism ensue. Your servant therefore requests that all persons possessing works of literature and discussions of the philosophers should destroy them. Those who have not destroyed them within thirty days after the issuing of the order are to be branded and work as convicts. Books to be spared from destruction will be those on medicine, agriculture, and divination. As for the persons who wish to study, let them take the officials as their teachers.

Qin Shi Huang Di approved the recommendation and the book burning occurred so as to "make the people ignorant" and to prevent "the use of the past to discredit the present." Even though Li Si's proposal was nothing less than an attempt to make knowledge an imperial monopoly, the proscription of books in Qin was not new. Shang Yang had already recommended this policy. What both he and Li Si wanted to do was to bring scholars under state control and thereby create a total conformity of political and intellectual outlook. They did not intend to destroy all scholarly traditions, since copies of proscribed books were deposited in the imperial library, but they had no tolerance for arguments aimed at curtailing a ruler's authority.

In spite of the early collapse of the Qin dynasty, the infamous burning of the books had a real effect on China. When, in 206 BC, the rebel army burned Xianyang, the conflagration engulfed the imperial collection of books and in many cases destroyed the sole surviving copies. The loss caused a definite break in consciousness, for when, under the patronage of the Former Han emperors, ancient texts were painfully reconstructed from memory and the badly tattered copies hidden at great personal risk, the feudal age seemed historically remote. Further opposition in 212 BC persuaded Qin Shi Huang Di to conduct a purge of scholars and 460 were condemned to be buried alive. Not even the protest of Crown Prince Fu Su could stem the rising tide of his fury at "alchemists who have wasted millions without obtaining any elixir and scholars who said that the dragon throne lacked virtue."

Li Si's motive for supporting the banishment of Fu Su was personal anxiety, which was skillfully exploited by the chief eunuch Zhao Gao.

Because he was unwilling to risk demotion, Li Si acquiesced in the installation of the worthless younger son Hu Hai as the second Qin emperor, Er Shi Huang Di, and pandered to Hu Hai's lust for power. In 209 BC Li Si told the new emperor: "The intelligent ruler makes decisions solely himself and does not let his authority lie in the hands of his ministers." Only then could he "devote himself to using the empire for his own pleasures."

The circumstances of Qin Shi Huang Di's death gave Li Si and Zhao Gao their chance. Having on a tour of inspection a dream of a sea god interpreted as an evil spirit keeping him from contact with the Immortals, Qin Shi Huang Di roamed the shore of Shandong province until he dispatched what was most likely a stranded whale with a repeater crossbow. Shortly afterwards he sickened and died, but Li Si and Zhao Gao suppressed the news and brought the imperial litter back to Xianyang behind a cartload of moldering fish in order to disguise the stench of the corpse. As a result of the terror inspired by the imperial title, there was neither an onlooker to question these arrangements for the homeward journey, nor on arrival in the capital an official to oppose the forged will they used to elevate Hu Hai. Neither of the conspirators, however, gained permanently from their actions. Zhao Gao engineered Li Si's execution in 208 BC, and in the ensuing year forced Er Shi Huang Di to take his own life, but the usurpation then attempted by the scheming eunuch was blocked. We are told:

> After Er Shi Huang Di had been at the Wangli palace for three days, Zhao Gao summoned the guard and commanded the soldiers to put on ordinary clothes. He then entered the palace and informed the emperor that bandits had arrived from the mountains. Having climbed up to a pavilion, Er Shi Huang Di saw the soldiers dressed in ordinary clothes and, believing them to be the bandits, he was overcome with fear. Zhao Gao seized the opportunity to force him to commit suicide. Then Zhao Gao took the imperial seal and hung it from his belt. But no official would accept his usurpation, and when he went to the audience chamber, three of them offered him harm. Realizing that Heaven had refused to grant him the mandate to rule the empire, and that the imperial bureaucracy would not cooperate with his desire, Zhao Gao summoned a nephew of Er Shi Huang Di and handed over the imperial seal.

Afterwards Zhao Gao strove to maintain his own position as best he could. He advised the new ruler to be content with the title of king, as Qin was once again one state among several. "Not until he became ruler of all the Chinese states did Qin Shi Huang Di assume imperial authority," Zhao

Gao said. "Now that these states have reasserted their independence and our territory has shrunk accordingly, it would be improper to retain an empty dignity."

Not that it really mattered which title was chosen. Early in 206 BC Qin Shi Huang Di's hapless nephew was the prisoner of Liu Bang, the first of the rebel leaders to reach Xianyang. The subsequent arrival of the main rebel force under the nobleman Xiang Yu brought death to the entire imperial family in the sack of Xianyang.

The violence was unprecedented. Liu Bang had treated the inhabitants of the surrendered imperial capital with restraint, forbidding his men from plundering its riches or taking captives. The devastation of spring 206 BC, and the subsequent division of China between the rebel leaders, was beyond Liu Bang's prevention, but in 203 BC he was ready to make a bid for the dragon throne. He blamed Xiang Yu for the unnecessary assault on Xianyang: "You fired the Qin palaces, you desecrated Qin Shi Huang Di's tomb, you stole the imperial treasure, and you executed the king of Qin, who had already surrendered. Your arrogance has plunged China into great turmoil." This accusation, and Liu Bang's subsequent occupation of the Wei River valley, took Xiang Yu by surprise.

Appreciating the advantages of the Wei River valley, its protective mountain ranges, and its fertile soil, Liu Bang used Qin as his base and from it repeated Qin Shi Huang Di's conquest of all China. While Xiang Yu dashed from one place to another in order to maintain his authority, and at the same time constantly suffered a shortage of supplies, Liu Bang drew on the agricultural resources of his stronghold, and awaited his opponent's collapse. This came in 202 BC. Never defeated on the battlefield, Xiang Yu found to his dismay that he had frittered away his strength. His belligerent attitude had cost him all support by the time he died that year in a cavalry engagement.

Thus humble Liu Bang outlasted aristocratic Xiang Yu. At the time it could not be foreseen that China under Liu Bang's dynasty would become a society divided by literacy, a prerequisite of success in the examination system for public office that his successors developed in order to recruit men of talent to manage the empire. Liu Bang, who adopted on his accession as the first Han emperor the title Gaozu, "High Ancestor," was barely literate himself. Yet as a result of his policies the fundamental social distinction in imperial times was always between the rulers and the ruled, between the educated gentry from which the officials were drawn and the peasants who could not read or write. The ruling class, however, was neither closed nor unchanging. Old families lost ground during the Former Han, while Later Han society was even more open to the rise of new ones. Below the ruling class were the mass of the peasants, living in villages, working owned or share-crop land, paying rents and taxes, providing manpower for public works and the army, surviving at subsistence level. The opening up of new lands, together with improvements in agricultural techniques, raised the population to fifty-three million, a total in excess of the Roman Empire.

Histories recall the distinctive physiognomy of Liu Bang, his prominent nose, "dragon forehead" and "the seventy-two black moles on his left thigh," as well as the scaly dragon that appeared to his mother at his conception, but they can neither disguise a peasant background nor a dislike of the excessive ceremony attached to learning. When some scholars came to him in formal costume, prior to his final victory in 202 BC, Liu Bang seized one of their elaborate hats and urinated in it. Yet this behavior was moderate in comparison with Xiang Yu's cruelty, for the good reason that Liu Bang knew how war-torn China yearned for peace. In order to set up a sound administration he turned for help to Confucian scholars untarnished by service under the Qin dynasty, a decision influenced by his court chamberlain Lu Jia. Dismissing quotations from history books as useless, the new emperor once commented on the fact that he had conquered the empire on horseback. Lu Jia replied: "That is correct, but Your Majesty will not be able to govern the Empire on horseback. If Qin had governed with humanity and righteousness, if it had followed the precepts of the sages, then Han would not have gained the Empire." At this Liu Bang blanched and said, "Explain to me the reasons for the fall of Qin and the rise of Han, as well as that which won and lost kingdoms of old." In obedience to this imperial wish, the chamberlain wrote a book about statecraft, and when Liu Bang listened to the Lu Jia reading aloud from it, he praised the ideas strongly. To bring order to the daily life of the imperial palace he asked Lu Jia to work out a new court ceremonial for his boisterous followers. His only instruction was "Make it easy."

Liu Bang's mildness seems to have been a genuine part of his character, a singular virtue in what was a violent age, and it made his rule popular. People felt he governed in their interests, unlike the dictatorial rulers of Qin. On the throne he neither aped aristocratic manners nor slackened his compassion for his poorer subjects, and his habit of squatting down, coupled with an earthy vocabulary, unsettled polite courtiers and accentuated the kindly attitude of the people towards him. But Liu Bang had the wit to appreciate the need for educated assistance even before Lu Jia explained to him the problems involved in ruling effectively.

During his struggle against Xiang Yu he relied on the organizational skills of Xiao He in the difficult task of supplying his army. When the fighting was over and the dynasty founded, Liu Bang awarded him the top rank in his court, despite the protests of other followers, who pointed out that Xiao He "never rode sweaty steeds in battle, but sat with brush and ink deliberating on questions of state rather than fighting." Liu Bang's obliged them to accept Xiao He's elevation and "his privilege of wearing a sword and shoes when he entered the audience chamber, and his exemption from the duty of hurrying when he was inside the palace."

This new imperial residence, the Eternal Palace, was situated in the southwestern corner of Former Han Chang'an. A second palace, to its east, was an expansion of a Qin summer resort and irregular in shape. Both were enclosed by earthen ramparts, as the new imperial capital still lacked a city wall. The Eternal Palace formed roughly a square, its east and west walls measuring 2,150 meters in length, its north and south 2,250 meters: the enclosed area was 5 square kilometers, about one-seventh the size of Chang'an itself. Xiao He was responsible for building the Eternal Palace, along with an arsenal and a storehouse.

Upon his return from his disastrous campaign against the Xiongnu, the ever-humble Liu Bang was livid about the size of the new palace. Xiao He managed to deflect his anger by pointing out the need for a Son of Heaven to demonstrate his authority by dwelling in magnificence. He also showed Liu Bang the newly built arsenal, recent excavation of which has revealed a two-court structure with extensive warehouses and offices, plus a very strong defensive wall.

Liu Bang, the Former Han dynasty founder, had settled for a political compromise after the repression of Qin rule: he allowed the restoration of certain feudal houses and granted fiefs to his own close relations, but these diminished holdings were intertwined with districts controlled by imperial officials. Although Liu Bang realized that Qin policy was correct in reducing everything "in a uniform manner," he was hesitant in his approach to government, for then China remained a confederation of recently independent states with still vigorous regional cultures. By rejecting the Legalism that underpinned Qin autocracy, though, Liu Bang paved the way for the emergence of a bureaucratic empire organized along Confucian lines. It is not a little ironic that the totalitarianism of Qin Shi Huang Di should be replaced by the Celestial Empire so admired by the European Enlightenment. "A remarkable fact and quite worthy as marking a difference from the West," the Jesuit missionary Matteo Ricci was to write seventeen hundred years later, "is that the entire kingdom is administered by the Order of the Learned, the Philosophers. The whole responsibility for orderly management of the entire realm is wholly and completely in their charge and care."

In reaction to Qin despotism, the Han system of government was based on the principle that no one person should have unlimited authority, and that all actions including those of the ruler should be open to scrutiny.

When the Eternal Palace was completed, Liu Bang summoned nobles and officials to a sumptuous reception in its front hall. There he raised his jade cup and proposed a toast to his father with these words: "You, my father, always used to consider me a worthless fellow who could never look after the family fortunes and had not the industry of my older brother. Now that my labors are over, which of us has accomplished most?" All present laughed and shouted "Long life!"

Their wish was not to be granted. In 195 BC, an arrow wound gave Liu Bang blood poisoning from which he died. Before announcing a period of mourning, his wife Empress Lu was frightened enough about the safety of the dynasty to propose the execution of Liu Bang's leading followers, as they like the deceased emperor had "all made their way up from the ranks of the common people" and were unlikely to acknowledge "a young master," his fifteen-year-old son. When this drastic proposal became known, the empress was compelled to admit her widowhood and immediately enthrone the young Hui Di. He ruled under Empress Lu's shadow until his early death in 188 BC. This formidable woman issued edicts on her own authority and did away with at least one puppet emperor during her regency, which lasted for another eight years after Hui Di's death. Learning that the first child emperor threatened to make trouble for her when he grew up, she gave out that he was gravely ill and unable to see any official. Then this puppet emperor was replaced by a second one who also failed to outlive her. The enlightened state system erected by Liu Bang could not prevent Empress Lu from becoming powerful, especially when many of Liu Bang's followers admired her contribution in establishing the dynasty, but it meant she was unable to act entirely on her own. She had to consult her officials when she changed child emperors.

Empress Lu herself died of a dog bite in 180 BC. Returning from a religious ceremony held outside Chang'an, Empress Lu was attacked by a blue dog, which disappeared after savagely biting her. Back in the Eternal Palace, a diviner called to interpret the event told the empress that the dog was "the ghost of a lord, turned into an evil spirit." She had in fact just starved to death a nobleman who preferred a concubine to his wife, who was a relation of Empress Lu. Consumed with jealousy, this woman slandered her husband to the empress dowager, alleging a plot against the imperial government. Now in great pain from the dog bite Empress Lu was convinced of her own end, which she believed had already been signaled in

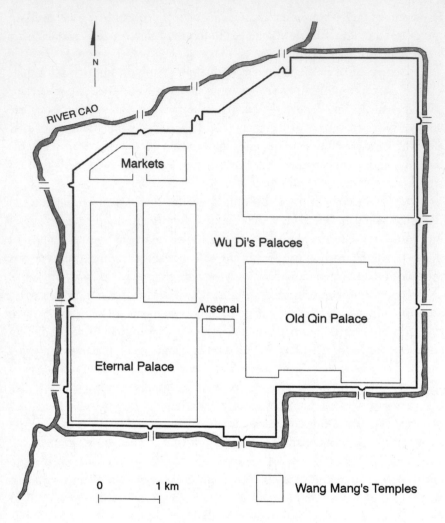

Map of the site of former Han Chang'an

a solar eclipse. On her deathbed she appointed two members of her family to the most senior official positions.

Encouraged by these promotions, the Lu family decided to destroy the Liu imperial house, but their plans were thwarted by Liu Bang's three surviving sons. They hunted down "the men and women of the Lu family and, without distinction of age or youth, beheaded them all." Styled kings, these brothers still held eastern fiefs that Liu Bang had awarded to members of the imperial family.

Empress Lu's successor, Wen Di, the fourth of Liu Bang's eight sons, was the first of the Former Han emperors to reign for longer than a decade.

His twenty-three-year reign provided the empire with a sense of continuity that it had previously lacked. Dynastic stability was further reinforced by the peaceful accession, in 156 BC, of his son Jing Di. And we are told that Wen Di "set an example in the simplicity of his way of life. In preparing his burial place he had pottery vessels throughout, not allowing gold, silver, copper, or tin to be used for ornamentation, and he did not have a mound raised over the tomb." What a contrast this funeral frugality was to the megalomania at Mount Li, where Qin Shi Huang Di had buried an army of life-size terracotta warriors, whose individually modeled faces were nothing less than actual portraits of men belonging to his personal body-guard.

Just how great was the importance attached to the welfare of the dead can be gauged in the strange, twenty-seven-day reign of Liu Ho, a grandson of the later emperor Wu Di. The successor of Jing Di, Wu Di had only three sons who survived him. This thinning out of the imperial clan meant that in the summer of 74 BC, when Wu Di's youngest son and successor Zao Di died childless, the highest officials summoned Liu Ho to the imperial capital by means of fire-beacons. In his enthusiasm to become the next ruler, the nineteen-year-old Liu Ho galloped all the way from his fief in present-day Shandong province to Chang'an. He and his friends rode a string of horses to death and, on their arrival in the imperial capital, Liu Ho forgot to observe the period of mourning prescribed for his predecessor. Instead of weeping as heir to the dragon throne, he was unable to control his excitement and threw extravagant parties in the Eternal Palace. Even worse, Liu Ho postponed visiting the ancestral temple of the dynasty's founder, Liu Bang, an absolutely essential feature of an imperial succession. Partying without thought for the proprieties of imperial ancestor worship, the teenage emperor sent out his close companions for chickens and pork when palace officials refused to assist him in breaking the taboo of a mourning fast. These officials were equally appalled at Liu Ho's importation of women, again brought in by his friends, flush with gold from the imperial treasury. Anyone who protested at this reckless behavior was warned to keep silent or suffer imprisonment. The height of insensibility, however, was to turn the Eternal Palace into a pleasure resort while his predecessor's coffin still stood there awaiting entombment.

To put a stop to this scandalous insult to the empire's customs, the experienced minister Huo Guang called the most senior officials together and proposed the removal of Liu Ho. A precedent for this unusual act was thought to be the decision by one of King Tang's ministers to imprison the unworthy successor of this great Shang ruler for three years, until he mended his ways. Once the wayward successor had repented his misbehavior, he was released from a prison situated near King Tang's tomb and restored to power. The officials were astounded at the proposal to dethrone Liu Ho, and did not dare to say anything until one of Huo Guang's closest colleagues threatened to kill anyone who spoke against it. Thereupon they agreed unanimously.

To accomplish the dethronement without arousing Liu Ho's suspicions, he was lured out of his private quarters by his mother, who technically had a degree of authority over him. Separated by the eunuchs from his companions, who were subsequently imprisoned, Liu Ho was received by his mother in the throne room, where she was attended by several hundred armed men. Then the officials filed into the chamber according to their rank and Liu Ho was ordered to prostrate himself and hear the proceedings. A memorial signed by Huo Guang and all the senior officials was read out, which listed the emperor's failings one by one, including his seduction of palace maids. When the reading got to this point, Liu Ho's mother cried out, "Stop. How could any subject or a son of mine behave in such a disorderly manner?" Then the official who was reading the memorial continued to its telling end, the point that Liu Ho had not yet bothered to present himself at the ancestral temple of Liu Bang so as to receive the heavenly mandate to rule. As he had also shown how unfit he was to continue the imperial line and maintain the sacrifices to the imperial ancestors, it was recommended that he should be dismissed and this news conveyed to the imperial ancestral temple. Then Huo Guang ordered Liu Ho to rise, bow, and accept the edict. When the baffled young emperor tried to protest, the imperial seals were forcibly taken from him and he was led away. Afterwards Liu Ho was stripped of all his titles and banished to his fief, where his sisters were given charge of his property. Years later, when he had proved to be utterly harmless, he was awarded one of the lower noble ranks.

This peaceful handling of dynastic discord is impressive in comparison with Empress Lu's violent methods. Perhaps Liu Ho's mother knew her son too well to do other than assist in his immediate deposition. She felt that she had no choice but go along with the plans of her grandfather Huo Guang. That the minister was prepared to abandon a ruler so closely related to himself reveals the real offense Liu Ho had caused at Chang'an through his utter disregard for in the rites of ancestor worship. It highlights, too, the power wielded by officials like Huo Guang, whose female relations had married into the imperial family. The minister, who died in 68 BC, was given a magnificent funeral: he was allowed a suit of jade, a burial item usually reserved for members of the imperial family. An imperial edict noted how Huo Guang had facilitated the smooth succession of the infant emperor Zhao Di following the unrest at the close of Wu Di's reign and acted as a loyal assistant to the current emperor Xuan Di, thereby giving "peace to the Ancestral Imperial Temple." The favor Xuan Di continued to show the Huo family, and especially Huo Guang's son, appears to have been its undoing. More demonstrative than the deceased minister, the Huo family members in high office soon united officials and courtiers alike in criticism of their arrogance and ostentation. Even the emperor came to see the folly of the family, which was eventually removed from office and eliminated.

On his accession as emperor in 141 BC the sixteen-year-old Wu Di met none of the opposition that had toppled the irreverent Liu Ho. Even more remarkable is the length of Wu Di's reign, which at fifty-four years it is one of the longest in Chinese imperial history. For the Former Han dynasty it represented a new departure in that consolidation gave way to expansion and reorganization. Efforts were made to improve the administration of the empire, reinforce control of its inhabitants, improve the economy, increase state revenues, and strengthen border defenses.

The chief problem was security. Along the northern frontier the Great Wall had ceased to be adequate against nomad attack, the raids of the Xiongnu becoming such a serious threat that China went over to the offensive between 134 and 91 BC. The emperor, whose title Wu Di means "Warrior Emperor," launched a series of campaigns to outflank and ultimately crush the Xiongnu. While these nomads were driven deep into the Gobi desert, other Chinese forces moved westwards into the Tarim basin, now a part of Xinjiang province. In 121 BC a favorite commander of Wu Di by the name of Huo Quling achieved the impossible when, after a six-day advance across the steppe with a cavalry force, he captured the Xiongnu leader and 40,000 of his followers. So pleased was the emperor with this exploit that on Huo Quling's early death five years later at the age of twenty-four, he accorded the general the honor of a state funeral adjacent to the imperial tombs north of Chang'an. On an artificial hill raised above the grave were placed a variety of stone carvings, executed by craftsmen in the imperial workshops. The purpose of these fabulous beasts, monsters, and horses trampling nomads was the perpetuation of Huo Quling's victories through the attraction of benevolent spirits.

The Chinese movement into Central Asia resulted from Zhang Qian's missions there. In 139 BC he was first dispatched to stir up the enemies of the Xiongnu, the Da Yuezhi, later known in India as the Kushan. Under pressure from the Xiongnu, they had migrated westwards, crossed the Oxus (or Amu Darya) River, and conquered the whole area up to the Hindu Kush. Unlike the Hunnish Xiongnu, the Da Yuezhi were not all pastoral nomads in their original homeland to the north of the Great Wall, and in the fertile valley of the Oxus most of them settled down as farmers. Unable to persuade them to ally themselves with China, Zhang Qian finally returned to Chang'an where the imperial court was staggered to hear about the existence of another settled community.

What most interested Wu Di in Zhang Qian's account of his travels were the large horses he had noticed, because they could be used to carry heavily armed men against the Xiongnu, who rode the smaller Mongolian pony. In 115 BC Zhang Qian was sent out again, this time on a diplomatic mission to the horse-breeding peoples of Central Asia. As a result one of the chieftains living near Lake Balkhash, in modern Kazakhstan, asked for the hand of a Chinese princess and sent a thousand horses as a betrothal present. The chieftain was given Liu Xijun, a princess of the imperial blood, who set off with a large retinue for the distant land. Ever since, the homesickness of the princess has proved a fascinating subject for painters as well as poets: she who yearned "to be the yellow swan that returns to its home." Wu Di soon became dissatisfied with indirect contacts and after a three-year campaign a Chinese general succeeded in conquering the Fergana basin and securing enough horses for stud purposes.

But Wu Di's northern war was never a great success. The problems he encountered in campaigning of the steppe are graphically illustrated in the surrender of one of the best Han field commanders, Li Ling. With a force of five thousand picked infantry, he was stationed near Dunhuang with the duty of defending the line of the extended Great Wall. When in 99 BC an advance was ordered against the Xiongnu, Li Ling got permission to mount a separate raid, although there was no cavalry immediately available to support him. Always before this occasion the Chinese had attacked the nomads on horseback, but Li Ling thought the crossbow, an ancient Chinese invention, would offer sufficient protection against the nomadic composite bow made from wood and horn. Wu Di seems to have appreciated Li Ling's need for protection and ordered a cavalry commander to meet him halfway on his return. Because this man held the rank of general, while Li Ling was only a chief commandant, he protested that such cooperation would make him appear subordinate to Li Ling.

Through the confusion caused by this dispute about rank Li Ling's force had to fight 30,000 Xiongnu horsemen on its own. When Li Ling positioned his crossbowmen behind a wall of shields and spears, the effect of their fire was devastating and several thousand Xiongnu fell before they fled. If Li Ling had chosen to withdraw at once to the line of the Great Wall, he would have probably saved his tiny force. A pursuit of the fleeing

Xiongnu left it dangerously exposed to a counter-attack, which soon came with the arrival of more nomad-archers. With crossbow bolts running low, Li Ling ordered his men to find their way back to China as best they could. Only 400 soldiers reached the safety of the Great Wall, Li Ling himself being taken prisoner. The Xiongnu had been informed by a Chinese traitor that there was no hope of cavalrymen coming to support Li Ling, and had screwed up their courage to attack once again.

When the news of the Xiongnu victory reached Chang'an, Wu Di hoped that Li Ling had died with his men, as was customary in the imperial army. Later Wu Di was furious on hearing of Li Ling's surrender to the Xiongnu. The historian-official Sima Qian wrote a memorial defending Li Ling, but the emperor took a different view and Sima Qian was charged with attempting to deceive the throne. After a perfunctory trial he was castrated. Eventually Wu Di recognized how he himself was to blame for not insisting that a cavalry column went to Li Ling's aid. The emperor sent for the chief commandant, but he refused to return to China and so his family was destroyed. For Sima Qian the whole sequence of events was a terrible humiliation, which must explain the absence of any direct discussion of Wu Di in his monumental history. That he refused to make a large payment to the imperial treasury in order to commute the punishment means that he was prepared to accept castration rather than impoverish his near relations.

Sima Qian's *Historical Records* is the first general account of China's history. It deals only with the knowable past. Sima Qian knew that mankind existed long before he began his narrative, but he refrained from speculation or comment on the grounds that the sources to hand were untrustworthy. Another characteristic that deserves sober notice is the unofficial nature of the *Historical Records*. Sima Qian compiled his history as a private person, in spite of his duty as a court astrologer to note any coincidence between the ruler's actions and natural phenomena, eclipses, comets, unseasonable falls of hail, drought, and floods; all these found their way into Sima Qian's writing, but for him the historical focus always remained the quality of the imperial government. What interested Sima Qian in 178 BC was the response of Wen Di to solar and lunar eclipses. This emperor said,

> I have been entrusted with the protection of the ancestral temples and, with my frail person, placed in a position above the common people, the nobles, and the feudal rulers. The order and disorder of the entire empire rests upon me, a single man, and upon the two or three ministers who, like arms and legs, assist me. But I have not succeeded in bringing order and aid to living creatures, so great is my lack of virtue!

This public acceptance of personal guilt is amazing. Equally surprising was the request the emperor then made for "all to give thought to my errors and consider in what way I have fallen short in understanding, vision, and ideas." He also called to Chang'an "wise and upright men who will speak frankly and reprimand me, that I may repair my shortcomings."

It could well be argued that Wen Di's sense of inadequacy helped to establish the Chinese system of bureaucratic government. Unlike other ancient rulers, no Chinese emperor ever considered the state to be his private property after the totalitarianism of Qin. The repressiveness of Qin taught China to distrust despots, with the result that Former Han emperors were frequently reminded that they were the inheritors of an empire founded by Liu Bang, the first ruler to summon "men of wisdom" and "men of virtue" to help in its administration. Even though Wen Di continued this practice, it was Wu Di's urgent need for reliable administrators to oversee his policies that really led to its permanent establishment. From 135 BC onwards would-be civil servants were expected to prove their abilities by answering questions which were set, in theory, by the emperor himself. Thus began the system of imperial examinations, the ultimate origin of present-day public testing. Its transfer to the world at large occurred in the nineteenth century. As Robert Inglis, a British resident in China, correctly noted in 1835: "The East India Company have adopted the principle and the full development in India of this Chinese invention is destined one day, perhaps, like those of gunpowder and printing, to work another great change in the states-system even of Europe."

Wu Di's interest in examination answers extended to individual grades, for he would revise the pass list whenever he spotted someone whose ideas he liked. The emperor also accepted a suggestion to found an imperial university in which the cleverest provincial students could study alongside the sons of top officials. The number of students was restricted to fifty under Wu Di, but it rose to ten thousand during Wang Mang's usurpation, and still more under the Later Han emperors. The curriculum of the imperial university entrenched Confucianism in government service, as there was a chair for each of the five classics—the *Book of Changes*, the *Book of History*, the *Book of Odes*, the *Book of Rites*, and the *Spring and Autumn Annals*. Wu Di proclaimed Confucianism as the recognized state cult. However, the revised form of Confucianism that Wu Di endorsed drew on both Legalist and Daoist concepts, not least because the emperor was unwilling to act as a passive ruler and he never abandoned his ambition of attracting the Immortals.

On Chang'an itself the emperor had visibly stamped his own authority with the construction of two new palaces, taking over large parts of the imperial capital. Although manpower shortages prevented him from under-taking all the projects he had in mind, a third palace was eventually com-pleted outside the city walls. Having concurred with Dong Zhongshu's pro-posed elevation of Confucius, Wu Di paid great attention to the ceremonies involved in the Sage of Lu's cult. Officials advised him to build a new hall for the worship of Heaven in Chang'an, but the emperor preferred to use the one on Mount Tai, where he could combine at one auspicious site both his Confucian and his Daoist rituals. Former Han Chang'an was now basi-cally complete, the only significant additions at the end of the dynasty being the temples commissioned by Wang Mang just outside its southern wall.

Between 92 and 90 BC the imperial capital was the scene of incredible unrest. Fear of black magic, and the hysterical response it evoked at the imperial court, led to the execution or enforced suicide of senior officials and members of the imperial family, while in the streets large numbers of people were killed in the fighting that broke out. The trouble started at Chang'an when Wu Di ordered a ten-day search for objects used in black magic. To prevent the escape of anyone connected with this sorcery the gates of Chang'an were kept closed. Whether or not the search turned up anything at all we do not know, but shortly afterwards arrests and execu-tions began. Some three hundred people were condemned to death, one of whom was the emperor's own daughter, accused of using witchcraft upon him. The sixty-six-year-old Wu Di, now hopelessly ill and impressionable, was at the mercy of those who reported such dark deeds. He seems to have been quite unaware that the growing turmoil was a consequence of rivalry between the families of his six consorts. By starting the practice of entrust-ing power to the relatives of his favorite women, Wu Di had sown the seeds of the dynasty's downfall.

The situation was made worse by the absence of the emperor from Chang'an. When the heir apparent was also accused of black magic, he felt that his only chance of survival was to seize power for himself. Soldiers sta-tioned in the imperial capital rallied to his cause, as did his numerous fol-lowers who were issued with weapons from the armory. The struggle between the emperor and the crown prince was decided by the refusal of the inspector of the northern armies to sanction the crown prince's use of their troops. Not that this military official got any thanks for his loyalty: Wu Di later accused him of waiting on events, and he was duly beheaded. In the meantime the heir apparent gained control of the imperial capital but, realizing that there was no possibility of holding Chang'an, he fled and later committed suicide. What he had no wish to suffer was the lingering death, a punishment that kept traitors alive over a number of days in order to inflict maximum pain. If the dreadful events in Chang'an exposed anything about imperial rule, it was the yawning gap between the Confucian ideal of moral government and the reality of political conflict inside the Eternal Palace.

The years immediately after Wu Di's death were a virtual regency of Huo Guang, the guardian of the infant emperor Zhao Di, who was only eight years old. Just before he passed away in 87 BC, Wu Di had selected his youngest son as his heir and given the minister full control of the imperial government. There was no constitutional provision for a regency, except for one by close relatives of an infant ruler. The choice of Huo Guang was fortunate for the Former Han dynasty, as the minister understood the workings of the imperial administration.

By the time young Zhao Di died childless in 74 BC the Chinese empire had largely recovered its strength. Another factor contributing to dynastic stability was the final victory of Confucianism over rival philosophical schools, an almost inevitable consequence of the promotion of graduates from the imperial university. From the moment Huo Guang sent the superintendent of the Eternal Palace to prepare Zhao Di's successor for his elevation to the dragon throne, the new emperor Xuan Di had cause to be thankful for the loyalty that Confucius's teachings encouraged. The superintendent respectfully "bathed his body, washed his hair, and dressed him in clothes taken from the imperial wardrobe," before Xuan Di was conveyed in a chariot to the palace, where he received "the imperial seal and sealcords and ascended the dragon throne, after paying his respects in the Temple of Gaozu," (Gaozu being the imperial title of dynasty founder-emperor Liu Bang).

Before the end of Xuan Di's reign in 49 BC all senior officials had undergone a Confucian training. Their common approach to running the imperial administration was valued by Xuan Di, but he was aware of the shortcomings of the Confucian emphasis on benevolent rule. The Later Han historian Ban Gu tells us how he reminded the heir apparent that the laws and customs of China derived from more than one school of philosophy. Xuan Di said that the Confucian principle of using moral persuasion to maintain order was unrealistic without punishment for those who refused to behave properly. The advice was well given, as his son Yuan Di was brought up in the Eternal Palace and had little contact with the outside world. When he came to the throne, Yuan Di immediately ignored this advice and initiated a whole series of Confucian reforms, which his successors were pleased to develop even more. This development later obliged the usurper Wang Mang to adopt all sorts of Confucian practices as he tried to secure public approval by being more Confucian than any of the Former Han emperors.

Wang Mang's family had been influential at the imperial court through marriage for two decades before his usurpation of the dragon throne. During the short reign of Ai Di, from 7 to 1 BC, the Wang family was in bitter competition with two other families, the Fu and the Ting, who were also maternal relatives of emperor Ai Di. This sickly young man attempted to imitate the strong government of Wu Di, but only succeeded in becoming the tool, first of his grandmother, the dowager empress Fu, and then of his constant companion, Dong Xian.

Dong Xian's meteoric rise and fall is an example of how a handsome, though worthless, young man could exploit imperial favor. After being made a gentleman by the emperor, this palace retainer soared upwards from one post to another and accumulated enormous wealth on the way. The infatuated emperor Ai Di had even proposed that he should abdicate in Dong Xian's favor. As it was, Dong Xian had already been entrusted with the construction of the emperor's tomb, a duty of immense ritual significance, while in the imperial court those who sought the emperor's favor adopted the fashion of the cut sleeve, henceforth an euphemism for homosexual passion. The fashion originated in a singular act of Ai Di himself. So great was his love for his favorite that, once when they were in bed together and the emperor wanted to get up, but found Dong Xian stretched across his sleeve, Ai Di cut it off rather than wake his lover. Their affair represents the high point in Chinese homosexuality. It by no means disappeared from either the imperial court or society at large, but never again would the Confucian emphasis on the importance of heterosexual marriage ever be so publicly challenged.

Dong Xian's temporary eclipse of the Wang family came to an end in 1 BC with the accession of Ping Di. A first cousin of Ai Di, this nine-year-old emperor was entirely under the control of Wang Mang, to whose daughter he was immediately married. Revenge was taken on the rival Fu and Ting families; their members were expelled from Chang'an and the empresses who had introduced them to positions of power in the Eternal Palace were posthumously downgraded in title to that of mother and concubine. In AD 5 Wang Mang had their tombs opened, their official seals removed and destroyed, and their bodies reburied in simple wooden coffins, like ordinary concubines. Even the mounds over their tombs were leveled and thorns planted there instead. Behind this drastic course of action may have been a desire to end the destructive squabbles of maternal relatives at the imperial court.

For that reason the sudden death of Ping Di would have taken Wang Mang by surprise. There was nothing to be gained in poisoning the young ruler, as his enemies liked to suggest had happened. If anyone other than a child sat on the dragon throne, Wang Mang's position could be threatened. He decided to risk the wrath of the imperial house by picking as Ping Di's successor the youngest of the possible candidates, the two-year-old Liu Ying. Although uprisings by imperial relatives swiftly ensued, Wang Mang easily defeated the insurgents, and his regency was accepted by practically all officials. He seems to have come to believe that the moment was right for a new dynasty, and to be fair to Wang Mang there were others who claimed such an event was about to happen. When auspicious omens were reported in AD 9, nothing stood in the way of Wang Mang's putting on the yellow robe and asserting his descent from the Yellow Emperor, that legendary paragon of virtue.

CHAPTER 3

A Restored Dynasty:
Later Han Luoyang

Here in Luoyang, what surging crowds!
Capped and belted ones forever rush
Along the narrow lanes and streets,
Avenues overflow with the mansions
Of princes and high officials,
While from afar silhouetted
Against the sky are the towers
Belonging to the two great palaces.

C HANG'AN ENJOYED A BRIEF REPRIEVE AS AN IMPERIAL CAPITAL UNDER
the Xin, the dynastic name which Wang Mang adopted in AD 9,
the year he finally ascended the dragon throne. The change in the
ambitious minister's status was accompanied by portents, hardly surprising
in light of the general expectation that the Han dynasty was coming to an
end. Because the rule of Qin, China's first imperial house, was so short-
lived, it was considered to have achieved supremacy without either securing
the heavenly mandate to rule or the assistance of the element of Water.
Constituting rather an interlude in the regular cycle of the Five Elements,
the reigns of Qin Shi Huang Di and his son Er Shi Huang Di were dismissed as an aberration, something quite outside the regular succession of
dynasties. Thus the Han dynasty now came to be regarded as the true successor of the Zhou kings, with a period of power that was calculated to end
in AD 4. When sixteen years earlier there was an eclipse of the sun on New
Year's day, followed by thunder without clouds in springtime and the
appearance of Haley's comet in the autumn, the imperial court became agi-
tated. The opinion of a leading interpreter of portents did nothing to still
its worries: he declared that the element of Earth was in the process of dis-

placing Water, the cosmic force on which the Han dynasty was said to rely. Added to the concern of the imperial house was the fact that its last three emperors had died without producing heirs. People naturally saw this extraordinary circumstance as another sign of Heaven's growing indifference to the dynasty.

Had Wang Mang founded a lasting dynasty, Chinese historians would have accorded him the heavenly mandate to rule and detailed with sympathy the policies of his reign. But with the collapse of his administration and his violent death, Wang Mang automatically became a usurper who was blamed for a whole series of unfortunate decisions. In *The History of the Former Han* the bias of its author, Ban Gu, is obvious:

> Wang Mang by nature was touchy and hot-tempered and could not bring himself to let things alone. Every time there was something that he initiated or invented, he always tried to justify it by reference to ancient custom . . . But his new measures for currency . . . buying and selling . . . price control . . . and state monopolies . . . caused hardship and suffering. And when the wealthy were not able to protect themselves and the poor had no way of keeping themselves alive, they arose and became thieves and bandits . . . Before Wang Mang was executed the population of the empire was reduced by half.

In this telescoped version of the disruption apparently caused by Wang Mang's policies we are given, nevertheless, the real reasons of his fall. While there can be no doubt that his reform program stimulated opposition, the imperial bureaucracy remained a loyal supporter almost to the end of his reign. Ultimately it was widespread peasant unrest which brought about a change in allegiance, and then only after the abortive imperial campaign of AD 23 against the Green Woodsmen, a rebel army at large in present-day Hebei province. The sending of four hundred thousand troops into a famine area turned the rebellion into a disaster, for the empty state granaries there obliged the hungry soldiers to relieve the peasantry of what little food was left. Added to this misery were the violent attacks of the Xiongnu. Ban Gu tells us that "the nomads made a great raid. As soldiers in this emergency Wang Mang enrolled convicts, prisoners, and domestic slaves, and he temporarily taxed both officials and ordinary people, taking one-thirtieth of their property."

The counter-attack saved China, but the effects of drought and large-scale mobilization weakened Wang Mang's authority, especially when he started to confiscate land from rich families in order to redistribute it to those without any land at all. What he sought to limit was the excessive wealth of the largest landlords, whose holdings were then on the increase by leaps and bounds. He also tried to alleviate the distress of the peasant-farmers, who were obliged to sell their land and pledge their service to the rich during famine years. The buying and selling of land was banned, and low-interest government loans were advanced to poor peasants in order to buy tools and seeds.

Perhaps the innovation which annoyed the wealthy as much as his land policy was the restriction Wang Mang placed on slavery. An edict announced, "Male and female slaves are to be known as private followers. No longer may they be bought or sold." The lowest group in society, the enslaved were never a significant feature of ancient China, unlike in the Greco-Roman world. Exactly how many slaves existed in Wang Mang's reign is impossible to calculate from the surviving evidence, but the number was a low one. In 44 we know there were around 100,000 government slaves, the majority of whom were engaged in looking after livestock. Only convicts are mentioned as working in iron mining and manufacture. Compulsory labor on public works provided the manpower necessary for water-conservancy projects, grain transportation, even the constant repair of the Great Wall. Slaves possessed civil rights and could not be killed at will; officials frequently complained about the uselessness of government slaves who "idle with folded hands" in contrast to the hard-working peasants. In the end, however, Wang Mang abandoned as unworkable the prohibition on buying and selling slaves, and instead imposed a stiff annual tax on each slave owned.

That Wang Mang was aware of the rising discontent in the provinces there can be no question, but he seems to have been less well informed about the political situation in Chang'an itself. Officials who were concerned about the way in which Wang Mang's policies drained the Chinese empire's wealth found their advice ignored in the Eternal Palace, with the result that the initial support his rule had attracted from the imperial bureaucracy gradually drained away, too. Even more careless was the treatment he meted out to relations as he executed, or ordered the suicide, of three of his four sons: the eldest because of an intrigue that opposed his policies; the second, for killing a slave; and the third, because of an act of adultery had put him in a position where the son was afraid he would be executed if he did not first assassinate his father. In prison Wang Mang "granted poison to this son, but he was unwilling to drink it. Instead, he stabbed himself to death. Afterwards Wang Mang granted the spirit a kingly set of clothes" (At ceremonies held for the dead, it was customary to place garments on a special chair reserved for the spirit of the deceased). Wang Mang's fourth son, who was mentally unstable, died before his father. The loss of all his sons led people to think it was a judgment from Heaven, so that many who might have supported Wang Mang in a crisis now began to desert him.

Even though he was never the devious bungler described by Ban Gu, Wang Mang does seem to have lost his political touch once he mounted the dragon throne. Resistance to the radical measures he introduced was irresistible when famine and mismanaged relief drove north China into a rebellion which was legitimized by declaring a member of the deposed Liu family the restored Later Han emperor. Yet even before the arrival of the rebels at Chang'an, in late 23, Wang Mang displayed some of the character traits associated with Qin Shi Huang Di, whose enthusiasm for Daoism had so amazed his officials. When someone said,

> "The Yellow Emperor built a richly decorated canopy in order that he might rise up as an Immortal," Wang Mang ordered a similar one to be constructed in nine layers, twenty-five meters tall. It stood on a carriage, with four wheels, and was drawn by six horses and three hundred strong men. On the carriage there was a man beating a drum. Those who pulled it called out, "He will mount up to become an Immortal." When Wang Mang went out, he ordered the carriage to go before him. Many officials commented secretly, "This is more like a funeral cart than a vehicle for an Immortal."

After the construction of the "funeral cart," the reaction of Wang Mang to an omen advising remarriage was even stranger. On learning that "the Yellow Emperor attained immortality after he had taken to wife one hundred and twenty girls," we are told, "he sent out forty-five officials to search the empire and select for him the same number of virtuous young women." Here we have, just before his downfall, an attempt to strengthen his spirit by going to bed with a bevy of girls. Daoist speculation on the magical power of sexual relations was already well known in the imperial court. Apart from the chemical solution offered in the elixir of life, Daoists held that there were sexual techniques capable of attaining the same goal, an approach that obviously appealed to Wang Mang. Through the correct exercise of his "jade stalk," the imperial member itself, the worried ruler hoped to restore both his health and his prestige. From later biographies of sexually active Immortals we know that detailed handbooks on the art of the bedchamber were already in existence. A collection of biographies made in the second century refers to a Later Han woman who achieved immortality through such a handbook. Apparently

> the woman was a wine merchant, famous for the excellent quality of her wines. One day an Immortal happened to visit her shop and drank some wine. As a security for future payment, he left with her a book that explained the art of sustaining health through sexual intercourse. The woman copied out the key sections and prepared a special bedroom, so that the handsome young men who drank her wine could stay overnight and practice with her the things described in the book. When she had done this for over thirty years, she looked as if she were only twenty years old. Several years later the Immortal returned. Smiling at her, he said: "To steal the Way by studying it without a master is like having wings and still being unable to fly." Hearing this, the woman left the shop and went away with the Immortal, no one knows where.

For Wang Mang this option was unavailable, no matter how convinced he was two months before his overthrow that an ancestral spirit had visited the Eternal Palace with an invitation for him to become an Immortal. Increasingly cut off from events, and in control of little more than the imperial capital itself, he could only throw himself into the pursuit of sexual immortality while awaiting the arrival of the rebel army. This force reached Chang'an in the autumn of 23. Having ransacked his family tombs outside the city walls, the rebels broke into the imperial capital and an utterly exhausted Wang Mang fled to a high tower with a few officials and guards. There Wang Mang was hacked to pieces. Although the Eternal Palace suffered damage in the attack, the remainder of Chang'an was still unharmed. Within a month, though, the imperial capital changed hands again and its new masters, the Red Eyebrows, a Daoist-inspired rebel force, looted its riches and terrorized its inhabitants.

Ban Gu's terse comment on the fate of the Qin and the Xin dynasties was: "They came to the same end by different paths. They were both dragons who flew too high and whose breath Heaven's decree cut short." What he might have added, but chose not to do so, was the role played by rebellious peasants in bringing about Wang Mang's death. In the twentieth century Mao Zedong was sure that his own strategy of "encircling the cities with the countryside" would lead to a communist triumph, because he appreciated the revolutionary dynamic inherent in the agrarian revolts which had punctuated imperial history. Just as the Red Eyebrows were a contributory factor in the collapse of Wang Mang's authority, so in the 180s another Daoist-inspired rebel movement, the Yellow Turbans, would undermine the Later Han dynasty, already fragmented by palace intrigue in Luoyang.

Ever since the third century BC philosopher Mencius had extended the concept of righteous opposition to unjust government into the right of the people to take up arms against wicked rulers, Chinese political theory possessed a means of explaining dynastic change. Whenever a ruler lost the goodwill of his subjects and resorted to oppression, the heavenly mandate to rule was said to have been withdrawn and the ruler's replacement on the dragon throne by a more suitable candidate fully justified.

In 23 the loyalty still owed to the Liu family was sufficiently strong for the great families to rally behind Liu Xiu, better known by his imperial title of Guangwu Di. He was not the sole pretender, as eleven others claimed the right to don the yellow robe, and a complicated civil war was fought before he won through in 36. One of his firmest supporters, the general Ma Yuan, commented: "In present times, it is not only the emperor who selects his subjects. The subjects select their emperor, too."

Devoted to the restored dynasty though Ma Yuan was, his view of events indicates how Guangwu Di was much less independent than previous rulers, not least because he had to rely on the big landowners during the protracted struggle against rival pretenders. In 39 they prevented him for conducting a survey of cultivated land for the purposes of reassessing the land tax, a sign that feudalism was returning to China. The peasants were once again tied to the land, either as sharecroppers or laborers, while artisans and scholars were compelled to associate themselves with local magnets powerful enough to offer protection against bandits or rebellious soldiers. After the abolition of conscription in 46 the imperial government was entirely dependent on regular troops and the retainers of the great families, an underlying military weakness that explains the less aggressive policy adopted on the northern frontier. Later Han emperors could not achieve victories over the Xiongnu without the aid of friendly nomads.

Guangwu Di's imperial capital was indeed almost frugal in comparison with Former Han Chang'an, although with a walled area of more than 10 square kilometers Luoyang was, after Rome, the second largest city in the world. While the walls of Chang'an were much longer, they were actually less massive because Luoyang's defenses were strengthened during Guangwu Di's protracted struggle to secure the dragon throne. The city gates of Luoyang were twelve in number, of which three stood on the west wall and three on the east, two on the north wall, and four on the south wall. The southernmost one on the west wall, called the Gate of Extending Light, seems to have been used for official farewells to those traveling westward. Here in 30 Guangwu

Di performed a sacrifice to the spirit of the roads and inspected troops being sent against one of his rivals. Similar rituals would have been performed at auspicious gateways on the other walls, in particular the Gate of Spreading Light, near the western corner of the south wall. According to a story about its repair, one night a pillar suddenly appeared and lodged on top. When a message arrived from another city to the effect that a pillar from its own southern gate had disappeared, Guangwu Di ordered an investigation and learned that the missing pillar was the one that had mysteriously vanished. Diviners advised that the pillar be firmly fixed so as to ensure that the virtue it obviously possessed should remain permanently located in Luoyang.

City gates were kept closed at nights and only opened for exceptional reasons. Even the emperor could be locked out by over-zealous officials. When Guangwu Di once returned after dark from a hunting expedition and sought admission through one of the northern entrances to the imperial capital, the gate's captain refused to recognize him, even though the emperor's face was illuminated by a torch. Guangwu Di had to gain admittance through another gate instead. The following morning the captain who had refused to open his gate presented a memorial complaining that the emperor placed amusement above duty to the state. In response to this Confucian rebuke, Guangwu Di sent him one hundred bolts of silk cloth and demoted the captain in charge of the gate that had let him back into Luoyang.

Outside the city walls there was a moat, partly man-made. Its water came from a small river which flowed along the north and east sides of the city. By digging a channel round the other two sides, Luoyang had a moat that could withstand summer drought. Though well defended by strong walls and a deep moat, this was not where the imperial capital ended, for there were sprawling suburbs outside, albeit divided into wards.

The total population of Luoyang was in excess of 500,000, of whom 30,000 were students at the imperial university. When Guangwu Di made the city his place of residence, he ordered the transfer of all books and documents from the imperial library in Chang'an. They were brought to Luoyang in two thousand vehicles, and housed in four libraries, the most famous of which was called the Eastern Lodge. Situated in the Southern Palace, Bang Gu toiled there on his official *History of the Former Han* until his summary execution in 92. The historian died in a purge of the Dou family, the faction he supported. Empress Dou controlled the imperial court during the minority of Ho Di but, once this emperor came of age, he conspired with a eunuch attendant to assert his independence.

Started by Bang Gu's father, the *History of the Former Han* was completed mainly by Bang Gu and his sister Bang Zhao. As Bang Gu uncritically espoused the doctrine of the heavenly mandate to rule, he criticized the adverse comments made by Sima Qian on Former Han rulers in his own private history. Instead of harping on the glory of antiquity, Ban Gu advised his contemporaries to be more appreciative of the accomplishments of the present imperial house, the Former Han and the restored Later Han.

Equally sure of the value of a settled government was his sister, whose rare access to a classical education allowed her to finish his history as well as compose the standard work on her own sex, *Lessons for Women*. Because of her learning, Ban Zhao was even appointed as the teacher of several empresses and their ladies-in-waiting. *Lessons for Women* assumed the subordination of women to men; they were expected to obey their fathers when they were children, their husbands when they married, and their sons when they were widowed. The ideal age to marry for girl was fifteen, but wedlock could not be countenanced between persons of the same surname, lest the couple have a common ancestor. There were naturally grounds for divorce, the chief of which was bareness. Others were disobedience to parents-in-law, adultery, jealousy, incurable disease, loquacity, and theft. It needs to be recalled that at this period a man could only have one wife. Concubines were not regarded as full members of the family and the status of a concubine was always inferior to that of a wife. Unfortunately for women in China, Ban Zhao's recommendation that they should receive the same Confucian training that she had enjoyed was generally ignored.

By this time the supremacy of Confucianism was unchallenged. Under Guangwu Di it became customary for the emperor to offer sacrifices to the philosopher as the one "who had given laws to the people." The following emperor, Ming Di, delighted in expositions of Confucian doctrine, in which discussions he was sufficiently learned to take a leading part, and he even visited the shrine of Confucius at Qufu in present-day Shandong province. Confucius's teachings had become a moral code, a yardstick for measuring the correctness of behavior, something ideally suited to the administration of "the Empire of All under Heaven." If the long struggle against the Xiongnu had any effect on China at all, it was to strengthen the confidence felt by cultivated Chinese in the scale of values on which their civilization rested.

The area of the two imperial residences in Luoyang, the Southern Palace and the Northern Palace, occupied a very much smaller proportion of the city than had been the case with Former Han palaces in Chang'an. At Chang'an the Eternal Palace had taken up one-seventh of the imperial capital on its own: by the time the Former Han Emperor Wu Di finished his construction program in the 90s BC half the city was covered by palatial buildings. At Luoyang no more than one-tenth of the area within the city walls was ever used for such a purpose. But in Luoyang the Southern Palace was connected to the Northern Palace by means of an elevated walk-way. Along it the emperor made his way on a middle path, which was slightly raised above the others, and officials followed to the left and right. Halfway between the two palaces, close to the centrally placed drum tower, a special building offered the emperor a place for rest. As the "flying gallery" bisected Luoyang into almost two equal halves, it marked the capital city's north-south axis, the cosmic alignment which geomancers believed concentrated the power of the Pole Star. It was here, on this axis, that "earth and sky met, wind and rain were gathered in, and the yin and the yang were in harmony."

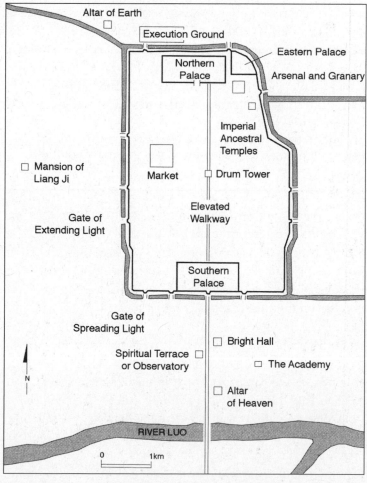

Map of the site of later Han Luoyang

Though the singular direction this link took clearly had ritual over-tones, it did not prevent conspirators from making use of the covered passageway when needed. In 125 eunuchs hurried the nineteen-year-old emperor Shun Di from his place of detention in the Northern Palace, pulling him in a hand-drawn carriage to the safety of the Southern Palace. There the majority of the civilian and military officials sided with Shun Di, and his enemies, the kinsmen of yet another dowager empress, were either executed or exiled to Vietnam, the northern part of which had been firmly incorporated into the empire's southern frontier. One of the generals who had supported the restoration of Guangwu Di, the outspoken Ma Yuan, put down a Vietnamese rebellion in 40 and then imposed direct rule in order to encourage economic development. Yet the general's military success could not save him from the baleful influence of court intrigue. His record of loyal service counted for nothing when Guangwu Di was persuaded of his corruption. The result was that Ma Yuan, who actually died on a campaign no other general would undertake, suffered posthumous demotion and his family dared not bury him in the ancestral plot. His widow, children, and nephew had an audience with the emperor and asked in vain for a pardon. Only after submitting six memorials were they finally allowed to give Ma Yuan a decent burial.

The central drum tower was a standard feature of Chinese cities. At a certain hour the drum was beaten to signal the close of ward gates within the city walls. In Luoyang, as elsewhere, the streets formed a grid and around each of its wards were walls controlling the movement of people. It is likely that there were also gates in the underpasses below the "flying gallery," allowing the authorities an easy method of dividing the imperial capital's inhabitants from each other at times of civil unrest. Although the rigidity of town planning was often relaxed as a result of population growth or under a weak dynasty, the Chinese city never managed through trade and industry to become sufficiently independent to challenge established political order.

Not that the lack of revolutionary activity meant an absence of crime. According to Wang Fu, who described himself as "the Hermit" because he was too honest to seek an official appointment, Luoyang was so overrun with criminals that the police force had no chance of keeping the imperial capital safe for law-abiding residents. Blaming the dire situation on too frequent amnesties, he relates how Luoyang's underworld had more business than it could handle. Amnesties must certainly have added to the difficulties of Luoyang's police force, because their announcement was so unpredictable. As droughts were especially associated with unjust trials and imprisonments, a worried emperor would suddenly order a general release of prisoners, making dry spells the last hope of the condemned.

In addition to the public prisons, there existed two palace jails. One of the palace prisons, the so-called Drying House, was used to accommodate divorced empresses who languished there till the end of their days. No prison was located in the Southern Palace, the seat of the first Later Han emperor Guangwu Di. Here he conducted audiences in a chamber next to an interior gateway, an entrance associated with the Pole Star. This great gate had lobbies each side for the shelter of subjects awaiting an audience. During the exorcism held in midwinter when the cosmic powers of death and decay were at their height, a torchlight procession passed out through this great gate, supposedly accompanying demons out of the palace precincts. Afterwards the torches were doused in the moat. As luck would have it, Zhang Heng's *Ode to the Eastern Capital* contains a detailed account of the exorcism ceremony. We are told that the chief exorcist donned an animal mask and led an assembly of officials through a series of purges aimed at eradicating twelve classes of demons, whose baleful influence ranged from personal illness to pestilence. Palace attendants clad in fur, feathers, and horns masqueraded as the evil demons themselves. As soon as the chief exorcist had expelled the demonic forces through incantation, the officials pretended to kill the disguised palace attendants. Extremes of the yin and yang were considered hazardous in the middle of winter and summer, and multicolored clothes were worn then in order to ward off roaming demons.

Through the same gate conscript guards marched for a final parade and a feast before their demobilization. Three thousand conscripts recruited from respectable families were responsible for the safety of the emperor, who feasted them after their one-year term of duty. Security in the imperial palace was maintained by a system of tallies authorizing entry. While permanent residents identified themselves with iron tallies, the other halves of which were kept at the entrance designated for their use, non-residents were issued with wooden credentials, and officials on business were announced by attendants. In an emergency the tallies were collected, which meant entry could be effected only by force.

The innermost part of the Southern Palace was reserved for the emperor and his women, access to which was denied to all except the eunuchs. These forbidden apartments were essentially the imperial harem, which in the mid-second century was at its largest, six thousand women strong. Though ritual ceremonies were conducted in the palace, the really significant ones took place within the city or outside its walls. One of Guangwu

Di's first decisions was to establish at Luoyang an ancestral temple for Liu Bang, the founding emperor of the dynasty. That a temple was urgently needed there could be no question, since an accession was not complete until the new emperor had been presented in the temple of the dynasty's founder. This declaration of legitimacy was invaluable to Guangwu Di at the start of his reign: he was only remotely related to the imperial line, and the outcome of the struggle with his rivals was then still very much in doubt. The ancestral tablets of the Former Han rulers were also brought from Chang'an and placed in the new temple. When Guangwu Di died in 57, a similar ancestral temple was built for him as the restorer of the imperial house. It was called the Temple of the Epochal Founder to distinguish it from that of the Eminent Founder, the name of Liu Bang's temple next door.

Besides the southern and northern palaces the Later Han emperors eventually constructed another palace in the northeastern corner of Luoyang. Almost an annex of the Northern Palace, it was named the Eastern Palace and belonged to the heir apparent, who was usually in residence there. The Later Han court resided in the Southern Palace until 65 and then moved to the Northern Palace for sixty years. The last rulers of the dynasty alternated between both palaces and the imperial court was in residence at the Southern Palace in 189, the year that witnessed the massacre of the eunuchs. In contrast to the Southern Palace, the Northern Palace possessed gardens and ponds in addition to halls and offices. The fact that Guangwu Di selected the Southern Palace as his residence implied that the Northern Palace was not in good repair, a deficiency corrected by Ming Di. Even though this emperor is recorded as having built it, much more probable is a thorough renovation in the early years of his reign, as an official felt obliged to warn him during a drought that the palace was becoming too splendid. Its most prestigious audience chamber was the Hall of Virtuous Light, a splendidly decorated room modest in its dimensions compared with the front hall of the Eternal Palace at Chang'an. A description of the Hall of Virtuous Light mentions pillars sheathed in red silk, and an elevated throne surrounded by a railing. The whole structure stood on a stone platform near a courtyard with a pond.

Most of the ponds and gardens were concentrated in the northeastern part of the Northern Palace, where there was a spring. Most ambitious of the gardens was that of the Sleek Dragon, a favorite place of recreation for Ming Di, who liked to throw parties there. It had a pond that was crossed by several bridges. The ruler who frequented the Garden of the Sleek Dragon most was Huan Di: in 166 he sacrificed there to Laozi. Though sacrifices were made in the same garden to the Buddha as well, his worship was still entwined with Daoism, as scholars interested in the teachings of Laozi and his followers reckoned that they had found a distant reflection of their own concerns in the doctrines of Mahayana Buddhism.

The earliest documented case of the Indian faith in China is its sponsorship by Liu Ying, one of Guangwu Di's sons. In 65 Emperor Ming Di addressed his half-brother Liu Ying as one "who recites the subtle words of Daoism and respectfully performs the gentle sacrifices of the Buddha." This characteristic mixture of the two beliefs derived as much from the circumstances of Buddhism's arrival in China as from the purposes to which its doctrines were put. Eclecticism was forced upon the Chinese by a shortage of scriptures, the small number of converts who could read them in the original Indian language, and competition between the different Buddhist sects. That Liu Ying was fascinated by Daoism as well as Buddhism, and surrounded himself with magicians as well as monks, shows that his goal was not the dragon throne, as spies reported to Luoyang, but immortality. He was denounced for sorcery in 70, and Ming Di received a strong official recommendation that his half-brother should be executed for treason. The emperor refused the advice, exiling Liu Ying instead to the Yangzi river valley, where his half-brother committed suicide the following year.

Study of Buddhist texts never constituted a criminal offence, and during the increasing political troubles that beset China towards the close of the Later Han dynasty many renowned scholars were drawn to them. They encountered in the first Chinese translations of Buddhist texts a ready use of Daoist expressions that caused Buddhism to be looked upon as a sect of Daoism. Daoist communities may indeed have served to spread certain Buddhist symbols and cults, thus playing a role analogous to that of Jewish communities that helped the spread of Christianity in the Roman Empire.

The public execution ground was situated at a short distance from the Northern Palace, outside the city wall. As freezing winter cold came from this direction, it is unsurprising that violent death was cosmologically associated with the Luoyang's bleak northern wall. This quarter of the imperial capital was an implacable place of retribution, as the sister of Guangwu Di was horrified to discover. She had taken a slave as her lover, protecting him even when he killed a man in broad daylight. Though the police were reluctant to arrest him when he sat beside her, the prefect of Luoyang intercepted her carriage in the northeastern part of the city, publicly criticized the moral shortcomings of the princess, and then executed the murderous slave on the spot.

It was an exemplary intervention for a moralist like Wang Fu, who accepted that extreme wickedness could not be corrected by reform. He said that the law had its function "to encourage the virtue of good people, and to make vicious people sorry for their bad actions." Being lenient with a criminal, Wang Fu argued, would be harmful for law-abiding people, as bad behavior would inevitably spread if the vicious were not eliminated. "When law and order operate properly, there will be good government; when law and order are by-passed, the Empire will be in disorder."

Close though this may seem to the harsh application of punishments favored by the short-lived Qin dynasty, Wang Fu was a realist who considered that society could not rely on moral influence alone. A ruler needed to set a virtuous example, as did his immediate relations like a sister, but this would not be sufficient to manage a city the size of Luoyang, let alone China. By the Later Han dynasty the worst punishments meted out to criminals under Qin Shi Huang Di had been abolished. No longer was mutilation commonplace: faces were not tattooed, neither were noses, hands, or feet cut off. The imperial authorities fixed five punishments for the guilty: beating with a light stick, beating with a heavy stick, penal servitude, life exile, and death. Beatings with the light stick were inflicted for trivial offences so as to shame the offender, the number of strokes ranging from ten to fifty. Beatings with the heavy stick started at sixty blows and progressed to a maximum of one hundred, a total that might kill a person with a weak constitution. Penal servitude involved forced labor for a definite period of time, anything between one and three years, while life exile meant banishment far away from one's home. An exile's womenfolk were also required to go into exile, but other relatives could stay behind if they wished. There were two kinds of death penalty, strangulation and decapitation. Though obviously more painful, strangulation was considered to be the less severe method of execution because it was thought that mutilation rendered the body unfit to receive the spirit again in the afterlife. There are instances of burial in ancestral graveyards being denied to kinsmen who had met violent ends.

Outside Luoyang's southern wall, there were several structures of note: the Spiritual Terrace, the Bright Hall, and the Academy. Constructed during Guangwu Di's reign, the Spiritual Terrace was a project dear to the heart of this frugal emperor, who personally consulted arcane books prior to ordering its construction. What is left of this earthen platform today suggests its dimensions were forty meters from east to west, fifty meters from north to south, and nearly ten meters in height. Corresponding to the months of the year, twelve gates gave access to the Spiritual Terrace, implying that it was once surrounded by a wall. The Terrace functioned as the imperial observatory, whose personnel were responsible to the court astrologer Zhang Heng, for keeping a watch on the movements of the stars and the planets. As they were also required to give early warning of heavenly displeasure, Zhang Heng's invention of the first practical seismograph comes as no surprise. It could not furnish a scientific reason for seismic disturbance, but the imperial observatory received immediate notice of a disaster and its direction from Luoyang. On its installation in 132 the "earthquake weathercock" was thought to be a supernatural device. Cast in bronze, it resembled a wine jar with a dome-like cover. Around the sides were eight dragon heads with bronze balls in their mouths, a reference to the pearl of wisdom an actual dragon held within its jaws. The outer surface was ornamented with antique seal-characters and designs of mountains, tortoises, birds, and animals. At the seismograph's base stood eight toads with their mouths open, ready to receive any ball the dragons might drop. The ingenious machinery inside vibrated whenever an earthquake occurred, with the result that a ball fell out of a dragon's mouth and was caught by a toad below. At the same instant a sharp sound alerted the observers on duty. According to the direction the dragon faced, an earthquake was indicated to have taken place at some point distant from the imperial capital in the same direction. On one occasion a dragon let fall a ball from its mouth without any shock being felt at Luoyang. Everyone was astonished by this strange happening. They were even more amazed by the arrival of a messenger with news of a very distant earthquake. "Nothing like this," an official commented, "had ever been heard of before."

The Bright Hall, built by Wang Mang when he was contemplating shifting the imperial court from Chang'an to Luoyang, was thoroughly renovated in 56. It stood slightly to the north of the Spiritual Terrace, not far from the Altar of Heaven, another important venue for imperial sacrifices. Ceremonies conducted in the Bright Hall invariably preceded the ruler's visits to the Spiritual Terrace. Although the nearby Academy was one of the very first projects of Guangwu Di's reign, subsequent Later Han emperors took less interest in its role as a recruitment ground for the imperial bureaucracy. Even a Confucian-minded ruler such as Ming Di toyed with the idea of closing this university down, while in the second century a shortfall in imperial funding brought about a gradual lowering of educational standards as well as physical conditions on the campus. But prior to the decline of civil service in the final years of the dynasty, the system that the Academy pioneered, with the aid of newly invented paper, laid the foundation of China's famous imperial examinations, which reached maturity under the Tang and Song emperors, from the seventh to the thirteenth centuries.

In comparison to their future operation, the Former and Later Han method of attracting talent was crude and corrupt, but somehow it provided the imperial government with enough competent officials. Throughout the provinces there were local schools maintained by the imperial government, and every year scholars recommended by local administrators were admitted to the imperial university at Luoyang. In 79 a conference was called of university teachers, officials, and scholars to "determine together the meaning of the Classics, so that students might better understand what they recited." The edict announcing the event quoted Confucius as saying: "Not to discuss thoroughly what is learnt is the thing I worry about." The emperor who called the conference in the Northern Palace was He Di, the fourth Later Han emperor. From his youth he had been an admirer of Confucian ideas, and his particular interest in old commentaries set the scene of the discussion. All kinds of topics were treated: ranks, names, deities, rites, music, the imperial capital, the Five Elements, the army, punishments, admonitions, retiring from office, education, marvels and portents, agriculture, sacrifice, inspection tours, examinations, demotion, divination, wisdom, trade, familial relationships, instinct and emotion, destiny, Heaven, the stars, clothes, marriage, and the passing of the Son of Heaven. So detailed is the record of the conference that we are well informed about all kinds of things which contemporaries took for granted, and otherwise made no mention. An example is the thickness for an imperial coffin, for we are told that

> the coffin of the Son of Heaven has nine layers. The inner coffin has four layers; the hides of a water buffalo and a rhinoceros, overlapping each other, serve as the innermost layer. Then there is a layer of white poplar, around which there are two layers of catalpa wood. Finally cypress boards form the five layers of the outer coffin.

There is no mention here of molten copper, which was poured to make the outer coffin for Qin Shi Huang Di. Here the conspicuous absence of metal may explain the reference to "barbarous Qin" in the edict inviting the learned to attend He Di's conference. Later Han imperial burials took place to the southeast of Luoyang, well beyond the suburbs. At the conference the view was expressed that seven months should elapse before a deceased Son of Heaven was buried. Unless empresses were divorced or disgraced, they shared the tomb of their husbands when in turn they died.

Beyond the suburbs were located the mansions of prominent families. The density of population was so high within the walls of Luoyang that even the wealthy had a restricted living area, though a courtyard, no matter how small, became something of a garden by means of plants and small trees in pots. A sense of seclusion was preserved by house design based on a central courtyard, the so-called "Well of Heaven." Even though substantial family dwellings were laid out around two or more such courtyards, the richest inhabitants maintained a residence inside the walled city as well as a large mansion outside.

The powerful Liang family owned a country mansion to the west of Luoyang and the assault launched on it was one of the most dramatic events at the imperial capital. In 141 the emperor Shun Di had appointed his brother-in-law Liang Ji to head the imperial administration, an appointment which allowed the minister to remain supreme for nearly two decades. When this ruler died and his fifteen-year-old successor, Huan Di, ascended the dragon throne five years later, the new emperor was at once obliged to take as his consort a younger sister of dowager empress. It was intended that this marriage to another relation would preserve Liang Ji's hold on the government. But the death of this second Liang empress, in 159, meant that the all-powerful minister had lost his vital ally in the private quarters of the imperial palace.

Huan Di seized the opportunity to rid himself of all of the Liang family. As he was surrounded by spies, the emperor withdrew to the toilet and there asked an attendant to identify the eunuchs he could really trust. Having assured himself of their loyalty, Huan Di acted swiftly to foil any Liang counter-attack. He ordered the defense of the palace and then sent a thousand men to surprise the Liang country mansion, where Liang Ji was advised of his demotion. The minister committed suicide the same day rather than suffer the disgrace. Elimination of the Liang family represented a victory for the eunuchs as much as the emperor and their influence grew in the imperial palace. A year after Huan Di's death in 168, a botched attempt was made to curb eunuch power by officials who tried to persuade the dowager empress to permit the execution of leading eunuchs. She was the third consort of Huan Di, who had died without an heir. At her instance a thirteen-year-old boy who took the title Ling Di, was declared the Son of Heaven. As guardian of this young ruler, the dowager empress realized that any weakening of the eunuchs would only lead to the rise of another powerful family, and she refused to co-operate with the officials. They acted on their own, but an order to arrest leading eunuchs was intercepted and made known to those threatened. Overnight the eunuchs seized control of the Northern Palace and the young emperor's person, before closing the elevated passageway to prevent any attack from the Southern Palace. With forged edicts they confused the soldiers stationed in Luoyang and overawed their opponents, who were either killed or exiled to Vietnam. And in spite of her conspicuous neutrality, the eunuchs kept the dowager empress under house arrest.

Ling Di's reign coincided with the rundown of the Later Han dynasty. Nomad incursions, peasant rebellions, and factional politics all weakened the ruling house, but it was Daoist-inspired uprisings that contributed most to the disorder, starting with that of the Yellow Turbans in 184.

The seriousness of the situation was lost on Ling Di, whom the eunuchs got to play games. We are also told how

> the Emperor was in the habit of hoarding money and treasure for himself. He collected all the valuable goods from the Empire and all the tribute sent in from the provinces, and he had them sent first to the inner palace, taking out a share for himself and calling it his own commission.

An official presented a memorial in protest, but its warning about the resentment this new practice would produce by "raising the burden of taxation and making life more difficult for the people" went unheeded. Given that avarice was a particular vice of the eunuchs throughout the history of the Chinese empire, Ling Di would have received no encouragement from them to desist. The amount of money collected can be gauged by the ease with which the emperor was able to fund extra military formations, once unrest necessitated the raising of extra troops. Ling Di appointed eight commanders for these forces, one of whom was Cao Cao, the father of the first ruler of the Wei dynasty, an imperial house which was destined to replace Later Han in 220.

Dislike as they might the appointment of military officials, the eunuchs could not block any of them during this time of acute danger. The sudden expansion of the imperial army was necessitated by the Yellow Turban revolt, and sustained by the rebellions that followed this northwestern peasant movement. All these uprisings were directed primarily by Daoists skilled in alchemy, herbalism, and faith-healing techniques. They assured their followers that the moment had come for the renewal of the world in "a great peace," the Taiping. So widespread was sympathy for the Yellow Turbans that the announcement of the new era of peace, written in white clay, even appeared on the outside walls of temples and official buildings in Luoyang.

The emperor did nothing to oppose the rebellion until it came to his notice that the Yellow Turbans had penetrated the imperial palace itself. Disaffected eunuchs were implicated in a plot masterminded by a Daoist adept, which aimed at installing the rebel leader Zhang Jiao as ruler. The court plotters were betrayed, the adept was captured and condemned to a terrible death. He was dismembered by being tied to two carts that were then driven in opposite directions. More than a thousand Yellow Turban sympathizers were seized in Luoyang and executed, a move that only served to spread the rebellion because Zhang Jiao called upon his followers to renew their efforts against the dynasty. Again Ling Di revealed his partiality to the eunuchs by including those who would have helped to depose him in a general amnesty. As if this was not enough to alienate his ministers, the emperor appeared indifferent to the defeats the Yellow Turbans inflicted on the imperial forces sent to destroy them. He was fortunate that one of his generals launched a surprise attack on the main rebel army and slew thirty thousand Yellow Turbans. The victory broke the back of the uprising, which may well have already faltered through the sudden death of Zhang Jiao. Learning of this event, the victors opened his coffin, cut off the corpse's head and sent it to the imperial capital.

On Ling Di's death, in 189, the commander-in-chief He Jin moved against the eunuchs. The seventeen-year-old emperor, Shao Di, was the son of Empress He, the general's sister. She became empress dowager and took over the imperial government the day Shao Di was enthroned, and He Jin was at last free to deal with the eunuchs. Having summoned reinforcements to Luoyang, he was preparing to strike when the news of his intentions leaked out. The dynastic history relates that

> He Jin went to the Southern Palace to see the Dowager Empress and requested that all the eunuchs be executed. Curious about this visit, because the general had apparently been too ill to attend the mourning of the deceased emperor, the eunuchs sent someone to hide and listen to what was said. As soon as they learned of He Jin's plan, the eunuchs gathered a group of armed men in a room near the palace door. The commander-in-chief came out, and they pretended to have the Dowager Empress's order to call him back, and so he went and sat in a waiting room. There a eunuch said to him: "The Empire's troubles were not our fault. When the late ruler was angry, each of us gave thousands and tens of thousands of our family wealth to bring harmony and pleasure to his mind. All we hoped for was the patronage of your family. And now you want to destroy us and our families, don't you?" Then another eunuch drew a sword and beheaded He Jin with a single stroke, while the armed men looked on. When worried senior officials asked to see the commander-in-chief, the eunuchs tossed his severed head outdoors saying, "He Jin planned to rebel, he has already been punished."

As soon as news of He Jin's murder became known, the soldiers under his command attacked the Southern Palace. As it went up in flames, the eunuchs escaped with the dowager empress and the young emperor along the elevated passageway to the Northern Palace. Their two distinguished hostages were told that the commander-in-chief's men were in revolt. But this ploy was of little avail, since the gates of the Northern Palace were soon broken down and the soldiers slaughtered all the eunuchs. Altogether two thousand people died. "Some men without beards," we are told, "were mistaken as eunuchs and also killed." With the massacre of the eunuchs, and the flight of Shao Di from Luoyang, one general after another tried to gain absolute power in an empire now dominated by rebellious troops and uncrushed rebels. The deposition of Shao Di did nothing to clarify the situation because his successor, Xian Di, the final Later Han emperor, was no more than a plaything of the rival warlords.

Luoyang was destroyed by Dong Zhou, initially the strongest contender for power. His soldiers were allowed to loot, rape, and kidnap, under the pretext that they were searching for provisions. Dong Zhou additionally permitted the looting of the imperial tombs, before taking the hapless Xian Di with him to Chang'an, where the ruthless warlord was himself killed two years later. The dynastic history reports:

> The palaces and mansions had all been consumed by fire. The various officials had to cut down brambles and live amongst bare walls. The governors of the provinces each had strong armies under their command and would not pay tribute. The court officials were starved and exhausted. Officials of lower rank had to go out and pick wild grains for food. Some of them starved to death or were killed by wandering soldiers.

This entry in the dynastic annals is for 196. That year Xian Di returned to Luoyang, living at first in a mansion and then in a newly built hall. Not every building had been wrecked because the emperor is recorded as visiting the ancestral temples of the dynasty's founder, Liu Bang, and that of its restorer, Guangwu Di. The telling detail of the 196 description is of course the non-arrival of tribute-grain at the imperial capital, making it impossible for courtiers and officials to live there.

Xian Di could have stayed on with an impoverished imperial court, rather like the last Zhou kings had done centuries earlier, and become an entirely nominal Son of Heaven during this period of strife. This option did not suit Cao Cao, who moved what was left of the imperial bureaucracy and the emperor to his own military base, the city of Xuchang, one hundred

kilometers south of Luoyang. The apparent restoration of the last Later
Han ruler at Xuchang was a turning point in the political fortunes of Cao
Cao. Henceforth this military adventurer could clothe his policies and
actions with the authority of decrees emanating from the Son of Heaven
himself. It also provided Cao Cao with the time-honored bureaucratic
means of recruiting talented young men to his own service and accommodating disillusioned officials and local magnets by appointing them to prestigious sinecures at the imperial court.

As head of the administration and the armed forces, Cao Cao defeated
his military rivals one by one until in 205 he dominated the whole of north
China. Three years later Cao Cao's attempted unification of the Chinese
empire failed when he invaded south China. At Chibi, in present-day Hubei
province, the superior nautical skills of the southerners discomforted his
army in an engagement fought along a river. After this setback, Cao Cao
was forced to consolidate his position in the north, though he still hoped to
conquer the southern provinces on his deathbed in 220.

Regarded by Chinese historians as the epitome of cynicism, Cao Cao
was no more than a product of his age. His infamous saying—"I would
betray the whole world rather than allow the world to betray me"—is a
reflection of uncertainties he had to contend with as China's second imperial house sank into oblivion. That he chose not to depose Xian Di was certainly a matter of policy and not sentiment, an awareness of the value of a
recognized political order. The Son of Heaven, no matter how insecurely he
sat on the dragon throne, remained a potent symbol of central authority for
the Chinese people. Once the last Han emperor was gone, there was nothing to stop rival houses in the south and southwest of China from claiming
the right to rule, too. For half a century the Chinese empire disintegrated:
the so-called Three Kingdoms returned the country to the internecine conflict which had crippled China prior to the reign of its first unifier, Qin Shi
Huang Di. Even though a legitimate line was supposedly traced through
Cao Cao's sons in the short-lived Wei dynasty, the political reality was
almost continuous warfare, for Cao Pi was opposed by Liu Pei, a distant relative of the deposed emperor, who established a separate state in the present-day province of Sichuan, and by the southerners who had defeated his
father at Chibi. They set up their own state in the lower Yangzi valley.

Because of its strategic location, Luoyang once again became an imperial capital, albeit the capital of only north China. Cao Pi, whose imperial
title became Wen Di, rebuilt parts of the Northern Palace, and his successor completed the task of reconstruction. The insecurity of the Wei dynasty
is evident in the fortress Cao Pi built at the northeastern corner of the city.

Its walls and ramparts were exceedingly strong and, because it stood on higher ground, the fortress commanded a view of all Luoyang. The overall dimensions were 1,000 meters from north to south and 250 meters from east to west.

In the final years of the Western Jin dynasty, which in 265 replaced the Wei, the fortress was fought over by those who were contending for control of Luoyang. The Western Jin dynasty came to power with Sima Yan, a soldier with an extraordinarily large and extended family. To its members he gave fiefs as rewards for their assistance in his seizure of power, a mistaken policy because his twenty-five sons soon turned their holdings of land into mini-kingdoms. After Sima Yan's death in 290, their mutual antagonism weakened the Western Jin house to such an extent that north China fragmented into a patchwork of small states. It was unfortunate that, ten years before he died, Sima Yan achieved the reunification of the Chinese empire, because this triumph was facilitated by the extra manpower he derived from nomad and semi-nomadic peoples who were permitted to settle within the Great Wall. This policy of barbarian settlement was to have the same dire military and political consequences it had for the western provinces of the Roman Empire.

The Western Jin dynasty lasted only till 316, the year in which most of the northern provinces passed into the hands of people from the steppe, and the remnants of Sima Yan's line fled southwards to Nanjing, where they founded the Eastern Jin dynasty.

CHAPTER 4

A Divided China:
Nanjing, Pingcheng, Luoyang

> Returning to Luoyang, I found the city walls had collapsed,
> palaces and houses were in ruins, Buddhist and Daoist temples
> reduced to ashes, and shrines and pagodas mere heaps of rubble.
> Creepers hung over walls and thorns filled the streets . . . To
> think that there had been once over a thousand temples, but now
> all are gone and the sound of their bells can be heard no more.

THIS DESCRIPTION OF LUOYANG WAS WRITTEN BY YANG YUANZHI, an official who passed by its ruins in 547. The city he had known was an extraordinary foundation: rebuilt at one ruler's bidding in 494, its population rose to little short of one million; in 534, Luoyang was emptied at three days' notice on another's order. How such a strange fate overtook this great city is one of the events we shall be recalling in this chapter, which looks at the three chief capitals of the twenty-six dynasties, Chinese and foreign, that ruled during the partition of China.

The Hunnish Xiongnu overwhelmed the Western Jin dynasty in a series of battles, the most significant defeat taking place at Luoyang in 311. For the first time an imperial capital and an emperor were both in foreign hands. The Xiongnu kept their imperial prisoner for a couple of years as a servant, but finally executed him because they were worried that he might become the focus of anti-foreign agitation. Then in 316 Chang'an was sacked like Luoyang, and the last Western Jin emperor became another prisoner-of-war. The Xiongnu now controlled all of north China, with the exception of the Liang state in the northwest and the Xianbei states in the northeast. The ethnicity of the tribal federation which the Chinese termed Xianbei remains something of a mystery: part Mongol, part Turkish, the Xianbei are here described as Turkish in order to distinguish them from the

Hunnish Xiongnu and the Mongols, who conquered the Chinese empire in the thirteenth century.

From Luoyang and Chang'an a great number of officials, scholars, and their families moved to the periphery of the empire. One exodus was to Liang, present-day Gansu province, where a Chinese bastion had been established astride the Silk Road. One of its governors had already secured its defenses against surrounding Turkish and Tibetan peoples, so that the arrival of refugees allowed the enclave to expand and prosper. With the disappearance of imperial authority from the northern provinces, there was no reason for its governor to hesitate in declaring himself the first ruler of the Former Liang dynasty. This ruling house was to last for sixty years, before Liang succumbed in turn to Tibetan, Turkish, Chinese, and Hunnish adventurers. Its last ruler was overthrown in 439 by the Tuoba Turkish emperor Tai Wu Di, a conquest which ended the fragmentation of north China, at its greatest extent into no fewer than sixteen separate states.

The second place of Chinese exodus was in the south, where on the southern bank of the Yangzi River at Jianye other refugees assisted in the restoration of the imperial house as the Eastern Jin dynasty. Nanjing, "the southern capital" as the riverside city was renamed, stood almost 500 kilometers southeast of Luoyang, entirely removed from the historical core of China. From this new imperial capital a Chinese emperor continued to rule and, despite the size of his diminished empire, he was seen as the true heir and preserver of imperial traditions.

Eastern Jin Nanjing was never a great city in the manner of Chang'an and Luoyang, but rather a provincial seat of the imperial government, as south China was then comparatively backward. The old native population, consisting of the Yao, Tai, and Yue, had to some extent combined with Chinese immigrants who arrived after the collapse of the Later Han dynasty, which meant that the people living there tended to look down on the comparative newcomers, who were just as dismissive of these southerners. Neither group was comfortable with the removal of the dragon throne to Nanjing, especially as extra taxes had to be levied and labor called up in order to construct the new imperial capital. The older immigrants were well entrenched in the southern economy: they owned large estates, dominated their tenants, who were usually of native descent, and they also engaged in trade. The sudden arrival of poorer northerners only tended to aggravate social tensions, since to an extent their interests still lay in the conquered north, where members of their families had remained. Why should the southerners pay for a brand-new capital and, worst still, the military effort required to regain north China?

Although there was no immediate uprising, a real sense of resentment typified the early years of Eastern Jin dynasty. This inauspicious beginning was not improved by the attitude of officials immigrating from the north: they regarded the south as colonial territory and, in consequence, preferred to live close to Nanjing where opportunities for leisure were only matched by those for intrigue. Trouble came in 321 with a rebellion headed by a provincial governor. So fearful was the first Eastern Jin emperor that he considered abdicating in the rebel leader's favor, but died before this drastic action proved necessary. Made of sterner stuff than his father, the second Eastern Jin emperor raised forces to oppose the insurgents, who were dispersed after two resounding defeats. It was the commander-in-chief Yu Liang who gained most from the fighting, however. The empress's brother, this general ran the imperial government for years to come, because the second Eastern Jin ruler also died early and his successor, Yu Liang's nephew, was still a child when he was styled the emperor Cheng Di.

Able though he was in military as well as civil matters, Yu Liang possessed a stubborn disposition that caused him to make unnecessary enemies. He even managed to offend the young emperor. Hearing from one of his spies a false report to the effect that a member of the imperial family was planning a rebellion, he had this elderly prince beheaded without any investigation. A few days later Cheng Di, who had been greatly attached to him, asked Yu Liang where the old gentleman with the white hair had gone. "A person said he was going to rebel," the general replied, "and so I had him executed." The young emperor shed tears and then asked pointedly: "If someone said that you were going to do the same thing, would your head be cut off?" Taken somewhat aback by this question, Yu Liang assured Cheng Di of his loyalty but failed to change his approach. By refusing to heed advice from his closest supporters, Yu Liang drove another commander to rebellion and temporarily lost control of Nanjing to the rebels, who even occupied the imperial palace. Loyal palace officials only just saved the emperor from harm when rebel soldiers rushed into his private apartments. On being told that ordinary people were forbidden to gaze upon the countenance of the Son of Heaven, they instantly withdrew, and waited to see what orders their commander had to give them, and whether he would now seize the throne himself. He chose to be appointed prime minister instead, claiming that the young emperor had need of a reliable guide, after being surrounded for so long by evil advisors. The inevitable counter-attack led by Yu Liang obliged the rebels to abandon Nanjing, because this imperial capital lacked the strong walls usually built for defense.

The Chinese five dynasties which ruled in the south, from 317 till 588, were safe from northern interference after the battle of Fei River. Fought in 383 on a river crossing in modern Anhui province, this engagement between two armies of very different sizes ended in a crushing Eastern Jin victory. Political rivalry between the various foreign conquerors of north China had already taken its toll on the military capability of the armies that northern rulers ordered to take the field. Continued efforts by southern commanders to recover lost territories were ignored until the Former Qin ruler Fu Jian ordered an advance on Nanjing. Of Tibetan stock, his dynasty had replaced the original Xiongnu rulers of north China some years before the battle took place. Fu Jian's invasion force is reported as comprising 600,000 foot soldiers and 270,000 cavalrymen. Against this host Nanjing could dispatch only 80,000 men, but they had better discipline and equipment than the northern army. Many of the northerners had been conscripted against their will: the Chinese officers and men in its ranks were notably half-hearted about the campaign, while both the Turkish Xianbei and Hunnish Xiongnu contingents had reasons of their own for not wanting a victory.

Had Fu Jian been aware of the confidence of the southern prime minister he might have called off the expedition. Well informed of the discord in the invading army, the prime minister was content to do nothing at all. An irate commander complained that "the prime minister, at this critical time, is hopelessly ignorant of military matters. He spends his hours picnicking in the hills or playing chess, and he makes me dismiss a detachment I have brought to defend the imperial capital".

When the northern invaders reached the Yangzi, they found the Eastern Jin army was deployed in a blocking position on one of that great river's tributaries, the Fei. Fu Jian observed this move and commented on the martial bearing and steadiness of the southern troops. He was equally impressed by Nanjing's absolute refusal to discuss terms, a point forcibly made by the prime minister himself. Allowing the Eastern Jin army to cross the Fei River was Fu Jian's tactical mistake, for it went straight into the attack and disrupted the front ranks of the northerners, who fell back in disarray. Even though a dispirited Fu Jian escaped the rout, his luck was not to last. Within two years he was killed by a rival Tibetan warlord and north China split into a number of separate states.

The repulse of Fu Jian's invasion marked the end of northern interest in south China for over a century. A line of partition was drawn along the northern boundary of the wet-rice growing area, countryside quite unsuited to the operation of nomad cavalry. To its south, the Chinese were free to carry on their lives and eat rice, a grain whose increase in popularity can be traced to this period.

Exploiting their victory, the Eastern Jin emperors launched a number of northern expeditions and regained some of the lost territories. In 417 one expedition managed to occupy Luoyang as well as Chang'an, but the success was short-lived. After the bulk of the army returned to the south, its commander-in-chief fell foul of his squabbling subordinates in Nanjing, and the re-conquered territories again passed under foreign domination. Three years later this man, Liu Yu, was strong enough to depose the last Eastern Jin emperor and set up his own dynasty. Known to Chinese historians as the Liu Song in order to distinguish it from the later Northern and Southern Song dynasties, Liu Yu's new imperial house looked for increased influence in the far south as much as in the foreign-dominated north.

Liu Yu was sixty-four years old on his accession, and he reigned for less than three years in Nanjing. His advanced age and anxiety about the future of his teenage heir was probably behind the decision to eliminate the Eastern Jin line. The deposed emperor was poisoned, mourned, and buried in splendid fashion. Yet this action did not save Liu Yu's son: he was killed after a one-year reign and replaced by an even younger brother. This third Liu Song emperor, Wen Di, patiently waited until he could assert his own independence from over-powerful ministers, then avenged his brother's murder. During his thirty years on the dragon throne, Wen Di gave attention to Confucian learning and built four colleges for the study of the classics. Although the revival in south China of the traditional curriculum pleased many scholars, as it was seen as a token of the return to proper relations between Wen Di and his officials, there were some learned men who still preferred to boycott the imperial examination system altogether. One such individual was Tao Qian, who died in 427. Coming from an impoverished landowning family, he astounded his contemporaries by refusing offers of government employment and choosing to live as a poor farmer instead. Admired though his poetry was in his own lifetime, the greatest impact that Tao Qian had on Nanjing was as a man of integrity, someone who preferred poverty and hardship to comfort and respectability when they could only be gained by compromising his principles.

To Tao Qian the lip service paid to the moral teachings of Confucius in the imperial administration was galling, as unscrupulous ministers, ambitious generals, and time-serving bureaucrats brought its workings into disrepute. Having once held a minor post, Tao Qian knew the extent of official corruption and simply could not tolerate the tasks that he was called upon to perform. "Hunger and cold may be sharp," he wrote, "but this going against myself really sickens me. When I was briefly an official, I realized how I was mortgaging myself to my mouth and belly, and this upset me

greatly. I was deeply ashamed that I had so compromised my principles."
Retiring to live on his small farm, Tao Qian soon learned to appreciate the
stolid strength of the peasants. Sharing their joys and sorrows, he glimpsed
the true foundation of traditional China, a hard-working peasantry now
lacking the leadership of decent imperial administrators. As he wrote:

> Here in the country visitors are few,
> On this narrow lane carriages seldom come.
> My wooden gate is forever closed,
> From my bare rooms dusty thoughts are banned.
> Now and then through the tall grass
> Like me, villagers come and go.
> When we met we speak of nothing else
> But how the crops we have planted grow.

So fond was the emperor of literature that, whenever he could, Wen Di
attended a new Confucian college he founded to learn from its distinguished head, a former hermit whom Wen Di had lured out of seclusion to
come and teach. The college was situated in a northern suburb of the imperial capital at a place with the improbable name of "chicken cage hill." All
four of Wen Di's colleges attracted a large number of students. Though
Daoism ideas were studied, too, Confucian learning received the emperor's
greatest favor. The colleges were an example of imperial as well as private
enterprise, because they appear to have been in existence as private schools
prior to their receipt of government aid. Whatever the hill was called, these
places of learning were no "wild chicken schools," the name the Chinese
use to describe establishments of dubious academic worth. On the contrary,
they were of such a high standard that, in 443, Wen Di was able to go on
and reopen the imperial university. Each of its five faculties was dedicated
to a specific field of study: Confucianism, Daoism, literature, history and
divination.

Apparently Wen Di's interest in learning was encouragement enough
for a mini-renaissance in classical learning at Nanjing. The emperor himself was said to have been the epitome of benevolence, openness, frugality,
and diligence. Unfortunately for the Chinese empire the praise heaped on
this ruler in the dynastic history is in part a consequence of the low caliber
of those who sat on the dragon throne after him. Wen Di was most unfortunate in his two eldest sons, drunken murderers who cared for nothing but
their own pleasures. When in 454 they became so unruly that Wen Di
decided to disinherit the eldest and put the second to death, they learned of

their father's intentions and in the company of drinking companions surprised him one night.

> Wen Di was with one of his trusted ministers, planning for the succession.
> The two men could put up little resistance against such a determined band
> of killers, although for a time the emperor managed to defend himself with
> a small table. Once his fingers had been chopped off, the table fell to the
> floor, and Wen Di was defenseless. He was cut down by the conspirators,
> who moved on to slay all senior officials known to be loyal to the mur-
> dered emperor. Nanjing was in uproar until Wen Di's third son, a twenty-
> four-year-old provincial governor, reached the imperial capital by a series
> of forced marches and restored order. No one lifted a finger to help the
> patricides and, at the head of his troops, the younger son entered the
> palace and executed his two brothers.

The avenger succeeded his father with the title of Xiao Wu Di, meaning
"Filial Warrior Emperor." A deceptive calm settled over Nanjing but was
soon disturbed by plots and rebellions within and without the imperial
family. The behavior of Xiao Wu Di did little to foster loyalty: hunting
and drinking were his chief concerns. The dynastic history cannot disguise
its disdain for his even more unsuitable son, whose title was Fei Di. It was
his pleasure

> to gather a large number of harem ladies in the palace gardens, making
> them strip off all their clothes before playing tag and other games togeth-
> er. A lady, more modest and brave than the others, refused one day to join
> in the improper fun. The furious emperor stabbed her to death on the
> spot. That same night the murdered woman appeared to him in a dream,
> reproaching him for his cruelty and warning him of an early death.
> Overwhelmed by terror, the Emperor sent for a Daoist magician and
> asked if he could prevent the danger to his life that the spirit of the harem
> lady he had killed now predicted. The magician explained that her angry
> spirit was lurking in the palace gardens close to the place where the mur-
> der was committed, but he agreed to drive it away at the Emperor's
> request. In order to do this the Emperor and a special number of ladies
> from his harem had to shoot arrows over the spot where the unfortunate
> woman fell. When this strange ritual, and what had necessitated its per-
> formance, became generally known in the imperial capital, opponents of
> the Emperor beheaded him not very far from the place where his victim
> had fallen.

The subsequent fall of the Liu Song dynasty was unavoidable. Again it was a minister with marriage ties to the imperial family who brought it to an end and, in 479, established instead the Southern Qi, the most unstable of all the southern Chinese dynasties. In twenty-two years, it was represented by seven different emperors, three of whom were either deposed or assassinated. In 502 a general by the name of Xiao Yan took advantage of the confusion and, after a two-month siege of Nanjing, he declared himself to be the first Liang emperor.

Although there was war with the northern Tuoba Turkish rulers till 515, Xiao Yan reigned for forty-eight years without embroiling Nanjing in unnecessary conflicts. One result of this long period of military inactivity was the reduction of imperial authority to little more than the lower Yangzi valley. Xiao Yan was thus at liberty to indulge his passion for Buddhism.

From the start of the Liang dynasty large numbers of Buddhist monks arrived by ship from India in order to propagate the new religion in south China. A parallel migration was taking place in the north, where Indian monks traveled eastwards in caravans along the Silk Road. One of the monks who arrived in Nanjing was Bodhidharma, the founder of the Chan sect, whose radical Buddhist teachings were later known in Korea as Son, in Japan as Zen. When asked by the emperor what merit he had acquired by good works, Bodhidharma replied, "No merit at all!" Amazed, he asked his visitor about the first principle of Buddhism. "There isn't one," was the reply, "since where all is emptiness, nothing can be called holy." After this rather splendid audience, Bodhidharma traveled to north China, where he advocated meditation by example: he spent his days gazing at a wall.

Already the question of how a Buddhist monk should behave at the imperial court had been hotly debated under the Eastern Jin dynasty. When the imperial bureaucracy failed to agree on what was appropriate, the advice of Huiyuan, Chinese equivalent of St. Augustine, was requested. Huiyuan gave his verdict in 403, a year before he died. He ruled that, because a monk has left behind family life and lodged beyond the earthly world, his ways are cut off from those of others. The doctrine by which he lives enables him to understand that sorrow and difficulties come from having a body, and that not maintaining a body ends all woes. By not encumbering his spirit with life, his spirit can become subtle and transcend everyday things. Thus he ignores the demands of existence, pays no homage to an emperor, and concentrates on his own salvation. That is why a monk is without rank and yet enjoys a ruler's kindness.

The profound indifference that informs Huiyuan's judgment was based on the Buddhist belief in the pointlessness of earthly striving. The Buddha had told his followers to isolate themselves from the ways of the world. A monk's saffron robe was indeed a badge showing society at large that he had elected to leave its toils, the color of this garment being the same as that worn by condemned men in ancient India on the day of their execution.

Huiyuan won the argument by acknowledging the loyalty of all Buddhists to the dragon throne, while at the same time insisting that its clergy could never be expected to go through the outward signs of obeisance. A monk should never be required to bow. The distinctive character of salvation in Chinese Buddhism derived primarily from Huiyuan's teachings, whose spiritual progress is reminiscent of his Roman contemporary St. Augustine. His early training was in the classics, which in old age he felt still contained the flower of Chinese thought. Along with this Confucian scholarship he developed a strong interest in Daoist philosophy, mastering its texts before his first exposure to Buddhism. Converted to this new faith, Huiyuan became a monk, studied and began to preach. About 380 he settled on a mountain in the Yangzi valley and formed a community of monks worshipping Amitabha (or Amida Buddha), in whose paradise of the Pure Land they sought to be reborn. To counter the charge of filial impiety, an inevitable accusation in a land dominated by the filial preoccupations of Confucianism, scriptures were translated that showed concern for the family. One text relates how a bodhisattva, "a being who is possessed of the Buddhahood," chose to be reborn as the son of a childless, blind couple who wanted to retire to the forest in order to lead a life of contemplation. This process of accommodation led to an eventual transformation: the Buddha became the dutiful Chinese son.

In 548 Xiao Yan left the imperial palace with the intention of spending the rest of his days in a monastery he had built at Nanjing. This was not the first occasion on which he had become a monk and needed to be ransomed by a huge donation to local Buddhist establishments. On this occasion, though, Xiao Yan seemed set on quitting the dragon throne for good, as he exchanged his imperial robes for a monk's cowl and contentedly slept on a bed with an earthen pillow. No longer addressed as "Bodhisattva Son of Heaven," Xiao Yan was treated as an ordinary monk until a crisis forced his return to the imperial palace. In 550 a northern general exploited the patent weakness of Liang dynasty to capture Nanjing. There was nothing the would-be monk could do but calmly await the conqueror in the audience chamber. When he arrived, Xiao Yan said, "I gained power through my own efforts, and now I have lost it through lack of exertion, so there is no reason to complain." Astounded by this remark, the northern general backed out, with his eyes on the ground, and confided in one of his officers:

"I have led thousands of men into battle, and I have charged the enemy at the head of my cavalry, and I have never felt the least fear. Today I was in terror when I met this old man. He is truly awe-inspiring, and I'll never venture into his presence again."

Afterwards Xiao Yan was kept a close prisoner in the imperial palace, where he starved to death. Even though the occupiers of the imperial capital were then ejected by southern troops under the command of Chen Baxian, this soldier chose not to restore the Liang imperial house, but instead declare himself the first Chen emperor. His successors ruled in Nanjing for thirty-two years, before the last Chinese emperor there succumbed to the forces of Yang Jian, later known as the Sui emperor Wen Di. Yang Jian's capture of Nanjing in 588 ended the period of disunity in China that had begun in 317.

During the period of partition the experience in the north was quite different from that in south China, notwithstanding more frequent changes of dynasty and more extreme political fragmentation. The chief reason for this was the impressive rise of the Tuoba Turks to power after the battle of Fei River. In 398 Tuoba Gui, a leading member of the Tuoba clan of the Xianbei people, established himself at Pingcheng, east of the modern city of Datong in Shanxi province, and the following year proclaimed the Northern Wei dynasty. Through a succession of able emperors it gradually defeated all rival princes until in 423 the Yellow River was crossed and Luoyang fell along with other cities. Six years later the Northern Wei emperor Tai Wu Di succeeded in overrunning Liang state in the northwest and brought about the unification of the whole of north China, although clashes between the different ethnic groups prevented the Northern Wei emperors from doing more than securing their position in the north. That the dynasty went through a series of title changes—Northern, Eastern, and Western Wei—reflects the power struggles that troubled each ruler. In 452 Emperor Tai Wu Di was murdered by a eunuch and his successor died at the hands of his own heir apparent. By the 490s, however, the Chinese at the Tuoba court formed the leading element, and they persuaded the emperor to move from Pingcheng to Luoyang, the old seat of the Western Jin, the last Chinese dynasty to have ruled from a northern capital. Shortly afterwards this emperor, Xiaowen Di, introduced further measures which were dictated by the administrative needs of what was now a very large state, stretching from Dunhuang in the west to Korea in the east. He prohibited Turkish speech, dress, and customs: henceforth Chinese culture was to be the standard for the imperial Tuoba court.

In unifying north China Tuoba Turkish rulers perfected the combination of tribal organization with a Chinese approach to government. Though they built on previous experience, inheriting administrators who knew how to make this delicate arrangement work, they also attracted the services of many Chinese scholars, who realized that there was an opportunity to gain influence by collaborating with a dynasty that required and rewarded civil officials. At their capital in Pingcheng, Northern Wei emperors were able to enhance their authority at the expense of tribal custom by relying more and more on a recruited Chinese bureaucracy. Already urbanized, the Tuoba Turks were pleased to settle on the arable land just inside the Great Wall, close to the Tuoba homeland. Forcible resettlement of subject peoples around Pingcheng did much to strengthen the local economy, freeing tribal warriors from the necessity of cultivation.

The population influx brought with it many adherents of the Buddhist faith, which was not met with open arms. The chief instigator of persecution appears to have been the Confucian minister Cui Hao, who came from a well-known northern Chinese family, his father having served as an official under the first two Northern Wei rulers. Cui Hao was respected in Pingcheng for his ability to make prophecies and interpret heavenly phenomena, but his enemies obliged him to retire and, returning home to seek solace in Daoism, he met the Daoist adept Kou Jianzhi.

Kou Jianzhi had the vision of establishing a Daoist empire with himself as its spiritual leader, and so he was delighted to make the acquaintance of the famous ex-minister, who could assist him in achieving his lofty aim. Cui Hao was just as pleased to meet the visionary, because he hoped that by backing Kou Jianzhi he might regain his official position. Both went to Pingcheng, where Cui Hao proudly boasted of the talents of his new friend. Emperor Tai Wu Di obligingly offered Kou Jianzhi an official post and soon restored Cui Hao to high office as well. Although the long-term objective of Cui Hao was the setting up of a Confucian state in order to sinicize the Tuoba Turks, he was prepared to promote Daoism against Buddhism, as Daoism was at least a Chinese belief. The emperor was won over to the cause, and in 438 a decree forbade those under fifty years of age from becoming a Buddhist monk or nun. When in the ensuing year it was reported to Tai Wu Di that Buddhist monks had fought against imperial troops, the emperor wanted to execute those who were taken prisoner, but Kou Jianzhi interceded on their behalf and they were conscripted as laborers on public works instead. In putting down another rebellion at Chang'an, Tai Wu Di was provoked into more drastic action when it was reported that a monastery there housed a very large store of weapons. The emperor condemned all its monks to death and, when it was also discovered that there existed hidden rooms where the monks had been secretly entertaining women, he accepted Cui Hao's recommendation that every monk should follow these corrupt men into the next world. The harsh decree was then proclaimed, and permanently lodged in the Chinese mind was the suspicion that celibacy would always prove to be an impossible vow for a Buddhist monk to keep.

In 488 Kou Jianzhi died, and two years after that Cui Hao met a violent end. The cause of his execution, and that of his entire family, was popular anger at the history he was writing of the Northern Wei dynasty. Having been entrusted with this task by Tai Wu Di, Cui Hao's account of its dynastic progress was read by the inhabitants of Pingcheng, when the tablets on which it was inscribed were being carried through the streets to the Temple of Heaven. Reference to the misdeeds of early rulers was unacceptable to the fiercely loyal Tuoba Turks, who had no sympathy with the frankness always expected of Chinese historians. Had the usual Chinese practice for compiling a dynastic history been followed, no uproar would have happened. Ever since the Former Han it was customary in China for specially appointed officials to compile a history of their own times, and no one but themselves was ever allowed to read what they had written. As each document was composed, it was deposited in an iron-bound chest, which remained locked until such time as the dynasty ceased to rule. Then at the order of a later ruler the chest would be opened and the documents it contained edited into a history of the previous dynasty. This method of storage had been devised to protect officials who might have to record facts unpleasant to the current occupant of the dragon throne. The instant Northern Wei history left Cui Hao with no protection at all.

With Cui Hao and Kou Jianzhi gone there was an easing of the Buddhist persecution, but monks and nuns were still subject to official interference. A gradual accommodation was helped by the carving in Pingcheng of a stone figure of the Buddha in the likeness of the emperor. After the statue was completed, it was found to have spots on the face and feet, corresponding exactly to black moles on the emperor's body. So remarkable was this coincidence that an edict gave permission "to chisel a stone wall in the mountainside west of the imperial capital, and open there five caves in each of which is to be carved a figure of the Buddha. The tallest statue is to be at least seventeen meters high, the next fifteen meters. The work is to be of such quality that it will be regarded as the crowning achievement of the whole world." For the next thirty years the Buddhist caves at Yungang were sculpted under imperial patronage, becoming the easternmost example of the great carved grottoes which stretch from Ajanta in India, through Bamiyan, Kucha, and Turfan in Central Asia, to

Dunhuang, at the western terminus of the Great Wall. It is hardly surprising that a modern visitor to Yungang is struck at once by the scale and splendor of the caves, since it is the pivotal site in the evolution of Buddhist art in China. The sheer number and variety of the carvings remain astonishing: there are fifty-three caves containing 51,000 sculptures. Some caves house colossal Buddhas in semi-darkness, others teem with lesser figures illustrating the Buddha's previous births, his ministry, and the lives of his closest followers, the bodhisattvas. As Mahayana was the form of Buddhism carried to China, this more developed form of the faith offered the artisans who worked on the sandstone ridge at Yungang an extensive pantheon to sculpt. The last recorded visit of a Northern Wei emperor to the site occurred in 483, when he came to witness the completion of several caves, one of which contained the largest figure of the Buddha carved there. At the same time as the Yungang caves were under construction, the Northern Wei built in Pingcheng lavish Buddhist temples and monasteries, adorning them with paintings and bronze sculptures.

Attractive as Buddhism may have been to the Tuoba Turks as a non-Chinese faith, its teachings afforded no protection for Turkish tribal customs, so that the rebuilding of the Northern Wei capital at Luoyang in 494 marked the final sinicization of the imperial Tuoba court. By this date many Confucian scholars had also converted to the Buddhist faith. Better translation of Buddhist manuscripts brought back from India by Chinese pilgrims, or introduced into China through the agency of foreign monks, drew their admiration once they emancipated Buddhist ideas from Daoism. Instrumental in clarifying the essence of Buddhism was the Central Asian monk Kumarajiva, who arrived in 401. Thanks to the efforts of Kumarajiva the concepts of Mahayana Buddhism were presented in the Chinese language with greater clarity and precision than ever before. In particular he rescued from Daoist influence the fundamental concept of sunyata, "emptiness," the unreality of all the elements of existence. Because Kumarajiva felt that translation could never reproduce the style of the original, he shortened texts so as to retain only the original meaning. For him the sole purpose of translation was to isolate the substance of each sutra, or "narrative scripture." Kumarajiva avoided falling into the trap of an unnecessarily eloquent manner of expression, unlike other translators who were concerned to make the Buddhist scriptures more readable, but differences between original and Chinese versions eventually led to another major round of translation. One reason for the famous Tang monk Xuanzang's pilgrimage to India in the 640s was to collect Buddhist manuscripts for the translation school at Chang'an.

The transfer of the Northern Wei court to Luoyang was a severe blow to the Tuoba Turk nobility. In the new capital the tribal leaders found themselves parted from their followers, with little or nothing to do, for virtually all official posts were by now occupied by Chinese. Nobles were poorer, too, because previously their herds and flocks had largely provisioned Pingcheng. To make even more transparent this anti-tribal bias, Emperor Xian Wen Di banned Turkish clothes and the Turkish language at the imperial court, encouraged the adoption of Chinese names, and rewarded those who married into the old landowning families of north China. In 496 a brief revolt among the frontier tribes slowed the pace of the reform, but the Northern Wei dynasty had to all intents and purposes become a non-Tuoba one. There is no question that the move to Luoyang drastically altered the relation of frontier garrisons to the dynasty: instead of being viewed as an integral part of Northern Wei strategy, the troops stationed there were often given inadequate supplies and, as the dynasty was soon to rue, accorded quite inadequate recognition. Even in the new imperial capital there were difficulties with Turkish soldiers. In 519 the imperial guard rioted when a Chinese official proposed that the military be excluded from the higher government posts. That the examination system for recruitment to the imperial bureaucracy was not then in operation only added insult to injury, since it appeared almost enough to be a member of an important Chinese family in order to obtain an official appointment. Families were indeed ranked in expectation of the public service their members would render the dynasty. Behind this idea was the assumption that educated individuals from families experienced in running the government would be able to take up official positions. Even though it coincided with Confucian belief in genealogy, this method of recruitment shifted the emphasis away from the value of learning, the traditional measure of worth for would-be officials.

When Emperor Xiaowen Di decided to relocate his court at Luoyang, he regarded himself not as a Turkish emperor ruling north China by force of arms, but rather the true successor of those who had sat upon the dragon

Giant Buddha sculptures at the Yungang cave complex

throne from Qin Shi Huang Di onwards. In order to realize this imperial dream he needed to rule from a predominantly Chinese area of settlement: hence the move to the old city of Luoyang. At Pingcheng the palace was never more than a great country house, surrounded by the mansions of the Tuoba nobility. The dynastic history speaks of the construction of palaces, ancestral temples and ceremonial altars, but to the eyes of visitors from south China it was still a foreign city. Horses and oxen were sacrificed in Turkish style while mounted musicians galloped around altars; officials with outlandish titles wore clothes better suited to riding and fighting than the business of government; and artisans were everywhere, some of them working on behalf of princes and nobles. Despite a regular city wall and internal walls dividing the city into wards, Pingcheng was never firmly under Northern Wei control. In 452 the city gates had to be closed for a three-day search in which hundreds of "evildoers and criminals" were arrested, while riotous drinking was such a serious problem that there were periodic bans on the brewing or selling of alcohol.

Dissatisfied with this state of affairs, the young emperor Xiaowen Di announced the removal of the imperial capital to Luoyang in late 493. At the time the only building of any worth left standing in Luoyang was the fortification in the northeastern corner of the city raised after the fall of the Later Han dynasty. Yet even this stronghold had ceased to be the prize it once was: following the Xiongnu takeover in 311, the days of Luoyang's glory seemed over forever. No one could have foreseen the complete rebuilding of the imperial city by the Tuoba Turks.

The site chosen for the new Northern Wei city was virtually that of the Later Han capital, the line of whose walls was followed closely. These inner city walls enclosed an inhabited area of around10 square kilometers. The purported million-man army Xiaowen Di had marched south was no doubt immediately put to work on these defenses. Apart from these soldiers, many of whom would have taken up residence in and around Luoyang, other people were moved there from adjacent lands as well as from Pingcheng in order to strengthen the local economy. All incomers were declared permanent residents of Luoyang, and even in death they were required to leave their bones in its cemeteries. The first couple of years were hard, as houses needed to be built, fields planted, and animals bred. Xiaowen Di's own palace was situated in the old fortress, where he died in 499. How much of the new capital he actually saw built is uncertain. Complaints were made about the shortage of offices for government departments, and there is evidence to suggest that Tuoba resistance to the move put a brake on Luoyang's initial development. It was not until 501, the second full year of the reign of Xiaowen Di's son, that all the palaces and official buildings were finished. And it was only in the same year that 55,000 convicts constructed the city's 220 walled wards.

That Xiaowen Di conceived his new capital on a grand scale is certain. Greater Luoyang extended over an area larger than Beijing, China's final imperial capital. This is incredible when one considers how it was planned from scratch in a single year, and most of it was constructed within a decade. Although the old Later Han city walls were sensibly repaired for the protection of the inner city, there were other walls newly built around the outer city, parallel to the inner ones. Like the inner city, outer Luoyang was organized on a grid pattern and divided into walled wards, but these wards differed greatly in character. The eastern ones were residential and had a small market of their own. The outer wards in the south stood on both banks of the Luo River and were altogether grander. They contained one of Luoyang's biggest monasteries, the Qingming, which was named after the supreme celebration of ancestor worship, since in 500 it was opened during that festival. Then filial piety was demonstrated by sweeping the ancestral tombs and the presentation of food. The *Record of the Monasteries of Luoyang* relates the monastery's charms:

> It faced the mountains to the south, and behind it was the wall of the inner city. The shade of its dark trees and the pattern of its green waters made it a beautiful and tranquil place. There were over one thousand rooms in its towered buildings. Their windows and gutters faced each other, and shaded terraces and purple pavilions were connected by flying passageways. No matter the season outside, it was never freezing cold or boiling hot inside the monastery. Beyond the eaves of its buildings were small hills and ponds, where reeds, rushes, water chestnuts and lotuses grew. Yellow turtles and purple fish could be seen among the waterweeds, while black ducks and white geese swam on the green waters. There were also water-powered rotary mills, pounders, and bolters in the Qingming, finest of all monasteries.

In this typical Chinese mixture of spiritual and commercial life we are given a rare insight into the economic role of Luoyang's leading religious foundation. Its array of grain-processing machinery must have provided the monks with a considerable income, because we know that the government-owned water mills to the north of the city were incapable of handling all the grain that was needed to feed the population. In spite of its commercial activities Qingming monastery was regarded as the center of Buddhist wor-

ship at Luoyang. At an annual ceremony each spring, all the Buddhist statues in the imperial capital were taken to the emperor for flowers to be scattered over them, a ritual in which he was assisted by the Qingming monks:

> The gold and the flowers dazzled in the sun, and the jeweled canopies
> floated like clouds. There were forests of banners and a fog of incense, and
> the Buddhist music of India shook earth and sky. Entertainers were mixed
> with monks holding their staves and the faithful carrying flowers.
> Horsemen and carriages were packed close together in an uncountable
> mass. When a monk from Central Asia saw all this, he proclaimed that
> China was truly the land of the Buddha.

Just how poor a relation Confucianism was to Buddhism can be gauged
in the Bright Hall, a building symbolizing the cosmic relationship between
Heaven, earth, and man. A quintessential Confucian place of worship, it
was not built until thirty years after the move to Luoyang and looked plain-
ly second-rate. Equally neglected was the Spiritual Terrace, now enclosed
by Luoyang's outer wall: Zhang Heng's old observatory had become the site
of a Buddhist pagoda. As Northern Wei rulers preferred to have Buddhist
monks explain the meaning of natural phenomena, there was no longer an
imperial astrologer of the Confucian persuasion to warn about heavenly
disapproval of government failings.

Many foreign merchants lived in the southern wards, but their homes
were restricted to those south of the Luo River. Zoning was deliberate in
Northern Wei Luoyang. Xiaowen Di listened to his Chinese ministers
when planning the new imperial capital and agreed that merchants should
be kept firmly in their place. In the outer western wards there were two
monasteries set aside for the accommodation of foreign monks. The majority of the people who lived here were the most socially respectable Turkish
nobles, who maintained large establishments and spent great sums on
entertainment. In the middle was Luoyang's largest market, ever ready to
meet the insatiable demand for luxury items. These select wards, which
covered an area the size of inner Luoyang, were known as Longevity Hills.

Inside the inner city wall were palaces, government offices, mansions,
and monasteries as well as nunneries. The main Northern Wei palace stood
in the northwestern corner, the old fortified section of the imperial capital.
We know little about the palace because the *Record of the Monasteries of
Luoyang* is only interested in religious foundations. At Eternal Peace
Monastery, near the southern gate of the inner city, a nine-story pagoda
built with a wooden frame rose to a height of 250 meters, with a golden

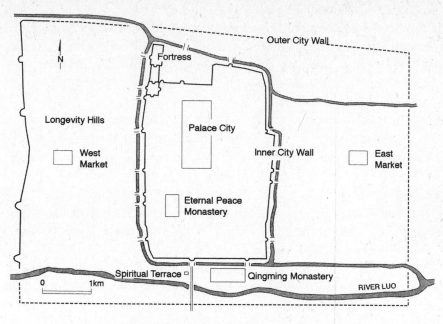

Map of the site of Northern Wei Luoyang

pole on its top. When it was being built in 516, the digging of the foundations revealed

> thirty gold statues, which were regarded as a god omen for the pagoda's
> construction . . . Bells were hung from all corners of the pagoda, in total
> 120. In each of its four sides were three doors and six windows all lac-
> quered red. On the leaves of the doors were five rows of golden studs,
> 5,400 in all, and in addition golden bells were mounted in holders. It was
> a triumph of building construction . . . North of the pagoda was a hall with
> a five-meter-high gold statue, ten man-sized gold statues, three statues
> studded with pearls, five statues woven from gold thread, and two jade
> statues—all of the Buddha. They were of exquisite craftsmanship. The
> monks' cells, the towers, and the pavilions comprised over 1,000 rooms.
> Their carved beams, painted walls, and elegant doors and windows were
> beyond description.

In this monastery were stored sutras foreign rulers had presented to the
Northern Wei emperors. Translators used this collection to verify texts and
search out commentaries on obscure points they had encountered. Here
the enigmatic Bodhidharma gazed at a wall. On his arrival in 526, he is sup-

posed to have commented: "In my one hundred and fifty years of existence, I have been everywhere and traveled in many countries, but a temple of this beauty cannot be found anywhere in all the lands of the Buddha." The assembly in the monastery of mutinous soldiers from the northern garrisons shortly afterwards was less auspicious, since their frustration was appeased in a bout of killing.

The troubles continued right down to the abandonment of the city in 534. As the last Northern Wei emperors were no more than the playthings of military commanders, the Turkish experiment in Chinese-style administration foundered and tribal rivalries reappeared. One emperor even prayed to the Buddha not to be reborn as a ruler, just before he was strangled. The great pagoda at the Eternal Peace Monastery caught fire amid a snowstorm, reducing the pride of the Buddhist church in Luoyang to ashes. As hungry soldiers were very well aware, expenditure on the pagoda had practically exhausted the imperial treasury. Almost as expensive, though more durable, were the rock carvings at the Longmen grottoes to the south of Luoyang. A present-day visitor cannot be unmoved by this second

The Longmen grottoes

Yungang and its even greater number of figures. Chinese images of the Buddha in museums around the world were inspired by Northern Wei delight in stone sculpture.

Rebuilt Luoyang enjoyed over twenty years of prosperity before the neglected northern garrisons began to mutiny in 523. Five years later they descended on the imperial capital and slew without mercy officials and courtiers, Chinese and Tuoba alike. After this massacre Luoyang ceased to be the effective political center of north China, which was divided between generals in command of forces stationed to its east and west. The strong man was the Chinese general Gao Huan. The murder of his close associate at the imperial court, on the orders of the last Northern Wei emperor, sealed the fate of both the dynasty and the city. In 534 Gao Huan occupied Luoyang, executed senior officials for failing to give the emperor better advice, and then evacuated the city's entire population. At three days' notice its inhabitants were required to accompany Gao Huan to his own base, the city of Ye in present-day Henan province, where he declared himself the first Eastern Wei emperor. Northern Wei Luoyang was left empty and three years later Gao Huan had its defenses pulled down, lest another dynasty use the deserted city as a base for military operations against him.

PART THREE

THE MIDDLE EMPIRE
589–1368

An example of Slender Gold calligraphy

CHAPTER 5

Reunification:
Sui and Tang Chang'an

Poor Chang'an looks like a chessboard,
Won and lost for a hundred years.
Now the mansions have new owners;
Another generation dons
The caps and robes of high office.

UNDER THE SUI AND TANG EMPERORS CHANG'AN WAS A CITY without rival in the world. The walls of the imperial city, excluding the Great Luminous Palace which was added in 634 as a northeastern extension to the city, covered an area of 70 square kilometers, as compared to 14 square kilometers enclosed within the Aurelian walls of Rome built in the late third century and the 12 square kilometers within the extended walls of Constantinople built around 447 by Theodosius II. The uniqueness of Chang'an is perhaps best illustrated by a comparison with Baghdad, then the largest city in existence beyond the boundaries of the Chinese empire. Baghdad covered 30 square kilometers, of which the walled city accounted for barely 5 square kilometers. Even though the construction of the Great Luminous Palace as a residence for the forcibly retired first Tang emperor destroyed the symmetry of Chang'an, the city founded by the Sui dynasty came closest of all imperial capitals to cosmological perfection.

The decision of Yang Jian, the first Sui emperor, Wen Di, to build a new imperial capital was a solemn one. When Yang Jian, a part-Turkish part-Chinese soldier who would eventually unify north and south China, took over from the Northern Zhou dynasty, he inherited a government in which Chinese titles obscured the realities of power, for military figures like himself determined policy. Before his elevation as the emperor of all China, he seems to have decided upon a more genuinely Chinese system of admin-

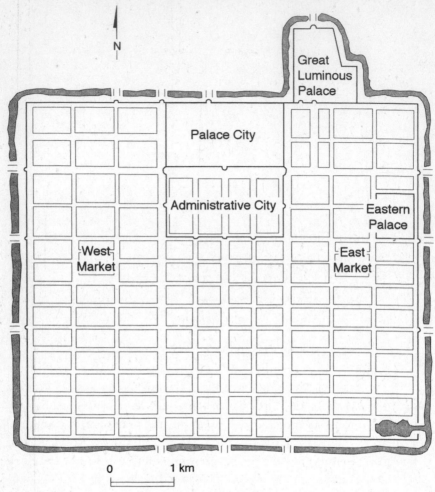

Site map of the Great Luminous Palace

istration recruited from worthy families across the empire. Yang Jian proclaimed his intention of following the precedent set by the Han emperors, the last rulers of a powerfully united China. That much of his official structure copied the Northern Wei administration goes to show how complete the Sino-Turkish synthesis was during the forty years when Luoyang acted as the capital of the northern provinces.

In accordance with the desire to resume traditional Chinese ways in government, it was natural that Sui Chang'an should be seen as the cosmic center of a renewed empire. Yang Jian placed in charge of its planning the architect and engineer Yuwen Kai, who not only oversaw the construction of the new imperial capital but also improved the Grand Canal, which linked north China with the key economic area of the lower Yangzi valley.

Along this waterway was transported the tax-grain needed to support Chang'an and Luoyang, the cities built respectively by the first and second Sui emperors. Yuwen Kai appreciated Yang Jian's desire for a city that symbolized the newly ordered empire. The location of the Former Han capital, the original Chang'an, therefore possessed a talismanic quality quite impossible to resist, and so Yuwen Kai recommended a site for the new imperial capital to the southeast of its ruins.

Since the fall of the Later Han dynasty in 220, old Chang'an had been sacked and rebuilt on numerous occasions as one ephemeral dynasty after another had taken and occupied it. In 582, the second year of his reign, Yang Jian accepted Yuwen Kai's recommendation and issued an edict announcing his decision to build a new Chang'an. The edict assured his subjects that divination had provided favorable results and that astronomical and geomantic considerations had been taken into full account when selecting the city's actual site. It asked the people to take on the burden of work in these terms: "Planning the new and getting rid of the old is like a farmer looking forward to autumn. Though the work is arduous he knows that after harvest he will enjoy food in plenty."

Yang Jian's Chang'an was built on such an unprecedented scale that the labor involved was indeed to prove arduous. On his return to the new imperial capital in 583, after an absence caused by a famine there, the emperor was delighted with the completion of his new palace, but besides himself with rage at the appalling cost in human lives.

> Finishing the palace, at a time of scarcity, entailed great sufferings on the part of the people. The superintendent of the work was a hard and unpitying master. When Yang Jian came to inspect the palace before he came to live in it, the superintendent had to hurriedly bury the bodies of the workmen who had died of exhaustion. Their corpses were lying about everywhere. Seeing the enormous pile of buildings that had been erected for him, the emperor pointed his finger at the superintendent and said: "In this extravagance you have given reason to the people of the Empire to hate me with bitterest hatred." Fearing for his life this man trembled but, once the Empress had seen the palace, the superintendent's fortunes improved. So pleased was she that, instead of losing his head, he was showered with presents from the grateful Empress.

Tough as Yang Jian was with those who served him, the first Sui emperor was in awe of his strong-willed Turkish wife. If she liked the palace of Long-lived Benevolence, then that was that. Yet Yang Jian was correct in anticipating trouble from an overburdened people, especially as his successor would even call up able-bodied women to labor on unfinished sections of the Grand Canal.

The labor required to build the earthen walls of Chang'an alone was immense. Inside its rectangular city wall, other walls were built for the palace and administrative cities as well as enclosing wards. In the center and backed up against the northern city wall stood the palace of Long-lived Benevolence, whose main audience hall was called the Palace of the Cosmic Ultimate. To its south, in another earthen enclosure, was situated the administrative city, with government offices laid out along internal streets. The concentration of the administration in this inner city was an innovation, because in previous imperial capitals ministries were scattered. Between the palace and administrative cities and the city walls were 108 rectangular walled compounds, of which all but two were residential wards served by two internal streets in the shape of a cross, with a gate in each of the four sides. The two non-residential wards comprised the markets, one in the west of the city and one in the east. 108 is a cosmological number, the product of multiplying 9, ordered space, by 12, ordered time. The main axis of Chang'an was the great north-south avenue that always divided imperial capitals into two equal halves: it was 147 meters wide. Lesser avenues measured 69 meters in width. The return to a strict grid-plan did more than satisfy a cosmological design, since it gave the imperial authorities control over the new city's inhabitants. No one was allowed to walk the main streets once the central bell tower had tolled the curfew.

In Chang'an the eastern side of the city was favored by wealthy people, whose large mansions could occupy as much as half a ward and house as many as three thousand people. Some of their gardens became so extensive that an edict of 779 ordered the destruction of those that had gone "beyond all former bounds in size and luxury of appointments." More spontaneous than either the geometrical arrangements favored in Europe or the stereotyped landscapes in Japan, the Chinese garden always had irregular and unexpected features that appealed more to the imagination than the reasoning faculty of the observer. The basic elements were the same as landscape painting: mountains and water, which could be interpreted simply as gnarled rocks and a pond.

Perhaps the most magnificent garden within the city walls of Chang'an belonged to Li Diyu, a minister whose checkered career overlapped with renowned Tang poet and fellow garden-lover Bai Juyi's. Li Diyu served under six emperors, alternating between trusted confidant of the ruler and banished critic of eunuch power, before dying in disgrace on the southern island of Hainan in 849. His garden in northeastern Chang'an was famous for its "fantastic stones and ancient pines, austere as those in any painting". But on the foundation of the imperial city, in 582, there were neither houses nor gardens. In order to fill the vast space within its earthen walls, Yang Jian launched a settlement campaign beginning with an order to his sons, the imperial princes, to build their mansions in the southwestern part of Chang'an in the hope that this would stimulate other building. The emperor also made gifts of land for religious purposes, and by his death in 604 there were over a hundred Buddhist and Daoist temples. There were still, however, many unoccupied wards on the fall of the Sui dynasty fourteen years later. The building of an imperial capital on such a scale early in the dynasty was a supreme act of faith, indicating confidence in the longevity of the new imperial house and its capacity to hold all China together within the empire. Confidence in the former was misplaced, but the next dynasty, the Tang, proved that it was possible to rule not only China but also much of Central Asia from Chang'an for more than a century.

Intending to restore the Chinese empire on a firm foundation, Yang Jian gave immediate attention to education. The revival of learning was an essential element in his drive to end hereditary privilege and to raise standards in the imperial administration. To do this he expected the examination system to recruit new men from outside the powerful families that had monopolized office for so long. At the imperial university in Chang'an he established two new faculties concerned with the teaching of calligraphy and mathematics. Practice in calligraphy was not new, but here we have the first mention of definite organized instruction in the art. It was something that developed further in the flowering of poetic composition under the Tang dynasty. Appreciation of calligraphy has always ranged from simply observing the calligrapher's skill in handling the brush to the pleasure that stems from a sense of the actual personality expressed in the individual strokes. The expressive character of a brushstroke can vary enormously according to the energy with which the calligrapher applies the ink.

In 604 Yang Guang probably hastened his father's death, thereby confirming Yang Jian's obsessive fear that one of his five sons would emerge as the leader of a court faction and replace him. Ironically, Yang Guang was the only son to have avoided suspicion due to his stay on official business in south China. There he embraced Buddhism with enthusiasm and took vows as a lay member of its community of believers. This was a shrewd move that endeared him to the southern Chinese, still smarting from the overthrow of the Chen dynasty at Nanjing. But Yang Guang's cultural strategy in the south was by no means limited to Buddhism, as he also showed favor to

Daoist and Confucian traditions.

Yang Guang's motive for getting rid of his hard-working father is difficult to fathom, because neither the dynastic history nor tales about this
"bad emperor" provide a precise picture of the events of 604. All that can
be accepted with any certainty is the conviction in Chang'an that Yang
Guang was guilty of arranging the murder. The problem with this is its
conformity to the stereotype of the power-mad ruler, whose grandiose
plans for the empire would brook no opposition. It is not impossible that
Yang Jian glimpsed such a danger in his designated successor and considered withdrawing his support for the succession. On the other hand, there
is evidence of Yang Guang's sensitivity to the finer things in life; his con-
noisseurship, his accomplished poetry and prose, his interest in both inherited and imported beliefs. And there was no reluctance to accept him as
emperor among the officials who had loyally served his father.

Between Yang Jian and Yang Guang, father and son, there was perhaps
only a difference of degree. Both rulers commissioned great public works,
the imperial capitals of Chang'an and Luoyang being their most obvious
monuments, but Yang Guang's restlessness gave him a reputation for
extravagance. Ostentatious though his tours of the provinces always were,
Yang Guang said in 609 that "from ancient times the Sons of Heaven have
carried out inspections. But the emperors in south China, during the time
when the empire was divided, mostly perpetuated womanly ways. They sat
in the innermost palace without meeting their people face to face. How
would you interpret their actions?" To which question a courtier replied,
"This is precisely why their hold on power slipped from them."

In the same year this conversation occurred, Yang Guang started to
become preoccupied with the conquest of Koguryo, a Korean state with its
capital at modern Pyongyang. Militarily Koguryo was a threat to China only
in alliance with its nomad neighbors, but Yang Guang magnified border
incidents so he could persist in squandering his armies there. Fortunately for
China exhaustion caused the king of Koguryo to end hostilities and in 614
he became a vassal. Though Yang Guang ordered the empire back to peaceful pursuits, the dynasty was already engulfed by peasant rebellion. One
courtier who tried to point out the extent of the unrest was beaten to death
in the audience chamber for his pains. Traveling to south China in 616,
where he stayed till his assassination two years later, a disappointed Yang
Guang left a power vacuum behind him, which was filled by Li Yuan, one of
the most powerful Sui commanders. He marched on Chang'an, overwhelmed its defenses, and was formally installed as the first Tang emperor.

Li Yuan had made his move in 618 at the prompting of his second son,

Li Shimin, the future Tang emperor Taizong. However, the exceptional military service rendered by Li Shimin in the struggle to secure the new dynasty provoked a crisis, as rivalry with the heir apparent cost Li Shimin's brothers their lives and nearly cost Li Shimin his. But he struck first, marching one of his trusted commanders, fully armed, into the imperial palace to announce to the startled emperor that Li Shimin was now in charge. The coup was a success.

Like the majority of rebel leaders who succeeded in founding imperial dynasties, Li Yuan was not a commoner but a nobleman whose family had served under several northern dynasties, including the Northern Wei. Notwithstanding the Li family's official lineage, it was actually Turkish in origin. Thoroughly sinicized through marriage and official service, the Lis never quite forgot their Turko-Chinese heritage and remained conscious of the danger posed by the warlike Turks. In 626 Li Shimin's familiarity with Turkish manners helped him when a large force approached Chang'an, presumably summoned by the heir apparent but arriving too late to prevent Li Shimin's seizure of power. Refusing to take refuge behind the walls of the city, Li Shimin rode out with only a handful of followers to parley with the Turkish leader. The dynastic history tells us that this bold action, coupled with the timely arrival of imperial reinforcements, persuaded the Turks to withdraw.

A year later the military strength of the Turks was undermined by inclement weather. Four feet of snow covered the ground, killing the herds and depriving the nomads of food. The heavy snow also precipitated a rebellion among their subject peoples. Although ministers urged immediate action, Li Shimin hesitated before ordering an offensive that surprised the main Turkish encampment deep in the steppe. Having captured an outpost of one thousand tents, the Chinese advanced without detection and launched a totally unexpected assault. As their vanguard of two hundred mounted archers approached through a mist, the Turkish leader was utterly unaware of danger until the cavalrymen actually reached his own tent. In the confused fighting, he escaped with a few followers, while the remaining nomads were either cut down or taken prisoner. News of the great victory was carried by a relay of riders to Chang'an, where Li Shimin proclaimed a general amnesty to celebrate this unexpected triumph of Chinese arms.

The youthful second Tang emperor—styled Taizong, meaning "Great Founder"—had achieved his first foreign policy success. Even though he could never benefit from the luster associated with the status of a founding emperor, Li Shimin's imperial title was an indication of his considered worth, for he possessed ample personal qualities and talents that by themselves would have assured him a place among the greatest Chinese emperors. Though we know little of Li Shimin's upbringing and education, his Turko-Chinese heritage ensured a schooling in both the arts of war and peace. He was a powerful archer and a superb rider: the bas-reliefs of six favorite steeds, which decorated his tomb, are still preserved. Though well versed in classical learning and a calligrapher of note, his career remained essentially a military one until he ascended the dragon throne.

For his time, Li Shimin appears to have been unusually free from superstition. Shortly after becoming emperor, when provincial officials started to report favorable omens to him, he retorted that whether the dynasty prospered or not depended on the quality of the administration and the actions of men, and nothing more. Instrumental in realizing Li Shimin's desire for good government was Wei Zheng, his most valued counselor. The military background of the Li family made the Li Shimin very sensitive to dangers from generals and led him, on Wei Zheng's recommendation, to shift the balance of power from the military to the civil arm of officialdom. He increased the number and frequency of examinations and instituted a scholarship system to promote learning. The northern aristocracy began to decline in influence under Li Shimin, when its place in government was gradually taken by professional bureaucrats recruited on the basis of personal talent and education.

The rise of officials committed to the service of the empire changed the position of the ruler: he was no longer the chief aristocrat whose pedigree, as in the case of the Li family, was modest; on the contrary, with no aristocracy to challenge his authority, and with a loyal and hard-working bureaucracy, the imperial family became set apart from ordinary people in quite a new way, and the emperor started to gather powers that could led to despotism. Wei Zheng set himself the task of resisting this dangerous political trend by insisting upon the joint ruler-minister approach. When asked, after Li Shimin had been on the dragon throne for a decade, whether government was better conducted than it had been before the emperor took over the administration, Wei Zheng replied:

> "In the beginning Your Majesty feared that we would not dare to tell you your mistakes; later you received our admonitions with pleasure; now one must say you accept them with difficulty."

At Li Shimin's request Wei Zheng gave specific instances of what he meant and the emperor remarked: "I would never have known my character was changing, unless Wei Zheng had proved it to me by these personal examples." Yet the ruler-minister relationship was not always as smooth as this exchange indicates, for Wei Zheng's opposition to some imperial schemes often threw Li Shimin into a towering rage. The minister was never awed by the emperor's powerful personality, however, and he was completely unafraid of him, even when he heard that Li Shimin had cried out: "I am going to have to kill that old country bumpkin!" Wei Zheng's daring independence rested on an unshakeable conviction that the fall of the previous Sui dynasty was attributable to its refusal to heed the advice of loyal officials. He believed that its inability to deal with internal difficulties resulted from a preoccupation with foreign conquest, a belief that led him in 640 to oppose an expansionist policy in Central Asia, much to Li Shimin's annoyance.

From Wei Zheng's rapid rise to the highest post in the official bureaucracy, and the reliance Li Shimin placed on him for seventeen of the twenty-three years he reigned, it might be thought that the minister really did enjoy a special relationship with the emperor. Nothing could be farther from the truth, if this is assumed to mean cordial personal relations. For the emperor's relations with Wei Zheng were often strained and stormy because whereas the minister stuck to principle, Li Shimin adopted only those principles that contributed to the success of his administration and the glory of his dynasty. He was frugal when China was poor, but once its economy had recovered, he was eager to embark on building projects inside and outside the imperial capital. He avoided foreign adventurism when China was militarily weak but later sought to bring far-flung peoples under Chinese influence.

The fame of Wei Zheng as an upright adviser was not unconnected with the relief Confucian officials felt at a return to a fully bureaucratic system of government. Li Shimin was a very self-conscious ruler, and a weapon that Wei Zheng was adept at deploying against his unwise policies was the judgment of posterity. On more than one occasion the emperor endeavored to influence the officials in charge of writing the dynastic history. When he asked about the possibility of examining documents before they were deposited in an iron-bound chest, he was respectfully told that "in recording a ruler's words and deeds, good and evil must be written down so that the ruler will not act improperly. For that reason they are never made available." Still worried about how the deaths of his brothers were being treated, Li Shimin appears to have asked Wei Zheng to intervene, and there is evidence that sections of the dynastic history dealing with this distressing episode were rewritten. But like Liu Bang, the first Han emperor, Li Shimin appreciated his own need for advice at the beginning of his reign. So just as Liu Bang turned to his chamberlain Lu Jia for guidance, Li

Shimin asked Wei Zheng to write a manual for him as well as his sons. It was entitled *A Record of Good and Evil Rulers since Antiquity*, and the examples Wei Zheng selected for discussion underscore his own view of responsible government, not least because he was keenly aware that during Li Shimin's reign precedents were being set that would affect the conduct of state affairs for generations to come.

In spite of his pragmatism, Li Shimin remained conscious of his subjects' awe of the spirit world, and a particularly severe earthquake gave him cause to pause. As a sign of self-blame, he ordered that a small palace in Luoyang be dismantled and its materials given to families who had suffered in a flood the previous year. Wei Zheng's suggestion that the earthquake was a heavenly criticism of imperial policy must have stung the emperor, since he rewarded the minister with gold and promised to mend his ways. But it was the last gift that Li Shimin bestowed on his faithful minister in 643, the year Wei Zheng died, that signified his tolerance of this official critic. On his final visit to the minister's home, the emperor brought along his sixteenth daughter to be presented to her future father-in-law. When Li Shimin asked Wei Zheng whether he was able to receive the princess, the minister was too feeble to reply. Next morning Wei Zheng passed away and, as a sign of respect, Li Shimin closed the imperial court for five days and ordered the imperial family and senior officials into mourning.

Li Shimin open-mindedness inaugurated what can only be described as a cultural renaissance. In Chang'an, and to a lesser extent in Luoyang, the Tang dynasty presided over a period of significant artistic and intellectual advance. Typical of Li Shimin's attitude was the audience he gave in 635 to a Christian missionary. An inscription set up in Chang'an records how a Nestorian monk was welcomed by the emperor, who commented:

> "The Way has more than one name. There is more than one Sage. Alopen, a man of great virtue, has brought images and books from afar to present them at the imperial capital. After examining his teachings, We find them profound and pacific, stressing what is good and important. This religion benefits all men. Let it be preached freely in Our Empire."

The inclusive habit of mind in evidence here, coupled with Confucian skepticism, has tended to keep religion and the priesthood as minor elements in China, with the result that religious persecution barely figures in the historical record. The severe, though short, repression in 845 can be seen therefore as an attempt to prevent a Buddhist church from securing a stranglehold over China's economy. Its method was confiscation of property and the compulsory laicization of supernumerary monks and nuns.

Another pilgrim to whom Li Shimin granted a personal interview was Xuanzang, on his return from India with Buddhist texts. Although the emperor inclined to Daoism, he supported Confucianism for the sake of the civil service, besides welcoming Buddhism and other foreign faiths. But he never provided the lavish support and patronage that the Buddhists had received from the Sui dynasty, as Chang'an was only allowed three Buddhist monasteries against the two allotted to the Daoists. One reason for Li Shimin's caution was an unfortunate interview he had in 637 with a monk, who dared to complain about the subordination of Buddhism to Daoism at the imperial court. When the monk went on to say that the Li family was misguided in claiming descent from Laozi, because the legendary founder of Daoism was the bastard son of a slave girl and everyone knew how Li Shimin's forbears were of Turko-Chinese stock, the audience chamber trembled in anticipation of the emperor's wrath over the slur on his ancestry. With great difficulty was he dissuaded from ordering the tactless monk's execution. By 645 Li Shimin had sufficiently recovered from the insult to receive Xuanzang. He only intended to give the monk a few minutes' audience, but he was so interested in the account Xuanzang gave of the countries through which he passed that Li Shimin asked him to become an adviser on foreign relations. Explaining how he had become a monk to study Buddhism in depth, Xuanzang told he emperor that "if I am ordered to return to secular life, it will be like dragging a boat from water to dry land." So Li Shimin agreed to Xuanzang's request to embark on his program of translation, and in return Xuanzang wrote for the emperor an account of his travels entitled *Record of the Western Regions*. At the end of his life Li Shimin seems to have turned to Xuanzang as a spiritual adviser, because the well-traveled monk was with him when he died in 649. After the accession of Li Zhi, Li Shimin's ninth son, Xuanzang boldly suggested that the new emperor should build a stone pagoda to house the Buddhist scriptures and images he had brought back from India. A seven-storied pagoda was built in brick "to show the magnificence of a great country and to be a monument to the Sakyamuni Buddha." The Big Wild Goose Pagoda, as it is called, still stands today in what was the Tang capital city of Chang'an, present-day Xi'an.

Li Shimin's doubts about the ability of the heir apparent, Li Zhi, to lead the Chinese empire effectively were well founded. In spite of efforts to prepare him for the dragon throne, the emperor Gaozong, as Li Zhi was titled, proved to be a well-meaning but weak ruler who was entirely overshadowed by his empress Wu Zhao. This attractive and talented woman was the exact

The Big Wild Goose Pagoda built by Tang Emperor Li Zhi.
The Pagoda still stands in modern Xi'an.

antithesis of the Confucian ideal. Her interference in public affairs, her pursuit of personal vendettas, her complete disregard for principle, and her exploitation of court factionalism has ensured that no sympathetic record of her actions now survives, so in fact we can be sure of very little about her. Her rise to supreme power began soon after the accession of Gaozong. Starting as a lowly concubine of Li Shimin, Wu Zhao had left the imperial harem on his death and entered a Buddhist nunnery in Chang'an. There Gaozong saw her and conceived such a deep passion that she returned to the imperial palace as one of his own concubines in 654. His first wife, Empress Wang, hoped that the arrival of a new woman would divert the emperor's attention from a favorite concubine, who had just borne him a son. What Empress Wang could never have anticipated was that within a year Gaozong would degrade her and raise up Wu Zhao in her place. At the time of her elevation few officials and courtiers appreciated the political skills of Gaozong's new empress, but it was not long before Wu Zhao revealed how effective, and how ruthless, were her methods of manipulation at the imperial court. Soon the ex-empress and the favorite concubine were brutally executed: they were left to drown in a wine vat, their arms and legs cut off. These peculiar injuries were probably intended to hinder their ghosts in seeking revenge on Wu Zhao. Officials who had tried to stop Gaozong from making her his chief consort were sent to the provinces where their careers ended. As the emperor's health deteriorated and he was forced to retire to a summer palace and to hold audiences on alternate days, there was every opportunity for Empress Wu and her supporters to consolidate their already powerful position. Empress Wu's authority became virtually impregnable in 660, when Gaozong suffered a stroke which left him partially paralyzed.

The regime of Empress Wu, however, did not solely rest on court intrigue. Her dominance also involved the formulation of new policies. One of the first was the designation late in 657 of Luoyang as a second imperial capital. Branches of every ministry and government agency were set up there, and in 662 an annex of the imperial university was established as well. Henceforth the imperial court often moved to Luoyang and, after Gaozong's death in 683, it stayed permanently there until 701. One reason for the transfer was political. In Chang'an there were too many supporters of the Tang dynasty for Empress Wu's liking, while in Luoyang newly appointed supporters from the northeastern provinces were closer to their family homes. Another reason was Empress Wu's unease in Chang'an, where her superstitious nature was sorely troubled by the ghosts of the two women she had had killed. Though obsessed with the spirit world, Empress

Wu was careful to ensure her own survival by strengthening her temporal relationship with the ruling class. Humbler official families, like her own, were raised in status and Confucian scholars of merit received her sponsorship. Some of the latter joined a secret secretariat, known as the Scholars of the Northern Gate, which processed for the empress memorials addressed to the emperor, and made policy decisions that were properly the duty of ministers. By the accession of the fourth Tang emperor, Zhongzong, there could be no doubt that Empress Wu ran the Chinese empire. When it became obvious that Zhongzong, her newly enthroned son, had ideas of his own, he was swiftly deposed in favor of his more compliant younger brother. Neither of these men played any role in government while their mother was alive, but after Empress Wu died in 705 both were briefly restored.

Allowing for the hatred of Confucian commentators towards her enthronement in 690, it is quite apparent that Empress Wu was a gifted ruler, even though her use of secret agents and sudden killings weakened the imperial bureaucracy, as did the freedom she allowed her favorites. It was indeed the scope that her personal rule gave for their crimes that most shocked her contemporaries, especially as the ageing ruler seems to have admitted these disreputable men to the imperial palace as her lovers. The worst were the two brothers Zhang, who gained Empress Wu's affection in 697, the year of her seventy-second birthday. Dressed in rich silks the Zhang brothers frequented the imperial court with powdered and rouged faces, exacting a deference greater than that accorded to princes of the blood. In order to give some semblance of respectability to these cock-sure favorites, they were officially commissioned to undertake literary work in company with noted scholars, but this deceived no one. In addition to the two favorites, there were other Zhang family members who shamelessly profited from the special relationship in order to enrich themselves. One openly accepted enormous bribes for arranging official appointments. On one occasion, he couldn't recall the first name of a Xie who had bribed him, and as a result all sixty Xies on the applicant list were given appointments.

After the return of the imperial court to Chang'an, the Zhang brothers became even more notorious. They tried to have the chief minister executed when he spoke out against their stranglehold over the imperial court. Forcibly retired, this official said to Empress Wu: "One day Your Majesty will certainly reflect on my case." Then turning to the Zhang brothers, he added: "Those brats will in the end be the cause of a revolution." The degradation of the chief minister had undermined her authority and given stimulus to the forces that had been slowly gathering in favor of a restoration of the Tang. At Luoyang again in 705 Empress Wu was aware that she needed to conciliate public opinion in view of the unpopularity of the Zhangs, but events were already moving too fast for her to avoid deposition herself. Officials and courtiers loyal to the Li family executed the two Zhang brothers in the courtyard of the imperial palace one night, before informing a disheveled Empress Wu that her half-century of power was now at an end.

The first decade of the Tang restoration witnessed a bitter power-struggle that lasted until the accession of the sixth Tang emperor, Xuanzong, a grandson of Empress Wu, in 712. The longest-reigning member of the Li family, Xuanzong restored the Chinese empire to its former greatness and is remembered as one of China's famous rulers. To return the imperial bureaucracy to its normal state of order, the new emperor streamlined the highest level of appointments and paid attention to the selection of candidates most suited to official posts. In 716, after complaints about the results of the latest examinations, Xuanzong summoned all those who had been appointed as district magistrates and examined them personally on their administrative views. Their answers were deemed to be so poor that nearly half of these graduates were sent back to their studies.

In recognition of the splendor and rich cultural life of the imperial capital, Xuanzong was styled Ming Huang, "the Brilliant Ruler." Poets, painters, and musicians thronged Chang'an's streets; architects were commissioned to enhance the beauty of the city; and, in the eyes of later generations, the tragic love of Xuanzong and his favorite concubine, Yang Yuhuan (or "Yang Guifei, "Precious Consort Yang"), lent a romantic glamour to the era. Every Chinese knows how the aging emperor fell deeply in love with a beautiful concubine named "Jade Ring," Yuhuan, who beguiled his mind. The disgruntled troops of the emperor's bodyguard claimed that Yang Yuhuan's great influence was a threat to the empire and demanded that she be executed; they backed their demand with a threatened mutiny. After the chief eunuch had strangled her in a Buddhist temple, Xuanzong was so sad that he no longer wished to be emperor. His grief moved many poets, for it happened that his reign overlapped with the golden age of Chinese poetry. The most famous treatment is that of Bai Juyi, whose *Everlasting Sorrow* captures something of the tragedy.

> The soldiers stopped, no one would stir
> Until their horses' hooves trampled
> Upon those elegant eyebrows.
> Ornate hairpins fell to the ground
> With tassels of the greenest jade.
> No one bent down to pick them up.

The Emperor could not save her,
He could only cover his face.
Later, when he turned back to look,
The place of running blood and tears
Was hidden in a cloud of dust.

This extract from Bai Juyi's semi-fictional version of events remains the enduring image of Xuanzong's sorrow.

"Precious Consort Yang" was not the first concubine that Xuanzong raised to the rank of highest consort, as the dynastic history makes good record. Shortly after the death of her predecessor in 736, the emperor ordered one of his sons to pass Yang Yuhuan onto him, although she was already that prince's wife. This un-Confucian demand shocked Chang'an, but Xuanzong was so taken with his son's sixteen-year-old bride on her presentation at the imperial court that he arranged for her ordination as a Daoist nun, as an intermediate stage in her transition from daughter-in-law to secondary wife. Two years later the emperor judged that enough time had elapsed for Yang Yuhuan to join his harem. The most virile of the Tang rulers, Xuanzong's wives bore him fifty-nine children during his reign, thirty sons and twenty-nine daughters. To relieve the monotony of harem life, he allowed his concubines to toss coins in order to compete for the privilege of his bedchamber. Otherwise they spent their solitary hours making clothes for troops stationed along the frontiers. A soldier once discovered a note in the sleeve of his coat on which the maker described her present life as having already passed, and expressed the hope that she might be united with him in their next life. He showed the note to his commanding officer, who sent it to the emperor. Xuanzong ordered the writer of the note to identify herself, and promised she would not be punished. When one of his harem ladies admitted her guilt, he was compassionate enough to let her marry the soldier.

Though Yang Yuhuan made little use of her needle, there were dramatic quarrels between her and the emperor. Expelled twice from the imperial palace, Yang Yuhuan was recalled when Xuanzong found he could not live without her. Thus she became the emperor's inseparable companion, sharing his musical interests by playing with him in the same orchestra, and going with him in winter to hot springs at present-day Lintong, near the mausoleum of the First Emperor at Mount Li. As Yang Yuhuan came from a large family of eight elder sisters and a younger brother, her elevation had an immediate impact on Chang'an society. Three of the sisters rivalled Xuanzong's new consort in beauty and they were conspicuous figures in the imperial capital. Recognizing the favored status they enjoyed, the Turkish general An Lushan assiduously cultivated them so that in 750, when the emperor presented An Lushan with a Chang'an mansion, the entire Yang family went to greet him at his new residence. So competitive were the sisters that, if one of them felt that a neighbor's home was superior to hers, she would order her place torn down and rebuilt in a more magnificent fashion. Once they even competed with one another to see whose carriage was best decorated. To the amazement of the city's inhabitants their carriages ended up with such heavy ornamentation that only oxen could pull them through the streets. Not only did Yang Yuhuan take a similar delight in display but, more dangerous for China, she shared her sisters' affection for An Lushan. The influence of Yang Yuhuan at the imperial court can be seen by the deferential way in which this soldier treated her there. In the audience chamber he once bowed to her first. The annoyed emperor asked the reason for this bizarre behavior and was informed that, "Your subject is a barbarian. A barbarian puts his mother first and his father afterwards." Xuanzong was amused by the reply and, at Yang Yuhuan's suggestion, allowed An Lushan the run of the imperial harem. How far matters went between her and the general we do not know, but his self-confidence in rebelling suggests he had the measure of Xuanzong's personal and political weaknesses. Along with Yang Yuhuan, her brother, sisters, and cousins were slain once An Lushan rebelled.

Luoyang fell to the rebels in 755. Having taken possession of the second largest city in China, An Lushan proclaimed himself emperor and set about forming an administration of his own. He had at his disposal a seasoned army of 200,000 men, including cavalry recruited from border peoples loyal to the Chinese empire. The government, by contrast, was ill-prepared, its immediate military strength being solely the imperial guard. The fall of Chang'an a year after Luoyang's capture seemed to have sealed the fate of the Tang dynasty. It was a terrific shock for the inhabitants of the imperial capital to see the government collapse so quickly, and even more to be deserted by their emperor, who had slipped away by night. Many members of great families fled to the southern provinces, some of them never to return. Already that mood of pessimism, the dominant trait of writers in the late eighth and early ninth centuries, had emerged in the verse of Du Fu, China's greatest poet. His *Song of a Prince Deposed* expresses perfectly the bewilderment felt in rebel-occupied Chang'an:

A Prince, in tears on a street-corner,

Using a false name. A poor man
In urgent need of employment.
Marks of a hundred days' hiding
In thorns show from his head to toe.
But the imperial hook-nose
Distinguishes this stray Dragon.
"O Prince, care for your sacred self!
I dare not speak more in the road."

The Tang reaction to An Lushan was slow as well as humiliating. Emperor Suzong, Xuanzong's successor, needed to call upon the help of Uighur Turkish cavalry from the northern steppe in order to recover Chang'an in 757. Difficulties arose with the Uighurs on the capture of Luoyang, where the heir apparent was believed to have shown the nomad leader insufficient respect. Several Chinese officials in his retinue were cruelly whipped to death, and then the incident was used as a pretext to plunder the environs of Luoyang. Despite this disagreement, the Sino-Uighur offensive put the rebels on the back foot, and An Lushan was killed by his son. Without either the will or strength to completely crush the rebels, the Tang court was obliged to settle for a compromise peace. In 762, the year the offending heir apparent became emperor Dezong, those rebel leaders who recognized the dynasty were permitted to continue as the semi-autonomous governors of the areas they controlled. Subsequent emperors never ceased to worry about how to reconcile their own claims of empire-wide authority with the political reality of the situation.

The Tang court, however, had no time to reflect on the nature of the peace, for a new external threat appeared in the form of the Tibetans. The withdrawal of the most effective elements of the Chinese garrisons in Central Asia to deal with An Lushan's rebellion had an immediate impact on the Tibetan presence there. A number of Chinese client regimes paid homage to the Tibetan king instead of the Tang emperor, and Tibetan envoys were sent to strengthen these new ties. But the main direction of Tibetan expansion was towards China itself. In 763 the Tibetans occupied Chang'an for two weeks, thoroughly looting the city. Tang forces soon re-entered the city, but for the next thirteen years the northwest was at the mercy of Tibetan arms. It was fortunate for the Chinese empire that Tibet was soon wracked by internal troubles, as a dispute between its king and the great Buddhist monasteries left the latter dominant in Tibetan society.

The Tang empire, though now much reduced, enjoyed another century of peace before popular revolts, those tell-tale signs of impending dynastic change, arose. The eunuchs became a power once again, a legacy of Empress Wu's attempt to circumvent uncooperative branches of the imperial bureaucracy; the Buddhist church almost gained a monopoly over religious belief; military commanders were harder to handle, making taxes more difficult to collect; the decline of central government caused a neglect of water-conservancy schemes, the traditional unifying force in Chinese history; and, beyond the imperial frontiers, pressure was already mounting on the steppes. When the last Tang emperor was dethroned in 907, the empire split into nearly a dozen separate states, a fragmentation possibly connected with the invention of gunpowder. But, prior to this breakup of China, Chang'an remained a great imperial capital during one of the most intriguing eras of Chinese history.

Wild Goose Pagoda

The Little Wild Goose Pagoda in modern Xi'an.

Huaqing

The famous hot springs at Huaqing, where Xuanzong often visited with his concubine Yang Yuhuan.

CHAPTER 6

Dynastic Decline: Late Tang Chang'an

How smugly arrogant they seem!
Their richly caparisoned steeds
Glittering brightly as they charge
Headlong through the dust of the streets.
Who are these distinguished riders?
People say they are all eunuchs
From the Imperial Palace,
Holders of high official rank,
Civil as well as military.
No wonder their horses hurry
Fiercely along like stormy clouds!

THE TROUBLES OF THE EIGHTH CENTURY WERE NOT DISASTROUS to Chang'an. An Lushan's occupation in 756 had left the imperial palace intact, while the Tibetans, who looted the city in 763, had fired only private residences. The imperial palace was still the grandest collection of buildings in China, despite suffering some damage in 783. That year soldiers destined for the frontier rioted when they learned that they were only to receive subsistence rations on their march. This mutiny was the concluding phrase of the separatist movements begun thirty years earlier by An Lushan. As provincial opposition to the Tang house still commanded sufficient support among the common people to sustain renewed rebellion, the imperial court made the grave error of stirring up conflict with semi-autonomous provincial governors before it was certain that imperial forces could win in the field. The emperor Dezong, Xuanzong's great-grandson, had to issue an edict pardoning and reinstating in their commands all the rebel leaders except his immediate adversary, a retired general living in Chang'an who assumed command of the mutineers there. This renegade was put down with the aid of the Tibetans, thanks to the signing of a peace treaty. Dezong was grateful for the aid of his newfound ally, despite their intervention turning into something of a Tibetan raid by its end.

The treaty of 783 between China and Tibet had not been concluded without difficulty. Negotiations had gone on for several years, in part because the Tibetan king demanded that the Chinese emperor treat him like an uncle, a superior relative. Once De Zong acceded to this un-Confucian demand, a date was set for the agreement to be ratified. Even then, the peace ceremony almost failed because of the deep sense of shame felt by the Chinese ambassador, an elderly Confucian official. The treaty was to be accompanied by a solemn blood oath, to be taken in the blood of a bull representing the agricultural Chinese and a stallion representing the Tibetan herdsmen. But the Chinese ambassador demanded that the ceremony be downgraded, suggesting the threefold sacrifice of a sheep, a pig, and a dog. As there were no pigs in the vicinity, they settled for a sheep, a goat, and a dog. The Tibetan envoy, after the oath was taken and the texts of the treaty exchanged, still remained uneasy about the Chinese attitude, and insisted that both parties should swear another oath before a Buddhist shrine.

For hard-pressed Dezong the peace treaty was concluded in the nick of time. He had to seek refuge in a northwestern town during the military mutiny, becoming the second Tang emperor to abandon Chang'an in haste. Yet Dezong returned to the imperial capital and sensibly accepted the existence of semi-autonomous provincial governors. He also agreed to a greater involvement of the eunuchs in running the imperial administration, since he only survived the mutiny through their protection. A notable feature of ninth-century Chang'an is the influence of the eunuchs. How such a relatively small number of palace servants, largely recruited from the non-Chinese inhabitants of the southern provinces, acquired so much power in a highly cultured and sophisticated city remains a mystery. To officials and courtiers alike, the eunuchs were no more than a necessary evil, the guardians of the imperial harem. The dynastic history relates the steady growth of eunuch power to a high point during the reign of Xianzong, the emperor whom the eunuchs both enthroned and murdered. In 806 they installed this twenty-eight-year-old after the abdication of his gravely ill father, who reigned for less than a year. Xianzong's father had been encouraged by senior officials to curb eunuch influence at the imperial court, and so the eunuchs made sure that the son was more sympathetic to their ambitions, at least at first. But in 820:

Xianzong, now totally preoccupied by death, became increasingly irritable when he took a potion the eunuchs prepared for him, and declared to be the elixir of life. The emperor was so bad tempered that the least thing offended him and for trivial offenses he ordered immediate execution. In this way many eunuchs lost their lives. One day news flew through Chang'an that Xianzong was dead. The popular belief was that he had been poisoned by the chief eunuch, who dreaded lest he and his fellows might fall victim to the emperor's caprice.

After the drug overdose killed Xianzong, the eunuchs arranged for his son to succeed him. Hereafter they played a key part in every transfer of imperial power. There are several reasons why the eunuchs were able to interfere so easily in the succession: the physical isolation of the imperial family; the growing control of the eunuchs over the transmission of important documents; their increased political strength through alliances with court factions; and, in the last resort, the presence of an army under eunuch command close to the imperial capital.

The isolated life of an emperor in the imperial palace was not a new phenomenon, but his increased dependence on eunuch assistance was an unusual development connected with the so-called Department of the Inner Palace. Originally charged with routine palace management, the department had slowly expanded its sphere of influence until it became a eunuch council, a power base at the very heart of the Chinese empire. Its members were solely responsible to the emperor who could use them as confidential courtiers, spies, and even administrators. Their usefulness in court politics only tended to enhance the role they came to play in decision-making at the highest levels. Added to this, there was the link they enjoyed with eunuch-led armies, which were financed from eunuch-controlled palace treasuries. These new central forces were invaluable to rulers who were unable to impose their will upon the provinces. As the Chinese never subscribed to primogeniture, there was plenty of scope for the eunuchs to determine which of the emperor's sons should sit upon the dragon throne. The eldest son of the principal consort was usually named heir apparent, but the political nature of the actual accession meant that this prince often failed to succeed. Fewer than half of the Tang emperors were in fact eldest sons. The control the eunuchs exercised over affairs in the imperial palace greatly worried ministers: the two attempts they made in 831 and 854 to end eunuch power failed, each setback only serving to strengthen the position of the eunuchs and further undermine the credibility of the Tang dynasty.

Just as trying for Confucian officials was Xianzong's keen interest in Buddhism. Compared with the Chinese dynasties in Nanjing during the Turkish partition of the empire, the Tang had a lukewarm attitude toward the Buddhist faith. Indeed, the ill-fated emperor Xuanzong had endeavored to bring some order to Buddhism prior to the rebellion of An Lushan. In 750, the painter-poet Wang Wei needed to seek special permission to turn his country house and garden into a Buddhist monastery. If old temples needed repairs, their sponsors were not allowed to undertake them without an official inspection. And small shrines were amalgamated with larger temples and monasteries, so that the land owned by them could be kept within reasonable limits. Monks and nuns were neither allowed to preach in the countryside nor to sell Buddhist scriptures and images in the streets. Finally, ordination involved the issue of official certificates from 747 onwards. These policies had the effect of slowing down the recruitment of monks and nuns, but Buddhism was too well established to be seriously hampered by such restrictions. With some justification, then, the Confucian official Han Yu chose to address his famous anti-Buddhist memorial to the enthusiastic Xianzong in 819. The occasion he chose was the emperor's annual welcoming of a finger bone of the Buddha usually housed in a temple outside the walls of Chang'an. What seems to have upset Han Yu most was the hysteria that always greeted the arrival of the relic in the imperial capital. His account tells how "a soldier cut off his left arm in front of the Buddha's bone, and while holding it in his right hand, he reverenced the relic each time he took a step, his blood sprinkling the ground all the while. As for those who walked on their elbows and knees, biting off their fingers or pulling out their hair, their numbers could not be counted."

The answer was quite simple, Han Yu contended: just allow the city authorities to destroy the bone. Whilst his memorial drew together criticisms previously voiced by worried officials, it was the intemperate manner in which Han Yu dared to express himself that startled contemporaries. It is quoted at length here as a prime example of remonstrance.

Your Majesty's subject humbly submits that Buddhism is merely a barbarian cult, which was introduced into China during the Later Han dynasty and which never existed in ancient times.

It was in the reign of Ming Di of the Han dynasty that Buddhism was first introduced into China, and yet this emperor was on the dragon throne for only eighteen years. Subsequently, disorder followed disorder, and rulers did not reign for long. From the Liu Song, Southern Qi, Liang, Chen, and Northern Wei dynasties onwards, while the worship of

Buddhism became increasingly fervent, the rulers were more and more short-lived, except Liang Wu Di, who reigned for forty-eight years. He even abased himself in the service of the Buddha. In sacrifices in the ancestral temple meat was avoided. He himself ate a single meal of vegetables and fruit each day. But ultimately he was dethroned and starved to death in Nanjing. His dynasty was brought to an end shortly afterwards. Thus, the worship of the Buddha, from which blessings are sought, only brought disaster instead. It is obvious then that the Buddha is not worthy of great devotion.

The Buddha was a barbarian. In his own tongue he could not have made himself understood here, and his clothes were quite different from ours. He did not speak with the wisdom of ancient kings, nor was his body clad like theirs. He did not know the proper relationship between ruler and ministers and affection between father and son. If the Buddha were still alive today and had been sent to the imperial capital as his country's envoy, Your Majesty would probably have granted him an audience, entertained him at a banquet, awarded him a suit of clothes and seen that he left our country's borders under guard, so that he might not have deluded the people. Now that he has been dead for a long time, why should we let this decayed and rotten bone, an ill-omened and disgusting relic enter the imperial palace?

"Reverence ghosts and spirits," said Confucius, "but keep them at a distance." When an ancient king presented his condolences, he sent a sorcerer ahead to ward off evil influences with a branch of peach-wood and a broomstick. But now Your Majesty for no apparent reason intends to watch this filthy object, without first sending a sorcerer and without making use of the peach-wood and broomstick, and none of your officials point out the error and none of your censors offer any criticism. Deeply ashamed, your humble subject begs that the bone be handed over to the city authorities to be consigned to water or fire, so that it may be destroyed forever. Then future generations will be relieved of their doubt and the people know how wise and far-seeing is their Emperor.

If the Buddha should have the power to inflict trouble, your subject would be prepared to endure anything visited upon him. With Heaven as his witness, he would have no regrets. It is with all sincerity that he hereby submits this memorial.

Xianzong was beside himself with rage at Han Yu's impertinence. "While I can tolerate Han Yu's assertion that I have been excessive in my worship of the Buddha," the emperor commented, "is it not absurd to assert that, since the Later Han dynasty, those rulers who have worshipped the Buddha have been short-lived? As an official, Han Yu's arrogant assertion is unpardonable." But such was the support the memorial writer received from other bureaucrats that Xianzong had to content himself with banishing Han Yu to the provinces instead of executing him.

From a Confucian point of view Han Yu had behaved responsibly. His frankness may have been foolhardy in terms of personal safety and his own career prospects, but it should be recalled that remonstrance was a peculiarly Chinese institution. Every official had the onerous task of pointing out any shortcomings to the dragon throne, including those of its current occupant. As he made clear in his memorial, Han Yu felt compelled to write in protest at Buddhist excess for the good reason that censors and ministers kept quiet. On arriving at his provincial post, Han Yu sent another memorial to Xianzong, expressing his appreciation of the emperor's magnanimity in sparing his life. Moved by this gesture, Xianzong told his senior officials: "The advice tendered by Han Yu before was evidently prompted by a profound love of me, but he should not have said that there can be no long life for Sons of Heaven who believe in Buddhism." Given the emperor's frantic search for the elixir of life, which culminated in a drug overdose the following year, it is obvious that Han Yu had touched a raw imperial nerve.

After Han Yu's recall to Chang'an, his resoluteness was deployed for the benefit of the next Tang ruler, whose hold on power was under threat from the start of his reign. Faced with the prospect of another provincial rebellion in the northeast, Han Yu went there in 822 as a special emissary of the imperial government to try moral persuasion. With only a token bodyguard, he visited the rebel camp and spoke his mind. His words made some impression on the rebel governor, but still more upon his men. As a result the governor, unsure of his support, was obliged to accept terms and the rebellion was over. Afterwards one soldier declared, "An official who is willing to burn the holy finger of Lord Buddha will not hesitate to chop off the heads of mere soldiers."

Although Han Yu's daring onslaught on Buddhism in 819 drew imperial disfavor upon himself, it helped set a climate of opinion among officials that led to the decrees of 845, which successively shut down country retreats, shrines, and monasteries, and finally the enormous temples situated in the cities. The persecution lasted nine months and left the Buddhist church in a subservient position within the Confucian state. The chief cause of the attack on Buddhism was economic rather than religious. Officials deplored the fact that monasteries not only removed good lands from the tax registers, but also sheltered able-bodied monks who otherwise would support the Chinese empire's economy by working and paying taxes. Far too much wealth was tied up in Buddhism for it to escape the clutches of the imperial exchequer.

An invaluable insight into Chinese Buddhism, and its disruption in 845, is the dairy kept by the Japanese monk Ennin, who had arrived as a member of an embassy. Although the Japanese monk observed China in one of its periodic eras of dynastic decline, his dealings with officials revealed the remarkable degree of centralized control which was still in operation: the meticulous attention paid to written instructions from higher authorities, the mountain of paper work involved in the smallest matter of administration. From the moment the Japanese embassy landed, Ennin was aware of the respect local officials had for the procedures of the imperial bureaucracy. He learned that "a minister had already petitioned the Emperor on the embassy's behalf and that it should await the arrival of an imperial order before setting out for Chang'an." Towards the end of his stay Ennin experienced the frustration of a visitor lacking proper papers. He was passed on from district to district, once a magistrate refused a request for temporary residence. No local official dared to allow him to stay for any length of time without central authorization. When the necessary document eventually caught up with Ennin, the official who received it told the Japanese monk "to be at ease."

On its way to the imperial capital in 838 the Japanese embassy was invited to participate in a national anniversary in honor of emperor Jingzong, who had been assassinated by a eunuch in 826. Even though the dynastic history regards this short-lived ruler as a hopeless reprobate who preferred to hunt and drink rather than fulfill his imperial duties, Jingzong had sat upon the dragon throne and so deserved to be remembered. Ennin writes that the local officials

> arranged a meal for five hundred monks. Early in the morning they waited for the arrival of a minister and a general, who entered the monastery side by side. Soldiers in ranks guarded them on all sides, and all the officials of the prefecture followed behind. They came as far as the steps in front of the lecture hall, and then the minister and the general parted, one going to the left, the other to the right. Having changed their shoes and washed their faces, they met again at the center door of the hall. Then they took their seats inside and worshipped the Buddha.

We happen to know that the minister who burned incense at this memorial feast was Li Diyu, whose splendid garden in Chang'an was mentioned in the previous chapter. A survivor of numerous palace plots, Li Diyu was accompanied by the commander of the local garrison. That the latter was a eunuch says a great deal about the minister's survival skills, because he often crossed swords with this eunuch general's at the imperial court.

During his stay in Chang'an from 840 to 845 Ennin lodged in several Buddhist establishments within the city walls. Soon after settling in, he went to see a powerful court eunuch whose duties included supervision of Buddhist monks and Daoist priests. From this official Ennin received permission to stay and study under a number of Buddhist teachers. The strict government control over the Buddhist church surprised him, especially as it extended to official permission being required for ordination. Perhaps the clearest instance of the strictness of government control over monks was the fate of a southern Indian monk named Ratnacandra. This scholarly cleric rashly presented a petition to the dragon throne asking to be allowed to return to his homeland, which caused the eunuch official whom Ennin had sensibly consulted in Chang'an to take offense. The unfortunate Indian monk "was imprisoned for five days on the charge of going over the heads of the responsible officials. And Ratnacandra's Chinese disciples were severely beaten," as they had failed to warn their teacher of the inappropriateness of his action. Worse still, Ennin tells us, "the Indian monk was not allowed to go home."

Against such a background the persecution of 845 is less unusual than it would otherwise appear. Anti-Buddhist sentiment had always been prevalent among officials, and the nationalist reaction against Buddhism became even more pronounced over the centuries following the collapse of the Tang, when the Chinese empire fought a slow and losing battle against nomad encroachment. The Daoists had also formed a national church of their own in competition with the Buddhists. Their indigenous beliefs were particularly attractive to Wuzong, in whose reign the all-out assault on Buddhism was launched.

The imperial edict of 845 still came as a shock to Ennin, a resident of Chang'an at the time of its proclamation. Over the five years he lived there the Japanese monk watched with dismay the growing coldness of the emperor towards the Buddhist faith, as victory after victory went to the Daoists in religious debates conducted in the imperial presence. Already the first moves against the monasteries had been taken as a consequence of Li Diyu's proposal for tighter regulation of monks and nuns. An imperial edict of 842 had ordered the weeding out of unregistered members of the Buddhist community, possibly laymen attached to monasteries, and had prohibited the admission of boys as novices. Ennin was fortunate not be deported, although the

eunuch in charge of foreign monks in Chang'an seems to have been sympathetic to their plight, even to the extent of calling all twenty-one of them to
his office and "personally laying their fears to rest."

This solicitude over the fate of foreign monks is an indication that not
the whole of the imperial court was in agreement about the new anti-
Buddhist measures. There was no mercy, however, for Manichaean priests
at this time: they were immediately killed, a drastic action connected with
the struggle against the Uighur Turks. They had once been the Tang
dynasty's staunchest allies, having given invaluable aid during the rebellion
of An Lushan, but they were now enemies and invaders of the empire.
Ennin reports the execution of hundreds of Uighurs in Chang'an, where
their Manichaean priests maintained a place of worship. Li Diyu's personal
motive for backing the persecution of foreign religions, and especially the
assault on Buddhism, would appear to have been political, because those
who most favored the Buddhist faith at the imperial court were his old enemies, the eunuchs. Officials of the Confucian persuasion rallied behind him
because, though they had mixed feelings about what was happening, there
was no doubt over their deep-seated disdain for the eunuchs. Anything that
weakened eunuch influence was welcome to them. The death of Ennin's
eunuch protector in 844, and the destruction of his household, revealed
how fast the tide was then flowing against Li Diyu's political opponents.
Ennin tells us that the eunuch's adopted son and heir

> got drunk and offended the Emperor by saying, "Although the Son of
> Heaven is so revered and noble, it was my father who put him on the drag-
> on throne." So angry was Wuzong that he killed this man on the spot, and
> ordered that his wife and womenfolk be sent, with their hair shaved off, as
> guardians of the imperial tombs. Then officials were sent to confiscate the
> family's wealth, Elephant tusks were found to fill storerooms, along with
> jewels, gold, silver, and silk beyond count. Each day for one whole month
> thirty carts transported the accumulated treasure to the imperial palace,
> where the Emperor exclaimed, "Never before has the palace seen such
> valuable things." The officials bowed their heads and said nothing.

Before Wuzong died in 846 at the age of thirty-three from the effects
of Daoist drugs of deathlessness, the Buddhist church was seriously under
pressure. With alarm Ennin noted the emperor's pursuit of immortality, the
oddest incident he relates being the construction of "the Terrace of the
Immortals" in the palace gardens. Already Wuzong's anxieties over his personal survival had been aggravated by a Daoist memorial claiming

Confucius had predicted a take-over of China by Buddhist monks. The emperor accepted this incredible prediction at face value, restricting the movement of Buddhist monks and nuns in Chang'an: they were neither allowed out in the streets during the middle of day, nor were they able to stay overnight in any other than their own monastery.

The imperial capital's inhabitants did not share Wuzong's worries and they expressed their annoyance when he transferred rich offerings from Buddhist temples to Daoist ones by refusing to come and see them on display in the latter. Even more bewildering was news of an intensive search of the city's medicine shops for the ingredients necessary to make an elixir of life. When these items proved unobtainable, the emperor ordered all the shopkeepers to be beaten with a heavy stick. If this irrational action was insufficient to cause the imperial capital to wonder about Wuzong's sanity, the building of a forty-five-meter high earthen terrace as a rendezvous for the Immortals definitely made heads shake. Ennin says

> the area at the top of the terrace is big enough to take a large building. People inside and outside the imperial palace can see the terrace from afar, soaring high like a solitary peak. On its sides are boulders brought from the mountains to give the appearance of cliffs, planted with rare trees. It is arranged most beautifully and the Emperor is overjoyed with its construction. Seven Daoist priests have been ordered to concoct an elixir and seek immortality on the terrace.

Whether it was this dramatic climax to Wuzong's quest for a longer life that finally unhinged him is open to debate, but his behavior on the terrace itself was quite extraordinary. While on its top

> the Emperor ordered a singer to push the Commander of the Left Army, a eunuch general, over the edge. The singer refused to do so and Wuzong asked him, "When We have told you to do this, why don't you obey?" The singer replied, "The Commander is an important official. I dare not push him down." Hearing these words, the Emperor became angry and gave him twenty strokes of the cane. On another occasion, while standing at the top, Wuzong asked the Daoist priests, "Twice We have mounted the terrace, but not a single one of you has as yet become immortal. Why is this?" To which the Daoist priests answered, "Because Buddhism exists alongside Daoism in the land, the elements are not balanced properly. Therefore it is impossible to mount to immortality."

Following this conversation the emperor issued an edict to the effect that "monks and nuns were all to be forced to return to lay life and to be sent back to their places of origin."

In order to avoid persecution Ennin informed the authorities by letter that he wished to return to Japan. Eventually permission came from the Board of Rites, but he was ordered to leave Chang'an without the copies he had made of Buddhist texts during his stay. On his journey home some 44,600 retreats, shrines, temples, and monasteries were closed, displacing over 260,000 registered monks and nuns. Few exemptions were granted, according to Ennin, who saw

> numerous monks and nuns being sent away with their heads wrapped up. The monasteries are destroyed, and their money, estates, and bells are confiscated by the government. An imperial decree says that the bronze and iron statues of the Buddha are to be smashed, weighed, and handed over to the Salt and Iron Bureau. Every action is reported to the Emperor.

Even though this persecution was mild compared to the later actions of military dictators in Korea and Japan, its swiftness caused considerable distress. As Ennin observes, "those who are returned to lay life lack clothes to wear and food to eat. They are forced to steal the property of others, and so in many places monks are under arrest." Those who escaped capture took up arms in the widespread peasant rebellions that preceded the fall of the dynasty.

The relaxation of persecution under Wuzong's successor, Xuanzong, stopped short of permitting the Buddhists to regain their former institutional strength. Even though monks and nuns no longer had to fear for their lives and could in many cases return to their religious vocation, the imperial bureaucracy took pains to forestall the resumption of private ordination, decreeing that only the Board of Rites could authorize the recruitment of new members to the monastic community.

The xenophobia unleashed by Wuzong's proscription of foreign faiths hit Chang'an hard, because a significant number of foreigners lived around its western market, including traders, craftsmen, and entertainers from Central Asia and the steppes to the north of the Great Wall. Prior to the disturbances of 845 the imperial capital was wide open to foreign influence, the Tang dynasty being the most cosmopolitan in Chinese history. Influences from abroad affected nearly every aspect of life, from food to festivities. One reason for this openness was Buddhism, the popularity of which had sent pilgrims like Xuanzang all the way to India to seek instruction in its sacred texts. Another factor was the nature of the ruling class itself. During the partition of the empire, which the Sui emperors ended in 589, a Sino-Turkish synthesis brought about a profound alteration in attitudes among the northern Chinese. Both the Sui and the Tang had Turkish ancestors, thoroughly sinicized though they were in their approach to ruling China. Notwithstanding the rationalism of Han Yu in his dislike for Buddhist relics or the superstitious Daoism of Wuzong's pursuit of the elixir of life, the Tang empire was remarkably self-confident and tolerant of foreign ways.

Under the Tang emperors the influence of the steppe peoples did not diminish, in spite of periodic conflict with the Turks. So keen was Li Shimin's eldest son on Turkish culture that he learned the language and wore Turkish clothes. He even chose to live in a tent in the palace gardens, where he and his attendants ate lambs roasted whole, carving their portions with swords. Li Shimin did not share this enthusiasm for camp life, although he was not averse to sweet and savory cakes introduced from Iran. A fruity and aromatic pastry of Iranian origin became the favorite snack of Chang'an during his reign. Imperial kitchen chefs investigated the culinary value of imported ingredients and brought to bear their long-standing expertise in food preparation. They gave considerable attention to cakes, and in particular fried and steamed varieties with sesame seeds. One of these cakes cooked with camel fat was believed to cure hemorrhoids.

Alcohol was a part of Chinese life from ancient times, its preparation for the rites of ancestor worship attested as early as the second millennium BC. A problem for translators is the use of a single word for all alcoholic beverages in the Chinese language: they have often failed to distinguish between distilled and non-distilled drinks, when referring to wine. Rice still formed the chief ingredient for making distilled "wine" in the Tang empire, although we know that wine made from grapes was also imported from Central Asia. Once a choice purple grape called "mare's teat" was successfully transplanted in the imperial gardens, knowledge of viniculture spread beyond Chang'an to the surrounding countryside. Xuanzong's favorite consort, Yang Yuhuan, always drank grape wine from a jeweled cup. No trouble or expense was spared in satisfying her gastronomic desires, whether her preference was tropical fruit from the far south of China or excellent wines from the far reaches of Central Asia. Perhaps her unusually plump figure had something to do with her drinking. In the 740s the poet Li Bai would have drunk all the wine available in the taverns of Chang'an: pepper- or flower-flavored rice wine, ginger wine, fruit wine, and grape wine. The Turkish habit of heavy drinking has encouraged speculation about Li Bai's ancestry, but his liking for wine remains very much within the tradition of the Chinese poet, inspired by a heavy draught. As he put it:

> From a full jug of wine I drank
> Alone, flowers my company.
> Till, raising a cup, I implored
> The bright moon to bring my shadow
> And make us three. Unhappily
> The moon could not enjoy a drink
> And my shadow just followed me.
> But with these two friends to cheer
> Me, I sang the whole night through.

Drinking parties in gardens were often enlivened by floating cups, a custom accidentally derived from picnics in the countryside. Cups of wine were floated down a winding stream to guests sitting along its banks. Whenever a cup touched the spot where a guest sat, he had to retrieve it, drink its contents, and then compose a poem. In the gardens of the richer residents of Chang'an specially designed channels were cut for the same purpose. Doubtless Li Bai knew the best place to sit.

Foreign influences had a profound effect on Tang fashions, too. To no avail the imperial court tried to regulate foreign borrowings by upper-class women, who enjoyed a freedom unmatched in the later Chinese empire. The practice of foot-binding had still to appear and there was no condemnation of remarriage by widows (both of these gender restrictions would be firmly in place by the time of the Southern Song). Upper-class Tang women, whether married or widowed, could come and go freely in public and dress as they pleased. A fashion for wearing foreign hats started in the imperial harem and was quickly taken up by women in Chang'an. By the 740s they were wearing hats that concealed nothing of the face, possibly because they wished to show off foreign styles of makeup. Some of these comprised painted beauty spots in the form of moons, crescents, birds, insects, flowers, and leaves: these temporary tattoos were not new in China, but they gained new vigor with the arrival of better pigments from Central Asia.

All this light-heartedness was cut short by the arrival in 880 of the peasant army of Huang Chao, who was described as "an educated bandit." Once again a Tang emperor was compelled to hurriedly quit Chang'an. Officials who had not fled with the imperial court came out to greet the triumphant rebel general, who arrived in a golden carriage. His uniformed soldiers quietly followed behind him. A proclamation was issued shortly afterwards claiming that Huang Chao had risen up on behalf of the common people, for whose welfare the Tang dynasty cared nothing. It was Huang Chao's misfortune that his followers were uninterested in his dynastic aspirations, since they already possessed what they wanted: the wealth of Chang'an. Looting by retreating imperial forces had begun before his own soldiers scrambled for their share. Unable to restore order, Huang Chao was obliged to witness the despoiling of the greatest city in the world. In this atmosphere of terror Huang Chao declared the establishment of his own dynasty and appointed an administration.

While he tried to rule like the Son of Heaven, the reality of his two-year reign in Chang'an was an appallingly harsh regime. When someone wrote a critical poem on the gate of a government building, the officials employed there were blinded and the soldiers who had guarded the gate were executed. Afterwards there was a purge of all who could write poetry. Apart from its frightfulness, this massacre of scholars destroyed any hope of gaining wider support for Huang Chao's rule. The rebel occupation had a devastating effect on Chang'an, which never really recovered.

Before we trace the death rattle of the dynasty down to 907, there are other aspects of life in Tang Chang'an that deserve notice. The first is the leisure and entertainment available to visitors and residents. In this instance we are lucky to possess *The Record of the Willow Quarter*, an account of the city's red-light district written around 884. It reveals how young scholars set the tone in this world of sensual pleasure. They studied the Confucian classics during the day in preparation for official examinations, but at night the moral teachings were forgotten. Those who failed completely in the examinations often frequented the Willow Quarter rather than return home and face their disappointed families. Even successful candidates with official appointments in the provinces would often recall with nostalgia the time they had spent with the Willow girls.

> Willow at the guest pavilion
> How green and fresh you looked then.
> Are you living there still today?
> Willow, though you may shed your tears,
> You must be crushed in another's arms.

The atmosphere in the Willow Quarter obviously led to emotional conflicts. Some visitors became accustomed to the rather frivolous, casual attitude to love, regarding it as no more than an elegant recreation, but others found it difficult to view their relationships with the girls in this detached manner.

The girls themselves ranged from illiterate prostitutes to accomplished courtesans skilled in music and dancing who might have some knowledge of literature as well. Most were recruited by purchase from poor families. Once in the Willow Quarter they lived in one of its walled compounds and learned their trade from an "adopted mother," whose method of instruction was sometimes reinforced by the cane. They could leave the quarter only when hired to entertain guests at a banquet, or on certain fixed occasions for attending services at a Buddhist temple. On these days of worship they never went unaccompanied as their fine clothes and deportment easily drew the attention of passersby. Eager crowds gathered to watch the Willow girls walking to and from their devotions. They were all registered with the city authorities for the good reason that, like every other aspect of life in the imperial capital, prostitution was strictly regulated.

Though it was a criminal offense to solicit without a license, some girls lived in private houses and disguised their activities. A Tang story about such a girl relates how she bewitched the son of a provincial governor and relieved him of all his money. After she disappeared along with her accomplices, the young scholar was too ashamed to admit his folly and became a mourner. So upset was he that his chants at funerals were sad enough to reduce everyone present to floods of tears. His renown as a professional mourner persuaded the city's undertakers to match him in a competition against the established champion. Prodigious betting, another popular Tang pastime, took place at the event staged in the Eastern Market. The story has a romantic ending, however. In spite of the lowly social position to which he had sunk as a funeral attendant, the girl who was responsible for his initial misfortune met him again, admitted her love, and then sponsored his studies. Grateful for her support and her continued affection, he proposed marriage with the result that she spent the rest of her life as the honored wife of a high provincial official. The storyteller marvels that "a singsong girl should have shown a degree of fidelity rarely surpassed by the heroines of old!" As a man could have any number of concubines, it was not unusual for someone with money to buy a girl out from the Willow Quarter. In the purchase price he would have to cover the initial cost of the girl's recruitment and training, plus the estimated loss of her future earnings.

The poet-official Bai Juyi had several of these girls at different times in his career, the climax of which was his governorship of Hangzhou. Factional conflict at the imperial court had made service in Chang'an very unsatisfactory for Bai Juyi and in 823 he requested a transfer to the provinces, although the appointment he got in Hangzhou exceeded his expectations. He went to this prosperous city determined to enjoy himself, taking with him two of the girls he had acquired in the imperial capital, the singer Fan Su and the dancer Little Barbarian. One possessed a "mouth like a cherry," the other a "waist like a willow." Already his health was not as robust as it should have been, but that did not stop him from entertaining friends, who enjoyed the performances of Fan Su and Little Barbarian. The former was still with him in 839, the year Bai Juyi had a stroke while living at Luoyang. Knowing that he would have to retire and manage on half-pay, he made a list of his current expenses with a view to effecting economies. It was obvious that he had better get rid of his horse, but the prospect of parting with Fan Su filled him with remorse. He wrote:

> Old horse, do not neigh,
> Dear Su, dry your tears.
> To the stall goes one,
> The Willow Quarter
> The other. Today
> I lose both my horse
> And my love. No more
> Will you sing for me
> As I pour out wine,
> Succor for sadness.

Bai Juyi's attachment to Fan Su was based on genuine affection, something quite separate from her purchase price. Even the austere Confucian scholar Han Yu had a dancing girl who was his inseparable companion. Because the girls bought out of the Willow Quarter were serious drinkers, they were regarded as good company. At banquets both men and women drank heavily, even in the imperial court where the emperor himself would take the lead in emptying his cup. Attitudes towards drinking only changed under the Ming and Qing emperors, from the fourteenth century onwards, when to be seen drinking in public was considered a disgrace. Foreign visitors to China then were favorably impressed by the fact that they never saw drunken people in the streets. Conversely, the Chinese were appalled at the drunkenness of European sailors, whose violent and ungovernable behavior gained them the title of "ocean devils."

Courtesans were not a new phenomenon in an imperial capital. There were troops of female entertainers from the start of the Chinese empire, but changing economic circumstances during the Tang era limited their permanent employment to the richest households. As only close relations of the imperial family could afford the upkeep of such expensive servants, the Willow Quarter met an unsatisfied demand for entertainment and provided girls to all who could afford to hire them. The role of courtesans was primarily a social one, its sexual aspects being of secondary importance. They were not prostitutes in the sense that they had to bestow their favors on anyone who paid for their company. This is the reason for so many Tang poems dealing with the subject of unrequited love. In some instances they were written by the courtesans themselves.

In Chang'an the high-class courtesans were controlled by the brothel-keepers guild. In return for belonging to this trade association, brothel keepers were entitled to the same degree of protection as other commercial enterprises. Amateur courtesans, like the one who featured in the story of the governor's son, worked outside official control and paid no taxes. But they were vulnerable, without any recourse to justice against either underworld thugs or corrupt policemen. That is why courtesans were usually content to be registered with the city authorities. Unlike low-class prostitutes, they suffered no social discrimination and went to the parties of the greatest men in the imperial capital. Girls who had to rely chiefly on their looks constituted the lowest class of courtesan. They lived together in crowded rooms under the strictest supervision. Those with other accomplishments were given rooms of their own and, although they remained bound to their brothel keepers, they could pick and choose their clients. It was in the interest of popular courtesans to be difficult in granting favors. As their reputation rose, so did the fees charged for their attendance at parties. Once they became really renowned for being unobtainable, the chance of a wealthy suitor buying them out greatly increased, to the advantage of the girls and their owners. Disease does not seem to have been a deterrent to the determined purchaser, possibly because syphilis was unknown in China until the sixteenth century, when Portuguese sailors brought the New World disease to Guangzhou. Tang treatments for other venereal diseases are evidence of the dangers hidden in the Willow Quarter, but these were never serious enough to discourage regular attendance.

In *The Record of the Willow Quarter* we encounter a bewildering array of courtesans and their suitors. The Biting Girl's amusement was trying to inflict flesh wounds on others. Not that this in any way diminished her appeal, even when her amorous victims were unable to conceal her scratches and bite-marks. A graduate who came out in first place in the civil service examinations had a raw cheek for several weeks after making fun of the Biting Girl at a congratulatory banquet. When this young scholar was forced to admit the reason for his scratched face to the chief examiner, this senior official burst out laughing. Another popular girl was Virgin Yu, who was bought out of the Willow Quarter to become a concubine of the emperor's son-in-law. Her purchaser was Yu Cong, the husband of not one but two princesses. Yu Cong's father-in-law annulled the first marriage when his wife broke her spoon and chopsticks during an imperial banquet in a fit of anger. The second marriage was altogether more satisfactory, as the second princess turned out to be a model wife. With her agreement Virgin Yu was placed in a separate apartment at their mansion, and the princess was even willing to forgive Virgin Yu's liaison with her nephew during the absence of Yu Cong on official business. She freed the ex-courtesan, gave her a dowry of one hundred pieces of gold, and married her to a minor official. As the newly weds squandered this fortune in less than a year, Virgin Yu was obliged to return to the Willow Quarter and once again earn her living there. When the rebels occupied Chang'an, an ill and weak Yu Cong was taken prisoner. His steadfast refusal to serve in Huang Chao's administration cost him his life. How Virgin Yu fared under the rebels we are not informed, but it is unlikely that she avoided the arson, pillage, and rape that then engulfed the imperial capital.

Yet even a courtesan was more fortunate than an inmate of the imperial harem. While she enjoyed the company of her admirers, there was always the possibility that she might end up as someone's concubine or wife. For the woman in the imperial harem there was no such escape. Precious Consort Yang, the favorite of Xuanzong, was petted and spoiled before her murder on the flight from Chang'an, but she was an exception in the length of time that an emperor remained under her spell. Although chosen because of her looks, a harem girl might through neglect or indifference on the part of the ruler live the life of a secular nun. An even more tragic fate awaited the inmates of a secondary harem, like the one maintained at Luoyang. As the sexual relations of the emperor were the subject of intense scrutiny, the ever-increasing number of women in the imperial harem made meticulous bookkeeping necessary. Eunuchs noted the date on which the emperor slept with a consort and carefully recorded the first sign of pregnancy. Harem women who received the emperor's favor were stamped on the arm with an indelible mark. In order to protect the Son of Heaven from danger in his bedchamber, all the doors of the inner apartments were heavily guarded, and so as to prevent an attack by a woman chosen to share his bed, she was carried naked except for a quilt on the back of a eunuch to the emperor's bedchamber. Thus she could conceal no weapon on her person. Precious Consort Yang was spared this indignity as Xuanzong's favorite.

Another aspect of life in the imperial capital that provided both instruction and amusement was the extensive calendar of festivals. Ennin's diary indicates how impressed he was by their magnificence as well as by the excitement these great public events generated among the residents of Chang'an. At the Lantern festival, the first celebration of the year, lamps were lighted at sunset along the streets and in the various temples to be viewed until late at night. It was customary for Buddhist monasteries to donate the oil necessary to keep the numerous lanterns burning for three nights. This represented a concession on the part of the city authorities, as travel after dark between wards was severely restricted. The punishment for ignoring the curfew, except in the case of official business or critical illness, was twenty strokes with a light cane.

Another highlight was All Souls: it was, according to Ennin, "a most flourishing festival with dramatic performances and puppet shows based on episodes in the holy scriptures." A reason for the excitement was its identification in the Chinese mind with the Confucian virtue of filial piety. During the Tang dynasty the All Souls remembrance festival was enlarged to a time for the lavish display of monastic wealth. This contrasted sharply with the traditional Confucian frugality of Chinese ancestor worship; Buddhist monasteries and temples in Chang'an were only too pleased to show off their most precious and valuable votive-offerings. There was even open competition among them to see which establishment had the most treasures, somewhat peculiar in light of the Buddhist notion of emptiness. While the Buddha preached eternal liberation by admonishing his disciples not to cling to material things, even he had to acknowledge the generosity of lay patrons whose donations supported monastic life. For the Buddhist clergy there always remained the problem of maintaining a spiritual authority based on separation and renunciation while at the same time attracting popular interest and worldly support. In Chang'an this seems to have become acute because there were so many affluent devotees who wished to purchase future blessings.

The festival that so annoyed Han Yu, the worship of the Buddha's finger bone, pulled the greatest crowds and caused the most frenzied outbursts of religious emotions. In 868 the unpopular emperor Yuzong used this relic festival to improve his own standing by ordering the erection of earthen incense posts along the route of the procession. When these richly decorated posts were seen to glow and tremble, it was regarded as an auspicious sign. Yizong personally welcomed the finger bone into the imperial palace, hoping thereby to gain most from the supernatural blessing. The attempt failed: the Tang dynasty was already living on borrowed time. After the defeat of Huang Chao, provincial governors set about establishing permanent power bases of their own, a renewed separatist movement that soon split the Chinese empire into nearly a dozen states.

The end of Tang Chang'an came in 907, when the northeastern strongman Zhu Wen decided to dismantle the imperial capital in order to build one of his own at Luoyang. His dynasty, the Liang, was the first of the Five Dynasties that ruled north China in the fifty-two years of disunity that separate the Tang and Song empires. Because Chinese dynastic historians were always concerned to trace a "legitimate" succession of ruling houses, irrespective of the territory they might control, only five of the ten houses then in existence receive attention. Zhu Wen beheaded the eunuchs, forced the last Tang emperor to abdicate in his favor, and moved the inhabitants of Chang'an to Luoyang. Twenty thousand carpenters were needed to reassemble the palaces, government buildings, mansions, and houses in Luoyang. What Zhu Wen could not transfer was the way of life of Tang Chang'an: three centuries of Chinese achievement in the world's greatest city were irrevocably lost, and the political center of the Chinese empire permanently shifted away from the northwest. Chang'an would never serve as an imperial capital again, although during the Boxer uprising of 1900 the Qing imperial house was obliged to flee Beijing and take up temporary residence in its successor city, which was renamed Xi'an, or "Safety of the West."

CHAPTER 7

Almost Paradise:
Northern Song Kaifeng

> Two huge frolicking dragons, covered with blue cloth and stuffed with straw, were placed on the left and the right of the palace gates. Each dragon was dotted with thousands of lanterns and candles. When these were lit, the writhing dragons appeared as if they were flying.

THE COLLAPSE OF TANG AUTHORITY LED TO THE FORMATION OF the Ten Kingdoms. The first of these independent states emerged in the lower Yangzi River valley, where accelerating economic development was stimulated by maritime trade along the south China coast. The half-century of stability achieved by their rulers contributed greatly to the distinctive character of the Song empire, whose foundation is dated to 960.

If many of the features of the Song are linked with economic events in the south, others are tied to the upheavals of north China. There the constant and ultimately overwhelming pressure on the northern frontier had been exacerbated by the internal conflicts of the final decades of Tang rule. It was not just the rebel occupation of Chang'an in 880, or the physical dismantlement of the city by Zhu Wen in 907, that signaled the eclipse of northwestern China as a political center, but rather the continued struggle between regional military commanders who established in turn each of the Five Dynasties. These so-called "imperial" houses were the Liang, Later Tang, Jin, Han, and Zhou; their wars of succession only added to the problem of national defense.

The first of the thirteen emperors that the Five Dynasties produced was Zhu Wen, a powerful northeastern general who dethroned the last Tang emperor and adopted Liang as his dynastic name. The Northern

Song historian Ouyang Xiu believed that the Liang emperors were not usurpers since they followed on from the Tang dynasty and for sixteen years ruled north China. Yet Ouyang Xiu's *Historical Records of the Five Dynasties* is in reality a description of the negative side of military government. He does not mince his words in drawing attention to its political and administrative shortcomings: "Because the rulers of the Five Dynasties all came from the ranks of military men, their fierce officers and men were free to appropriate land and titles for themselves. How is this different from having wolves shepherd men?" As he pointed out, the lack of popular support for any of the Five Dynasties meant that the military coup replaced the peasant rebellion as the primary route to imperial power.

Zhu Wen and his successors were no more than throw-backs to the warlord era that accompanied the disintegration of the Han empire at the beginning of the third century. They were quite incapable of taking China forward, and compared badly with the other rulers of the Ten Kingdoms. Zhu Wen had begun his rise to power as a lieutenant of the rebel Huang Chao. After Huang Chao's defeat, he allied himself with the officials against the eunuchs and was rewarded with a northeastern governorship. His murder of the last Tang emperor left Zhu Wen supreme in north China. While Ouyang Xiu describes the Liang dynasty as "despised by the world," he acknowledges that this was the inevitable outcome of a reliance on strong-arm measures.

Even the imperial family was consumed by violence, Zhu Wen himself succumbing in 912 to a palace intrigue. Zhu Wen's disembowelment was the work of an illegitimate son, the product of an "amorous affair with a married woman." Tipped off by his wife that he was being excluded from the succession, this man entered the imperial palace one night along with a band of sympathetic guards and "tore out the bowels" of his father, and then stabbed to death the newly designated heir apparent. The usurpation lasted only half a year, falling to a conspiracy organized by Zhu Wen's third son. Moral bankruptcy probably explains Ouyang Xiu's reluctance to discuss any of the political feats of the Five Dynasties, but Zhu Wen did achieve a critical success in ending eunuch influence at the imperial court.

In his comments on the Later Tang emperor Mingzong, Ouyang Xiu does concede that his reign from 926 to 933 was both humane and orderly. This emperor is recorded as saying, "To fatten war horses, I have to starve my people—such a policy would shame me!" Mingzong's successors proved less capable so that in 937 the Later Tang house fell to nomadic cousins. Their dynasty, the Jin, was terminated a decade later by the Qidans, who captured the Jin capital at Kaifeng. Although they were unable to hold on to all their conquests in north China at the time, the Qidans carved out a kingdom for themselves in the northeast before the foundation of the Northern Song dynasty. Surviving examples of the Qidan language, mainly in the form of names and titles, are unhelpful in determining ethnic origins, so that all we can be sure about is the Manchurian homeland from which the Qidans moved south.

After the capture of Kaifeng they occupied with the agreement of the Han, the penultimate imperial house of the Five Dynasties, a large tract of present-day Hebei province, including what is now Beijing. The Qidans called their state Liao, a sinicized name, and absorbed Chinese culture. As admiration is not the same as absorption, the Hebei cession remained outside the empire for centuries until through it came the Mongols to conquer all China. Neither the last two of the Five Dynasties fared well in north China, even though Ouyang Xiu takes pleasure in recounting how the final one, the Zhou, represents the return of Chinese rule after three decades of foreign dominance. Its extinction in 960 was the result of a mutiny by troops sent to fight the Qidans.

That year Zhao Kuangyin seized power in north China and declared himself the first Song emperor Taizu, naming his dynasty after a district he had governed in modern Henan province. While he advanced on the dragon throne in the same manner as the emperors who had immediately preceded him, the new imperial house did not disappear as quickly as the Five Dynasties. When one of the rulers of the Ten Kingdoms begged for independence, the first Song emperor asked, "What wrong have your people done to be excluded from the Empire?" En route to deal with the troublesome Qidans, Zhao Kuangyin was startled to be hailed as emperor by his officers and men. He had been appointed as commander-in-chief because of his rectitude and respect for learning: these qualities, it was hoped by the Zhou imperial court, would make him the trusted protector of the seven-year-old emperor, but the plan took no account of the temper of the soldiers. "While Zhao Kuangyin was still recovering from the effects of a drinking session," the dynastic history relates, "a party of officers burst into his tent and hastily wrapped a yellow robe around him. Once the soldiers heard that he had been saluted as the Son of Heaven, they also acclaimed him." But the next morning Zhao Kuangyin would only agree to their wishes if the lives of the existing imperial family and senior officials were spared, the imperial treasury was not robbed, and the question of rewards was left to him to decide.

Once on the throne, Zhao Kuangyin ended the vicious circle of suspicion and military revolution that had raised and toppled the Five Dynasties. He told his senior commanders at a banquet how uneasy he was. When everyone assured the emperor that his position was secure, Zhao Kuangyin reminded his guests of his own unexpected elevation. So the senior officers asked him to take whatever steps he felt necessary. At which the first Song emperor said:

> "The life of man is short. Happiness consists of the means to enjoy life, and then bequeath the same to one's descendants. Now what I propose is that you should all resign your military appointments, retire to the provinces, and there select for yourselves the best estates: on these you will be able to live at ease, drinking day and night, in the knowledge that you have provided for your descendants. Any man that is willing to accept my proposal I shall treat as a friend and ally our families through marriage."

The next day all the commanders tendered their resignations on grounds of ill health, and Zhao Kuangyin kept his part of the bargain, ennobling them and generously distributing lands and wealth. This action was in fact the first step in placing the army under the direct control of the civil bureaucracy.

Of equal significance for the future of the Chinese empire was Zhao Kuangyin's decision to retain Kaifeng as the imperial capital. He toyed with the idea of moving it back to Luoyang, which had better natural defenses, but finally settled upon Kaifeng. Its only line of defense against attackers from the north was the Yellow River itself, a circumstance that accounts for the concentration of soldiers there from the start of the Northern Song dynasty. Zhao Kuangyin's dynasty is known as the Northern Song because in 1127 the nomadic Jin, having disposed of the Qidans, fell upon Kaifeng and drove his successors south to Hangzhou, where as the Southern Song they lasted till 1279. Apart from the Liao kingdom of the Qidans, and then their Jin successors, the northern frontier was also threatened by the partially sinicized Tibetan state of Xia. In 1044 an annual gift of silver and silk to Xia was agreed as the price of peace.

In striking contrast to the Han and Tang empires, Song foreign policy was never expansionist but aimed at containment of the northern peoples. Foreign invasion remained a constant threat and was the cause of the ultimate overthrow of the Song empire, but the subjection of military officials to civilian control reflects the pacific tenor of this truly remarkable era of imperial history, one in which many later Chinese would have chosen to live. To them Kaifeng seemed almost a paradise.

It is then a paradox that the Song dynasty's first capital remains the imperial city with the least surviving monuments today, and yet we know more about its appearance and daily life than any other early capital. There is no great Buddhist cave complex to greet the modern visitor, like those carved at Pingcheng and Luoyang. Nor does any equivalent of the Big Wild Goose Pagoda at Xi'an rise majestically above the skyline of present-day Kaifeng.

An even greater difference would be evident if we compare the historical remains of Kaifeng with those of Constantinople. These two contemporary cities had much in common. Each was the capital of an extensive empire, a place where higher education flourished, and a major center for international trade. Both cities fell to foreign warriors who originated on the Asian steppe, having assimilated enough from settled civilization to make their nomadic ferocity all the more overpowering. But modern Istanbul is still filled with visual reminders of Constantinople's splendor, its cathedral-turned-mosque, Hagia Sophia, churches, hippodrome, underground cistern, and city walls. Kaifeng is just the opposite. Hardly anything from the Northern Song imperial capital can be seen now. One factor in this destruction is the Yellow River, which has inundated Kaifeng on several occasions since the city's capture by the Jin in 1127.

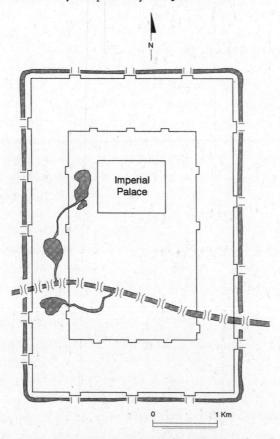

Site map of Northern Song Kaifeng

Another is the materials used in traditional Chinese architecture, and especially rammed earth. As walls were never weight-bearing, Chinese architecture relied on wooden frames to hold a structure together and on generously overhanging eves to protect it from inclement weather. A scarcity of stone in parts of north China doubtless encouraged this singular approach, but the prevalence of earthquakes always obliged the Chinese to devise safe building methods. Just how unimpressive the ex-Northern Song imperial capital seemed to early modern tourists is evident in William Edgar Gill's *Eighteen Capitals of China*, published in 1911. Writes Gill,

> Kaifeng is a has-been . . . It has no streets, only broad straight stretches which on rainy days are seas of mud, on dry days clouds of dust. "It has no trade," said a disappointed commercial traveler; no manufactures, no imports of any consequence; a local market-town it may well be, but it seems to have the value of a big, casual village. It is not far from the Yellow River, and is below its level, but the people fear to tap it and get a reasonable supply of water.

So tumble-down Kaifeng, which the American author tells us means "Opening the Seals," was rated a serious disappointment. "If it does not take care and dreg the Yellow River till the river flows below city level," Gill concludes, "it is likely to become a used-to-be."

Although the local Chinese authorities presented him with a set of "fifty-five volumes, not only beautifully bound in silk, but dealing with a variety of subjects," Gill failed to appreciate that they contained the work of some of China's foremost writers, the ex-residents of imperial Kaifeng. Our knowledge of this once-great city derives from a mass of poetry and prose, as well as a famous painting by Zhang Zeduan entitled *Spring Festival on the River*. Its panoramic view of Kaifeng brilliantly depicts outdoor scenes both inside and outside the city walls. Copied by later artists because of its vibrant representation of urban life in eleventh-century China, the scroll is an incredible eleven and a half meters in length. Kaifeng is also preserved in the plentiful nostalgia of scholars who fled Kaifeng for the southern refuge of Hangzhou, where they spent a great deal of their time recalling and writing about the Northern Song capital.

Kaifeng was roughly the shape of Northern Wei Luoyang. It also possessed inner and outer defensive walls, which enclosed altogether an inhabited area of more than 20 square kilometers. The outer city wall had sixteen gates, the inner one twelve. Northern Song Kaifeng also recalled

Northern Wei Luoyang in having a river flow through the southern quarter of the city. This waterway was a handy means of provisioning the imperial capital, and a scene from *Spring Festival on the River* shows a near accident as a cargo vessel barely avoids one of its fourteen bridges. Boatmen with poles struggle to steer safely beneath a semi-circular bridge, while spectators shout advice and prepare to jump into the water. The strong current would seem to have turned the cargo vessel sideways across the river. Blissfully unaware of any danger are the people on the bridge; pedestrians, riders, sedan-chair carriers, hawkers, stall holders, wheelbarrow men, in fact a whole host of Kaifeng residents going about their daily business.

Zhang Zeduan's eye for detail makes everything he portrays in this scroll an unforgettable insight into the lives of the Northern Song Chinese. We are shown people watching a dramatic performance next to a Buddhist temple; kite enthusiasts as well as fishermen along the riverbank; a bride on her way to her wedding feast accompanied by a band; officials greeting each other on the road; examination candidates chatting outside a city gate; resting laborers by a wayside food stall; anchored cargo boats swarming with stevedores; a Daoist magician ready to proffer advice; shops selling medicine, food, antiques, paintings, jewelry and other luxury goods;

a hall for mastering the martial arts; a quarrel between water carriers at a well; elaborate city gardens with gnarled rocks, water features, and pavilions; officials setting off for posts in the provinces; an artist painting a scroll; pleasure boats going along the river; men delivering furniture, firewood, wine, rice, even building materials; printers' and paper-makers' workshops; artisans coming and going from their places of work; street vendors of tea and snacks; an acrobatic troop with its monkey; storytellers with attentive audiences; garden designers transporting a tree; oxen, mules, camels moving slowly along the streets; a wagon repair shop; fortune tellers, conjurors, musicians, and dancers; a farmer taking a bath from a tree dipping into the river; ferrymen with their passengers; tea and rice pavilions serving light meals; and children everywhere, including two standing on the back of a docile water buffalo in order to get a better view of a wrestling match. By no means an exhaustive list, these examples should give an idea of the richness of Zhang Zeduan's composition. When the architectural detail is also considered, *Spring Festival on the River* is unmatched in the amount of information it gives about a twelfth-century city anywhere in the world.

Zhang Zeduan's approach is unlike any cityscape we are used to in Europe. It has nothing in common with Wenceslaus Hollar's "true and

exact prospect of the famous city of London before and after the Great
Fire of 1666." That Charles II appointed the Czech artist as a scenogra-
pher should be enough to point up the fundamental difference. Whereas
Hollar "proportionally measured" buildings according to a ground plan
in order to obtain an exact likeness, Zhang Zeduan was more imaginative
in his treatment of Kaifeng's waterfront. He painted lively scenes that
appealed to him, the buildings entirely incidental to the inhabitants of
the imperial capital. The choice of the festival for the time of his composition indicates Zhang Zeduan's intention, as the streets and roads
were crowded with people on their way to visit the ancestral tombs. Even
though this was an occasion on which women went abroad, the majority
of them in *Spring Festival on the River* are shown either within houses or
gardens. The freedom that Tang women enjoyed in Chang'an has
already begun to disappear under the impact of a revived version of
Confucius's teachings, which under the Southern Song emperors were to
receive their classic restatement in the writings of Zhu Xi. In his *Family
Rituals*, a manual for the performance of rites of passage, weddings,
funerals and ancestor worship, Zhu Xi fixed the place of women firmly
in the home, in the inner quarters of the larger houses. Women are told
not to intrude into the affairs of men, who run the world outside the

home. "Do not allow the disaster of the hen announcing the dawn," he wrote. So firm were Zhu Xi's views as regards propriety that he even found the Confucian historian Ouyang Xiu deficient in his morals. As the historian had freely partaken of life's pleasures in Kaifeng, Zhu Xi criticized this lifestyle, saying he "cultivated his literary works but made no effort to cultivate his personality. All day long he sang songs, drank wine, and sought to enjoy himself." Such conduct was unworthy of a true follower of Confucius.

It is impossible to tell whether *Spring Festival on the River* features any of the wine shops that Ouyang Xiu frequented. If enjoying himself meant sex, then he would have visited a

Hermitage Wine House. These establishments provide women as well as wine for the guests. On the second floor there are secretly installed beds for that purpose. Such special wine shops have bamboo lamps of red silk suspended on their front doors. Because they are protected with plaited bamboo leaves, they can be displayed in both dry and rainy weather. For it is by these red lights such special wine shops are recognized. The larger wine houses provide only girls to keep the guests company while drinking; only regular customers are allowed to go upstairs with these women.

Kaifeng also possessed its own Willow Quarter, named after the famous brothel-quarter of Tang Chang'an, with its high-class courtesans and singing-girls, but special wine shops like the ones described above were distributed throughout the imperial city. Within the Willow Quarter there were definite rituals for guests to observe. On arrival a guest was given an expensive cup of tea, and only after paying this entrance fee was he introduced to the girls, from whom he could choose companions for the elaborate feast to follow. Besides the cost of the entertainment, there were tips to be paid out during every stage of the visit. Everything in the Willow Quarter spoke of luxurious living: the comfort of rooms heated by coal braziers in winter, or cooled by basins filled with blocks of ice in summer; antique furniture and elegant drinking cups; even the finest clothes for an extravagant guest to rent. It was a costly world of make-believe divorced from Kaifeng's daily life.

The abiding impression of *Spring Festival on the River* is the bustle of the imperial capital. The majority of the activities depicted are undertaken by ordinary residents, which explains the esteem Zhang Zeduan's painting enjoys in the People's Republic today. He is the earliest Chinese painter to focus attention on the common people. In *Spring Festival on the River* there is a striking sense of the democratic character of Kaifeng's streets, a notable mingling of the classes in the pursuit of shopping and entertainment. Scholars found the relaxed atmosphere conducive to leisure activities and preparation for the expanded examination system. Like Ouyang Xiu, they could visit a whole range of wine shops, teahouses, restaurants, and snack bars. Even Huizong, the eighth Northern Song emperor, was unable to resist such popular pleasures. As a senior official worriedly remarked in 1120,

> "Your Majesty is bored by life in the imperial palace, so you often ride in a small carriage and visit markets, streets, suburbs, and the countryside. You come back only after you have had enough fun. At first, gossips in Kaifeng kept quiet, but now the talk is of nothing else."

Unmentioned in this tactful rebuke was the emperor's habit of returning in the company of a courtesan. Tongues wagged so much that Huizong set up a replica of Kaifeng's street life inside the imperial palace, where harem women acted as shopkeepers and wine sellers while the emperor himself impersonated a beggar. Remembered as a ruler preoccupied with frivolous pursuits, Huizong was a more complex personality than his critics have chosen to recognize. According to the dynastic history, "he was a man of naturally good abilities, but wanting in perspective at a moment of crisis for China." The crisis was the impending Jin capture of Kaifeng in 1127, eighteen months after Huizong abdicated in favor of his son.

What seems to have driven Huizong during his twenty-five-year reign was a love of beauty, artistic as well as sensual:

> He had a passion for beautiful artifacts, which were collected from all parts of the empire and placed in a specially built gallery. His whole energies were bent on adding to this collection, and men were rewarded for informing him of any curiosity that had been discovered. As a result of his enthusiasm, owners of any article of antiquity either handed it over at once or hid it in the ground, for no house was safe from the prying eyes of imperial agents.

This may explain the offer of a "magic" rock by the great calligrapher Mi Fu. Aware of Huizong's interest in both omens and beautiful objects, Mi Fu reported his discovery of a gnarled rock with eighty-one holes, a significant number for Daoists. Rather ingeniously in his address to the emperor the calligrapher presented himself as an undiscovered sage living contentedly on a small patch of land, but managed to suggest at the same time that he ought to be invited to take up residence in the imperial capital. As Huizong inclined to Daoist beliefs and he appreciated Mi Fu's knowledge of the arts, the calligrapher was swiftly admitted to the imperial court as a ceremonial official. The reason for the advancement of Mi Fu was his calligraphy, an art in which Huizong excelled as well. The emperor's wiry yet graceful style of writing was called "Slender Gold." Like the Tang poet Li Bai, Mi Fu did not manage to hold onto his court appointment for long, but at least he left for the provinces as an official and not a vagabond.

Before Mi Fu's death in 1107, the poet-official Su Shi had commented: "If a man is not praiseworthy, then even if his calligraphy is skillful, it is not valued." Mi Fu was aware of this subtle distinction between surface skill and inner strength, between the accomplished artisan and the real artist. And he knew what his contemporaries thought of his own lifestyle. "Because he is unwilling to be constrained by the conventions of society," a senior official wrote on Mi Fu's departure from Kaifeng, "scholars regard him as mad." A mania for cleanliness, a character trait he shared with the reforming minister Wang Anshi, certainly set Mi Fu apart from his colleagues. "In preparation for the annual ceremony held at the Imperial Ancestral Temple," we are told, "Mi Fu scrubbed his official robes so hard that the embroidery frayed." Yet it was his calligraphy which was given pride of place in Hangzhou, when Huizong's younger son, the first Southern Song emperor Gaozong, started to rebuild the imperial art collection there. In the eyes of this young emperor, who ruled a severely truncated Chinese empire, the free-spirit so evident in Mi Fu's brushwork summed up all that had been lost on the fall of Kaifeng.

A location that Mi Fu and Huizong would have been delighted to roam is depicted on the extreme left of *Spring Festival on the River*; it is the imperial park, a watery garden entirely surrounded by a wall. An extensive lake permits leisurely boating, meandering bridges and walkways pleasant strolls, and airy buildings comfortable places to take in the view. As Huizong was a keen painter of birds, insects, and flowers, we can imagine the calligrapher and the imperial artist examining the trees and bushes artfully planted in this park. Huizong's flawlessly accurate technique transformed the bird-and-flower school of painting into a movement concerned as much with true representation as a personal expression of delight in natural things. As one of the compilers of the catalogue for Huizong's collection of paintings tartly remarked of an earlier artist in this genre, he "showed an excessive reliance on his own wit."

Under the patronage of Huizong such individuality would have been discouraged in the interests of accuracy, for the emperor liked to arrange painting competitions as tests of observation, criticizing the smallest mistakes he could find in the completed works. When he judged a painting to be perfect, Huizong would add a poem of his own to the composition. By so doing the emperor combined "the Three Perfections" of painting, poetry, and calligraphy. Already would-be officials were allowed to offer painting as one of their subjects in the palace civil service examinations. The examination question, closely modeled upon that in the literary paper, consisted of a line or phrase from the classics or a well-known poem, which had to be illustrated in an original way. An interpretation of springtime, judged to be brilliant, depicted a group of butterflies chasing after a horse's hooves to which clung the fragrance of flowers. It is difficult to tell whether Huizong's aesthetic dictatorship had an adverse influence on Chinese art in general, although among some of the artists living in Kaifeng there are signs that the emphasis placed on technique was at the expense of genuine feeling.

The emperor's own preference for bird-and-flower painting, however, seems to have left artists in other fields free to develop their own styles of expression. Nowhere is this clearer than in the painting of the landscape, which started to replace figure-and-animal painting as the cherished form towards the end of the Five Dynasties. Although China abounds with splendid scenery, the Tang poets were the first to make fashionable the pleasures of the hermit in his remote hut, thereby ensuring that a romantic appreciation of the landscape became common among scholars. A handbook on gardening points out that in a well-situated and planned garden one could live as a hermit even in the middle of a city, provided all noise ceases when the garden gate was shut. This cautionary note is sounded because of the relaxation of the ward system in Kaifeng, an innovation Zhang Zeduan records. The high walls surrounding the residential quarters was gone, as crowd control was now maintained by strong wooden gates situated at the ends of main thoroughfares.

Everything about this unusual painting underlines the fundamental role of the street, the pulsing artery of urban life. Therefore it is unlikely that the peace and quiet of a hermitage was typical of the small garden Zhang Zeduan depicted close to a city gate. It belonged to a house squeezed between a chemist's shop and a large building devoted to the sale of furniture. The chief feature in the garden was a small pond surrounded by trees and bamboo. Though an urban garden at its simplest, this tiny retreat would have provided its owner with some respite from Kaifeng's noisy streets. After all, as the gardening treatise notes, "a single stone may evoke many feelings," even though this symbolic mountain might be no more than an irregularly shaped rock. Often it was enough that leaves should be framed in a window, or the roots of a pine be seen to force their way through the crevices of hollow stones. The creation of a private garden, no matter how small, was an opportunity to indulge the owner's Daoist dreams.

Interest in gardening as an art ran parallel to that of landscape painting. Both were aids to meditation. Landscape painters, for instance, regarded a winding path as not merely a pictorial device but a symbol of mankind's search for truth. Usually a path ends at a thatched hut in which a man sits rapt in thought or two men are deep in conversation. One such landscape by the Northern Song painter Ju Ran is entitled *Asking the Way to the Mountains*, the implication being that the way is not so much the right direction in which to walk as "the Way" of Daoism, the path trodden by the Immortals.

An older contemporary, the painter and art critic Guo Xi, believed that one could refresh the spirit by taking imaginary journeys through a landscape painting whenever the artist had succeeded in combining stunning beauty with the profound silence of the natural world. A favorite of Shenzong, the sixth Northern Song emperor, Guo Xi was asked to paint enormous landscapes in order to decorate the walls of the imperial palace. Large-scale landscape painting was put into temporary eclipse by Huizong's preference for bird-and-flower compositions. When he became emperor in 1100, Huizong had all of the paintings of Gao Xi removed, and so low did this great landscape painter's reputation sink that a servant was found using a Gao Xi landscape as a duster!

The revival of landscape culminated in the work of Xia Gui, who died in 1230. He was deeply influenced by the daring brushwork of the Chan Buddhist masters, who dwelt close to the Southern Song capital of Hangzhou, their monasteries bordering the city's beautiful West Lake. The unmistakable quality of Xia Gui is a profound sense of wonder at the lowly place of mankind in the great sweep of the natural world. A tiny figure crossing a fragile footbridge beneath a towering rock reminds the viewer that neither Kaifeng nor Hangzhou could ever be the center of the universe, no matter what cosmological theory might say about the pivotal role of the Son of Heaven.

Emperor Huizong did not have opinions on art alone. He also pronounced on tea, a beverage much favored in Kaifeng. As this city of the senses was preoccupied with food and drink, the treatise the emperor wrote in 1107 quickly became the arbiter of taste for tea drinking. Although the Chinese did not bother to develop an intricate tea ceremony like the Japanese, there was a definite art of tea in Song China, which embraced the brewing of fine teas to extract the maximum flavor and aroma, an appreciation of the choicest teapots and cups, and knowledge of stories and poems which related to tea. A rich connoisseur would go to the length of building a private teahouse in a landscaped garden, where he could entertain his friends. For fun he might even arrange tea-tasting competitions and brew a rare tea with pure water carried from a mountain spring. The person who correctly identified the beverage would be declared a "tea master," an accolade soon known throughout polite society in Kaifeng. The imperial tea treatise may have been printed in Kaifeng. Under the Five Dynasties the Confucian classics had been block-printed, but after 1040 the invention of movable type allowed the Song emperors to sponsor a revolution in consciousness through the government publication of standard works.

Learning, as enshrined in the civil service examinations, formed the basis of the Song achievement. Not only were more students allowed to pass their final examinations and take up an official appointment, but also there was a significant widening of the curriculum. During the ascendancy of the reformer Wang Anshi technical and scientific subjects could be offered for the first time. Though concerned with contemporary problems, the questions previously set were expected to be answered within the context of orthodox Confucian literature and philosophy. Subjects such as engineering and medicine did not long survive the fall of Wang Anshi in 1076, but this extension of official knowledge reflects the contemporary rise in scientific understanding among educated people. Wang Anshi's humble background may account for his concern for labor-saving devices, but no country could then compare with China in the application of science to practical human needs. The Song empire reached the edge of modern science and underwent a minor industrial revolution. The world's first mechanized industry was born at the same time that the printing of books facilitated the exchange of scientific knowledge derived from observation and experiment.

The first book known to be printed with a claim to copyright dates from 1190. The publisher inserted a notice to the effect that the work "is already registered with the authorities. Reprinting is forbidden." Such publishers' notices not only claimed protection against unauthorized reprints, but even attempted on occasion to reserve the author's right against unauthorized abridgements and alterations to the text. We hear of greedy publishers making a quick profit by printing mangled extracts from popular books, or even selling ghosted writings as the original work of well-known authors.

Faced with an enormous output of books, the Song emperors made constant efforts to regulate publication while maintaining a state monopoly over literature. Calendars, state documents, legal judgments, and collections of model examination essays were reserved for official publication. This approach naturally gave encouragement to black-market printing, and especially of miniature editions of essays that could be easily smuggled into examinations. By the end of the eleventh century all manuscripts were read by officials before approval for publication was granted. This attempt at censorship was of course doomed to failure once publishing houses came into existence in cities other than the imperial capital. Copyright continued for a couple more centuries, but the Ming emperors found both censorship and copyright impossible to enforce by 1500. Afterwards the very concept of copyright disappeared from the Chinese empire.

An unexpected bonus of printing in Kaifeng was paper money. In 1123 a special bureau for the issue of paper money was set up, and a government monopoly declared over the printing of such notes. This amazing ability to multiply the currency proved too much for the Northern

Song emperors and chronic inflation quickly necessitated the repeated devaluation of notes.

The shrinking freedom of women during the Song empire fortunately was balanced by access to knowledge through the medium of the printed book, which gave women unprecedented scope for self-cultivation. Well-to-do wives and daughters read widely, wrote poetry, and became proficient in calligraphy as well as painting. Many a wife of an official took an active interest in the literary and artistic activities of her husband. A community of interest provided, maybe for the first time in richer families, a solid foundation for a married life, since from then on Chinese historians extol the happy marriages of couples united by a shared love of literature and the arts.

The most famously successful Northern Song couple were the poetess Li Qingzhao and the antiquarian Zhao Mingcheng, who married when she was nineteen and he twenty-one. They enjoyed an exceptionally close intellectual relationship built upon Zhao Mingcheng's great ambition to compile a comprehensive account of all extant inscriptions on bronze and stone. After he obtained an official post, he devoted all his leisure hours to these studies. "Whenever we got a book," she wrote, "we would immediately look at it together and make notes. When we got a painting, calligraphy, or a bronze vessel, we would view it, discussing merits and shortcomings until the candle burned out." After Kaifeng fell the couple fled south but Zhao Mingcheng died before reaching Hangzhou. In this city his sad but devoted widow preserved what she could of his collection and finished his study of inscriptions. In a postscript Li Qingzhao recalls the simple pleasures of her husband's student days and the not very different delights they enjoyed after his official appointment. Here is an abridged version of what she wrote:

> As both of our families were poor, we led a quiet life, spending the little money we had carefully. Sometimes my husband pawned some clothes and we would buy in the market a few copies of old inscriptions together with some fruit. Back home we would go over these documents, munching fruit all the while, and we felt as happy as if were living in the Abode of the Immortals. Later, when my husband's official salary meant our food was assured, we could gather documents far and wide, enjoying together each new addition to the collection. Though never well off, our spirits were always free.

The marriage of Li Qingzhao and Zhao Mingcheng caught people's imagination. For all the social forces then working against married women's developing their talents, it revealed how a meeting of minds was an alternative ideal.

Kaifeng's interest in the good life stemmed from the first Song emperor's decision to concentrate power in the hands of the imperial bureaucracy. The number of officials living there was so great that houses had to be built outside the imperial city's two walls. Consumer demand within the city and its growing suburbs led to a gradual relaxation of regulation on trade. New firms sprang up and soon made Kaifeng the richest city in China, if not the world. It yielded five times as much commercial tax as its nearest rival, the southern city of Hangzhou.

Prior to the Northern Song dynasty the traditional Chinese city had only a limited commercial role because it was essentially a political creation, the headquarters of the local administration. All this changed with the shift of the empire's center of gravity southwards, and even more notably after the Southern Song emperors were obliged to reside in Hangzhou, a long-established center of trade. If there had been international tourism in the eleventh century, any traveler to China would have been struck with the general sense of prosperity and peace. Little suggested that the empire was already in critical condition.

Yet many prominent officials felt China was militarily vulnerable. What they feared was that the Qidan and the Tibetan states on the northern frontier would invade whenever the situation favored an attack. Furthermore, they saw how the maintenance of large armies to meet this potential threat overburdened the empire's finances and pressed down hardest on the peasants, who were increasingly driven to look for employment in towns and cities. A desire for reform was one thing, a reform program quite another. Thus Wang Anshi's new laws of 1070 split the would-be reformers and converted differences of opinion into downright disdain. An issue that annoyed most officials was Wang Anshi's assault on amateurism—he argued that men should be placed in positions for which they had special qualifications, and proposed reforms to the examination system accordingly. It was seen as nothing less than a condemnation on the current officialdom. Implicit in this challenge to Confucian orthodoxy was a Legist approach to administration, a philosophy forever associated with the excesses of Qin Shi Huang Di's rule. Wang Anshi wrote in a memorial to Shenzong:

> I propose that those whom Your Majesty has found by experience to be of good character and great ability, and to whom Your Majesty has committed important responsibilities, should be entrusted with the task of selecting men of like qualifications. Also that these should be given an ade-

quate period of probation as officials, after which they should be allowed
to make policy recommendations as well. When this has been done, and
when the recommended men have been found worthy, rank, salary, and
promotion should be conferred as a way of reward.

Such a modern agenda did not go down well with Wang Anshi's senior colleagues at the imperial court. Nor did his call for state intervention in the
empire's economy, which a growing commercial sector and heavy government expenditure seems to have seriously unbalanced.

The setting up of a commission to recommend fiscal changes was
anathema to conservatives like Sima Guang. This minister gave up a long
and distinguished career in protest at Wang Anshi's new laws, and devoted
himself to writing his monumental history of China. As he later advised on
his return to power, the government should keep in force only those new
laws "which are of advantage to the people and of benefit to the Empire so
that everyone will appreciate how much the Emperor is moved by paternal
affection." What went unsaid was that the Wang Anshi's effort to make
sense of the Song monetary revolution failed because it had struck at the
position of the propertied classes, from whose ranks officials were
recruited. Sima Guang attacked practical measures, like the technical subjects introduced into the civil service examinations, as dangerous lapses
from traditional standards, but Confucian rhetoric could not disguise
entirely the self-interest of the large landowners whose surplus wealth was
available for buying out struggling peasant-farmers. Wang Anshi suffered
the additional handicap of corruption amongst the officials he was obliged
to employ in running the economy. The austerity of his own life was not
enough to persuade others that a radical change was necessary. In vain
Wang Anshi stood against the growing affluence of the cities, before the
loss of Shenzong's confidence drove him from office in 1076.

Wang Anshi's new laws were concerned with six aspects of imperial policy. Apart from overall financial supervision and bringing the curriculum of
the examination system up-to-date, he sought to improve government pur-
chasing procedures, free farmers from the grip of money-lenders by advanc-
ing cheap government loans, allow a money payment in lieu of compulsory
labor on pubic works, and require a group of families to provide soldiers in
an emergency and to guarantee peace in their neighborhood. None of these
policies, with the exception of the education reform, were really new, but
their critics united around a dislike of government interference in daily life.

The willingness of Song emperors to listen to unpalatable advice was
remarkable. So receptive were these rulers that senior officials were encour-

aged to think deeply about the welfare of the Chinese empire and, as a result of the free exchange of ideas in the imperial court, the Song added more names to the roll of China's illustrious statesmen and scholars than any other dynasty. All that Wang Anshi wanted was freedom to adapt the highest principles to present needs. That is the reason for his emphasis upon improving the condition of the people, so that their wealth might increase and their lives become less harsh. Wang Anshi, who was uninterested in enhancing the powers of the dragon throne, intended a more rational method of handling economic problems, not any great increase in the power of central government. Wang Anshi grasped that a commercial transformation was taking place in China.

An intriguing historical fact is that imperial China, in spite of being so far ahead of other countries between the first and the fourteenth centuries, did not turn commercial development under the Song emperors into anything that resembled the rise of capitalism in Europe. China instead continued on its own distinct course, a society dominated by the scholar-bureaucrat. Only in the late nineteenth century would the educated classes became convinced that the Chinese empire needed to engage in international trade and import modern technology, the early stages of which had been acquired by the West, albeit indirectly, from China. The major information flow occurred after the end of the Southern Song, when Mongol conquest of all between modern-day Moscow and Hanoi facilitated overland trade and travel. By the thirteenth century Europeans were using Chinese inventions such as the magnetic compass, the stern-post rudder, and the windmill, and in the next century others like mechanical clocks, water-powered textile machinery, blast furnaces, gunpowder, segmental-arch bridges, and paper and block printing. While the exact origin of these inventions was unknown to the inhabitants of Europe, their significance as agents of social change was not missed. In the early 1600s Francis Bacon was fully aware that the metamorphosis of the continent stemmed from the application of these inventions. He wrote:

> It is well to observe the force and virtue and consequences of discoveries. These are to be seen nowhere more conspicuously than in those three which were unknown to the ancients, and of which the origin, though recent, is obscure; namely, printing, gunpowder, and the magnet. For these three have changed the whole face and state of things throughout the world, the first in literature, the second in warfare, the third in navigation: whence have followed innumerable changes: insomuch that

no empire, no sect, no state seems to have exerted greater power and influence in human affairs than these mechanical devices.

What he was pointing out was a crucial watershed in European history, the divide between medieval and modern times. Knowledge became readily available in printed form, whereas previously only the very rich layman could afford the long, tedious, and expensive process of hand-copied manuscripts. The Renaissance and the Reformation followed. Gunpowder eclipsed both knight and castle and in the Thirty Years' War inaugurated conflict on a continental scale, while the magnetic compass sent Columbus to America in 1492 and helped Magellan circumnavigate the globe in 1520.

Nothing akin to this great change occurred in the Chinese empire despite an enormous increase in commercial activity. Merchants were never permitted to acquire lasting influence in the direction of state affairs, although the Northern Song emperors eased the prohibition against merchants' sons sitting the civil service examinations. Neither were cities free as in the mercantile centers of Europe, nor had guilds any effective social standing. The imperial government's own direct revenues were enhanced by the introduction of advanced technology because of its monopoly over industry.

Not untypical of a Northern Song official's career was that of Su Shi, a determined opponent of the reforms that Wang Anshi introduced. Born in 1037, Su Shi was educated by his parents as well as at a private school run by a Daoist priest, and by 1056 he felt confident enough to go to Kaifeng to take the civil service examinations. His father had taken them earlier and failed, but within three years Su Shi had passed, along with his brother, the highest examination in the imperial capital. The purpose of this very highest examination was to discover and promote unusual ability regardless of previous service or qualification. A candidate had to be sponsored by an official, submit fifty essays to the emperor on both historical themes and current imperial policies, be examined on his understanding of six classical passages, and finally write an essay on a topic chosen by the emperor himself. Su Shi was sponsored by Ouyang Xiu and his brother Su Che by Sima Guang. Quite incredibly at this first attempt, the two brothers passed, Su Shi with a third grade and Su Che with a fourth. To gauge how outstanding this achievement was we should note that only 39 candidates passed this highest examination during the 167 years of the Northern Song dynasty, while 22,000 gained the qualification for entry to the civil service. First and second grades were never awarded, while third grade was unusual, and fourth grade the common passing performance. Su Che almost failed because two of the examiners felt strongly that his criticism of the imperial court was impertinent. He was given a fourth grade on the insistence of the emperor, who said that it was wrong to encourage candidates to present a remonstrance and then punish them for having done so.

Successful candidates could expect to advance their official careers by about ten years. Su Shi received an immediate appointment as a district magistrate, but Su Che had to hang around Kaifeng before receiving a similar post. The official who refused to sign the necessary papers was none other than Wang Anshi, who said, "Su Che has spoken like a chief minister and intentionally criticized the Emperor." Rumor also circulated concerning Wang Anshi's dislike of Su Shi's ideas, but there was nothing he could do to block the career path of "a third-grader." Possibly the future reformer took exception to his belief in sticking to traditional values. Lacking superior insight, Su Shi had written, it is best not to claim great knowledge, for Confucius himself had "never attempted to establish standards of right and wrong with mean theories." Customary practice should always act as the rudder of the Chinese empire.

Su Shi's opposition to the new laws introduced in 1070, then, is unsurprising. He and his brother had returned from their provincial appointments a couple of years before Wang Anshi gained Emperor Sengzong's ear. Like the Su brothers, the reputation of Wang Anshi as an efficient administrator had led to rapid promotion, especially as the empire's finances grew steadily worse. But the approaches of Wang Anshi and Su Shi to an admitted economic problem could not have been more diverse. Some of Su Shi's most thoughtful memorials were directed against Wang Anshi's education reforms. He was appalled at the proposal to remove literary composition from the civil service examinations and introduce qualifications in law and technology so as to encourage professional skills among officials. Not without reason, Su Shi suggested that an insistence on relevance could turn the examination hall into a place of partisan conflict and discourage critical opinion. "Institutions follow changes of custom like the flow of a great river," he informed the emperor. "When one attempts to influence in the direction it wishes to go, that is easy. But it is very difficult to force the flow against its natural direction."

Emperor Sengzong was impressed by the common sense of Su Shi's argument, and gave him an audience to explain in more detail his concern about the new laws. When the ruler wished to give Su Shi an appointment in the imperial secretariat, Wang Anshi argued against it and he was placed in the metropolitan judiciary instead. Within a year Su Shi was transferred to a provincial appointment because Wang Anshi simply could not afford to let the emperor have second thoughts about reform. From 1071 till 1085 Su Shi remained at a distance from Kaifeng, except for his brief return as a prisoner in 1079. His arrest on the charge of slandering the emperor was based not on his memorials but his poetry. Su Shi was judged innocent of evil intent but exiled. Under the Song emperors, senior officials who had outstayed their welcome in the imperial capital or bombarded the dragon throne with inconvenient memorials suffered a distant posting or an enforced retirement in south China. Under some earlier dynasties they would have lost their heads. Su Shi wrote a letter to a close friend at the time of his arrest in which he accepted that some of the new laws could be implemented to the benefit of the people. He frankly admitted that "when the new policies were first announced, certainly we were too prejudiced. We spoke impulsively and rarely hit upon the truth."

In his place of exile, an isolated district close to the Yangzi River in present-day Hubei province, Su Shi led a quiet life enlivened by occasional dinners with the district magistrate. It was during this period that he adopted his literary name Su Dungpo; he actually began calling himself the layman of Dongpo, "the Eastern Slope." As he reflected,

> Why mind being sent away?
> Other poets suffered so.
> Too bad I no longer serve
> The government, but I am
> Still well paid in old wine sacks.

The sacks came from factories run by the imperial wine monopoly. Lesser officials were sometimes given sacks that had been used for pressing wine, which could be sold or bartered. A good many of Su Shi's surviving 2,400 poems were written before his recall to Kaifeng. With Sima Guang chief minister once again and all the reformers in exile, Su Shi was in 1085 bound to be restored to active political life as an official. His provincial experience was not forgotten and he argued for the retention of the cash payment substituted for compulsory labor on public works, a reform of Wang Anshi that he had previously opposed. Wang Anshi had insisted that this duty was detrimental to agriculture, since it took the peasants off their land at critical moments during the farming year. Better to tax the farmers in order to hire vagrant laborers. Even though Su Shi came to the same conclusion, this change of view did not save him from a second exile in 1094, when the seventh Northern Song emperor, Zhezong, embraced a revived reform program. Accused again of disrespect for the dragon throne, Su Shi was banished to a town near present-day Guangzhou, and then to the southern island of Hainan. He knew the exact reason for his exile:

> It's strange—I can't keep quiet.
> As I grow older my mouth
> Refuses to stay tight shut.

Recalled in 1100, Su Shi did not live long enough to enjoy this final rehabilitation. He died the following year at the age of sixty-six, attended by a Buddhist monk. When the monk asked him to pray to the Buddha, Su Shi replied that there might be a heavenly paradise, but he was not prepared "to chant for it." He was buried near the house of his brother, with whom he had hoped to share many years of retirement.

Su Shi was fortunate not to witness the calamity that art-loving Huizong brought down on Kaifeng. Noting the weakness of the Qidans, this emperor concluded an alliance with the restive Jin for a joint attack on the state of Liao. Until 1114 the nomadic Jin had been Qidan subjects, but from this date onwards they gradually became the strongest people in north China. Chinese co-operation with the Jin was incredibly shortsighted, as the defeat of the Qidan state of Liao removed a buffer from the Northern Song frontier and exposed Kaifeng to a direct Jin attack. Huizong's abdication failed to improve the situation because his son, the last Northern Song emperor, Qinzong, had no stomach at all for a fight. On the fall of Kaifeng in 1127, one Song imperial prince refused to accept Qinzong's abdication in favor of the Jin ruler and rallied populous south China against the northern invaders.

CHAPTER 8

Holding On:
Southern Song Hangzhou

At the end of three days you reach the noble and magnificent city of Kinsai, which means "the celestial city." It well merits this name, because it is without doubt the finest and most splendid city in the world, in point of grandeur and beauty, as well as abundant delights, which might lead an inhabitant to imagine himself in paradise.

ARCO POLO'S DESCRIPTION OF THIRTEENTH-CENTURY HANG-zhou is the reason why Cathay is such an evocative word in the English language. It retains something of the wonder felt by this Venetian traveler when he encountered at first hand the magnificence of Kublai Khan, the far-reaching and cosmopolitan nature of the Mongol empire, and the wealth and civilization of China. "On one side of the city," Marco Polo tells us, "there is a lake of fresh water, very clear. On the other side is a huge river, which entering by many channels spread across the city, carries away all filth and then flows into the lake, from which it flows out towards the sea. This makes the air very wholesome." He noted how these waterways were spanned by twelve thousand bridges, in contrast to his native Venice, which would not boast the famous Rialto until the sixteenth century. Their arches were "so high, and are built with so much skill, that vessels with their masts can pass underneath them, whilst at the same time, carts and horses are passing over their heads—so well is the slope from the street adapted to the height of the bridge." The richness of the description carried over into the minds of his contemporaries in Europe a marvelous image of China during the reign of Kublai Khan.

Yet this impression could not have been more partial and one-sided if a deliberate attempt had been made to undervalue the Chinese cultural achievement. Although Marco Polo served in the Mongol civil service from 1271 to 1294, the year Kublai Khan died, he remained unaware of the recent triumphs of the Song dynasty, whose last capital he called Kinsai. He did not realize that Kinsai was a corruption of "temporary residence," the only title the Southern Song emperors could bring themselves to confer on Hangzhou, despite the charm and attractiveness of its environs. Employment in government service gave Marco Polo a unique opportunity for collecting information about the Mongol empire, and his account of his experiences in *The Travels* does provide us with detail about Mongol rule, but it lacks real insight concerning the situation of the Chinese, for their discontent with the foreign regime was entirely missed.

That Marco Polo could believe "the natural disposition of the native inhabitants of Kinsai is pacific" could not have been wider of the mark. It was not true that "by the example of their former kings, who were themselves unwarlike, they have become accustomed to the habits of tranquility." Only the last two Northern Song emperors, the painter Huizong and his son Qinzong, were unwilling to defend China against northern invaders. Qingzong's younger brother refused to accept defeat by the Jin and he declared himself the Southern Song emperor Gaozong, meaning "High Ancestor." Settling finally in Lin'an, as Hangzhou was then called, Gaozong secured the independence of south China during his thirty-year reign. Equally unappreciated by Marco Polo was the determined resistance put up by the Southern Song to the Mongols. Nearly thirty years of war was necessary before in 1279 the last member of the imperial house perished in a sea battle off present-day Hong Kong.

The choice of Hangzhou as the new imperial capital was not solely a matter of chance, as the location was safer than that of other Yangzi River valley cities. Its approach was dotted with lakes, rivers, streams, and paddy fields, formidable obstacles to the deployment of Jin cavalry. Summer heat and rain also caused problems for these steppe-warriors and in 1130 they gave up their pursuit of Gaozong: he had sailed to an offshore island, only returning to Hangzhou on news of the Jin withdrawal north of the Yangzi. Neither the first Southern Song emperor nor his six successors showed any enthusiasm at all for living at Hangzhou. But they had to make the best of it, because at the very least the city's economy was capable of sustaining the imperial court. Even then, it was not until the middle of the twelfth century that a permanent palace was built. The influx of courtiers, officials and scholars altered the character of Hangzhou, though by no means eradicating its commercial role. It still remained the greatest trading city in south China.

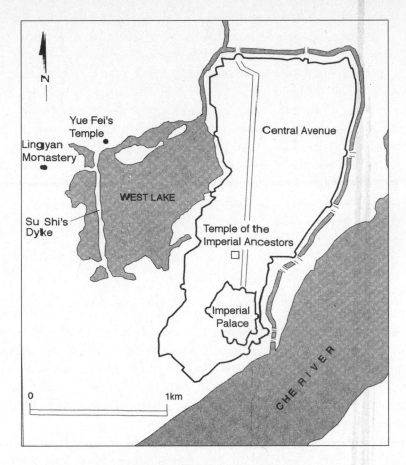

Map of the site of Southern Song Hangzhou

That the imperial court had to settle there was an annoyance, but more serious cosmologically was the restricted nature of the site itself, squeezed on a neck of land, less than a kilometer in width, between West Lake and the Che River. In spite of chronic congestion, a central avenue or imperial way was driven north-south through the middle of Hangzhou, which ended at the gates of the imperial palace, unusually constructed near the city's southern wall. Cosmology alone was not the reason for asserting the axial predominance of this great thoroughfare. In the 1130s there was concern about the maintenance of order in what was the most populous city in the world. A memorial submitted to Gaozong drew attention to the unsatisfactory situation:

Within the city and without the walls are many bandits. Also there are many refugees living in thatched huts easily consumed by fire. Although patrols are supposed to be in operation, the system is defective. Those responsible are appointed in name only. Let the Bureau of Military Affairs order patrols inside and outside the city. Divide the city into four main wards, each having its own patrolling inspector, and provisionally appoint talented commanders to these posts. In the wards, assess the need for police posts and then assign six soldiers and an officer to each post established. At night they can use a water clock and strike the drums. They can also prepare fire equipment. When legal cases are brought to the patrolling inspectors, they will be forwarded to the city authorities. A daily security report should be kept. If it is discovered that bandits are still active, then the responsible patrolling inspector and his subordinates should suffer punishment in accordance with the law of the capital.

This proposal was approved. Over one hundred police posts were set up, the number doubling over the next half-century as it proved difficult to keep crime in check. There were even complaints about the soldiers becoming "too familiar with the streets and alleys they patrolled, so that they often got into trouble themselves." Better arrangements for tours of duty helped to solve the discipline problem, as did the requirement for officers to stand surety for their men.

Overpopulation seems to have been at the root of the trouble; more than a million people lived in Hangzhou. House frontages were so restricted that buildings rose to compensate for the lack of space. The Francisan Odoric of Pordenone, who visited Hangzhou in the 1320s, was impressed by the multi-story houses, which gave the city a compact appearance. He mentions eight or ten stories occupied by as many families, presumably with one family housed on each floor. In these crowded conditions groups of families were charged with sorting out the lowest level of disorder, a method of social control suited to the family-oriented Chinese. When they were unable to resolve a case, they passed it on to a police post for further action. Mutual security units, sometimes called patrolling societies, also took to the streets in order to support the soldiers when the situation was deemed to be dangerous. All these measures were a response to the disappearance of walled wards, a change recorded in Zhang Zeduan's panorama of Kaifeng: *Spring Festival on the River* shows that even in the Northern Song capital the traditional model of a tightly regulated city had already broken down. Urban life had

A pleasure boat on Hangzhou's West Lake

become increasingly free from official interference and there was little chance of imposing strict supervision on Hangzhou, whose size and shape obliged the Southern Song emperors to find new ways of dealing with crime prevention, fire fighting, and the administration of justice.

The most overcrowded sections of Hangzhou were situated to the north of the imperial palace, in the low-lying part of the city. There was indeed a striking contrast between the spaciousness of the imperial way, the great avenue that ran through Hangzhou's center, and the congested streets on either side. From the start these lesser thoroughfares were smaller than those of Kaifeng and much smaller than those of Tang Chang'an. Fires had become a problem under the Northern Song emperors, but for the Southern Song they were a menace. In 1132, some 13,000 houses were destroyed in three separate fires. The victims were given permission to camp in two Buddhist monasteries near Hangzhou, rice was distributed to the needy, and building materials were made exempt from taxation. Five years later another fire consumed more than 10,000 houses before it was brought under control by two thousand soldiers. When Marco Polo wrote about Hangzhou, fire-fighting precautions had combined with the night curfew to make it an offense to show any light or fire burning after dark. Prior to the Mongol occupation, however, the streets bordering the imperial way were illuminated by multi-colored lanterns into the morning hours. Here stood the best restaurants, tea houses, and taverns. Establishments in the back streets and lanes catered for the less welloff. As in Kaifeng, many of them provided more than food and drink for customers; even government-owned wine bars had girls available on their premises. In theory the latter were reserved for higher education students but wealthy young men could gain admission as well.

The Mongols, stricter in public morals than the Southern Song Chinese, were to expel prostitutes from their capital at Beijing. Ladies of the town were obliged to ply their trade outside its walls. But later on at Hangzhou the Mongols made little headway with the regulation of prostitutes, as Marco Polo noted with amazement. "In certain streets," he wrote, "there are hundreds of such women. They are extremely accomplished in all the arts of allurement, and readily adapt their conversation to all sorts of persons, insomuch that strangers who have enjoyed their attractions seem enslaved, and so taken with their fascinating ways that they can never forget the experience." What Marco Polo missed was the Daoist lore that continued to be associated with sex. A belief in the life-sustaining function of sexual activity is by no means absent from the modern Chinese mind. In Southern Song times it was taken for granted. As one commentator said,

> princes and nobles now keep large numbers of consorts and concubines as a kind of medicine. They use them to seek "the true essence" so as to strengthen their vital power. But this is really no good for them and, on the contrary, it often ruins their health. Yet even a Confucian of Han Yu's stature could not resist these Daoist teachings, for it is hard to control one's passionate desires. Thus countless scholars are harmed by those with powdered faces and painted eyebrows.

He might have added tiny feet, since excessively small, pointed feet had become an essential feature of the attractive woman.

Chinese authors are vague about the origins of foot-binding. The new fashion probably started during the Later Tang, the second of the Five Dynasties. An imperial concubine is credited with winding bands of cloth around her feet to make them small and curled up at the toes like "the sickle moon." The practice could have developed from dancers who bound their feet to make them stronger and more elegant-looking. It is said that the concubine's bandaged feet excited such general admiration that other court ladies followed her example. Although we cannot be sure whether this was the actu-

A view from a West Lake boat

al origin of foot-binding, both literary and archaeological evidence points to the tenth century as the start of the fashion. By the Southern Song era foot-binding was no longer a practice confined to dancers or concubines. Well-to-do families found nothing strange in wives and daughters having bound feet. Poets praised tiny feet as "moons forever new," thereafter making them the most intimate part of a woman's body, the very spring of her sex-appeal. Touching them was soon the preliminary to love making. If a couple were eating together, the man would deliberately drop a chopstick on the floor, and when stooping to retrieve it, he would touch the woman's feet as a final test of her interest in him. If she did not get angry, then the man was being given permission to press his suit without restrain. It has to be recognized, though, that such an encounter could only happen with a lady of dubious virtue.

In a wealthy house, bound feet remained a private matter and reserved for the family quarters. In public they were hidden by floor-length skirts. The only surviving depictions of women with bound feet show actresses and courtesans. Nineteenth-century European visitors to China were appalled to discover foot-binding, quite forgetting the health problems caused to women back home through the tight-lacing of their waists. Given our current use of plastic surgery, the alteration of feet seems less drastic than it did to these early observers of the practice, although it permanently restricted the role that bound-feet women could play in society, since they became housebound.

Apart from foot-binding, there were other differences in attitude to female beauty under the Southern Song emperors. Whereas the Tang Chang'an was relaxed about women showing their shoulders, back, and neck, in Hangzhou polite society found such exposure indecent and adopted the high-collared jacket. Women's clothes were, however, always more colorful than those worn by men, who favored garments in a single color and hid their hair beneath a hat. Capping or the putting on of a hat was indeed the first sign of manhood, a key ritual according to Confucian propagandists such as Zhu Xi. Even though this morally outraged scholar did not revive Confucius's teachings single-handed, his contribution was profound.

Adopting the argument that the empire was in harmony with a preordained pattern in the natural world, Zhu Xi placed emphasis both on the understanding of this relationship and the pursuit of moral perfection. But arguing that the universe and men are one and the same did not lead Zhu Xi into pantheism, as he denied the immortality of the soul and the existence of a deity. "There is," he remarked succinctly, "no man in the heavens judging sin." Yet Zhu Xi's skepticism was never indifference, because his strong social conscience reflected a belief that life could only reach fulfillment within the family. As a result of this Confucian viewpoint, the free association of men and women began to be more restricted. Zhu Xi stressed the inferiority of women and the strict separation of the sexes, and condemned husbands who sought sexual gratification outside the home. His *Family Rituals* is a guide for the conduct of the family from the cradle to the grave. It gives perfect expression to Confucius's idea that virtue comprised self-control and ritualized behavior. As the mutual dependence of the living and the dead, of ancestors and their descendants, had been a central part of Chinese civilization from ancient times, it is to be expected that *Family Rituals* was meant to establish the correct pattern of observance for cappings, weddings, funerals, and ancestral rites. "The most serious instance of filial impiety," Zhu Xi insisted, "is depriving our family of posterity." Reprinted many times, *Family Rituals* was gradually expanded by commentary until it became the late Chinese empire's standard guide to social conduct.

Zhu Xi repeatedly declined official appointments. His refusal, and the disinclination of other strict Neo-Confucians to serve what they regarded as a corrupt imperial government, was seized upon by their critics as evidence of empty talk and administrative weakness. All that appeared to interest them was the correct observance of archaic rites. In a way the criticism was justified: Neo-Confucians like Zhu Xi took an almost puritan pleasure in solemnity. They dressed in what they took to be pre-Song fashion, a tall hat with a pointed top, a gown with wide sleeves, and shirt underneath. Their whole demeanor was grave and dignified: they sat squarely, walked in measured steps, and bowed deeply or knelt in greeting. Zhu Xi himself was incredibly frugal in all his habits. Typically, his first action each morning, well before daylight, was the worship of his ancestors. In 1179, at the age of forty, Zhu Xi finally accepted an official appointment. By then he had written thirteen works, which established him as a leading philosopher. He seems to have yielded to pressure from his closest adherents who were already concerned that continued refusal to accept office would discredit the moral teachings for which he stood. Appointed as prefect at Nanjing, Zhu Xi was diligent in his duties but still managed to promote learning in the city. His sharply worded memorials to the dragon throne so displeased Xiaozong, the second Southern Song emperor, that he was dissuaded with difficulty from punishing this righteous critic. What Zhu Xi disliked most in contemporary political life was its disregard of ethical standards in the pursuit of personal advancement.

In 1189 a broken-down Xiaozong abdicated in favor of his son, who became Emperor Guangzong. Unwell when he succeeded his father, the new ruler was in turn forced to make way five years later for Ningzong, his own son. Zhu Xi warned Ningzong about the dangers of factionalism and for a while it seemed that his ideas might prevail in the imperial palace, but the philosopher's enemies launched a ferocious assault, even demanding the death penalty for an amazing range of offenses, including lack of filial piety, disrespect for the emperor, intriguing at court, immorality, and damaging religious belief. Though Zhu Xi's access to the emperor was blocked, and his followers persecuted for their loyalty to his cause, he was not unhappy to spend the final years teaching and writing. His funeral in 1200 was dubbed a "gathering of scoundrels mourning the teacher of rebellious falsehood." Yet within forty years a reassessment of Zhu Xi's teachings had accorded him sacrifices in Confucian temples.

Defense against northern enemies had exercised the Southern Song dynasty from the moment it settled at Hangzhou. After their capture of Kaifeng in 1127, the Jin tried repeatedly to gain strategic footholds south of the Yangzi River, these attacks only ceasing after the counter-offensive of Yue Fei in 1134-35. This determined commander had assembled an army of great striking power: its formidable reputation was reflected in the popular saying that "it is easier to move a mountain than defeat Yue Fei's men." Although considerable areas of lost territory north of the Yangzi were reconquered, the first Southern Song emperor remained nervous about further operations against the Jin. The narrow escape he had made to an offshore island left a deep impression on Gaozong, as did feelings of guilt over the failure to rescue his father and elder brother from Jin captivity. As he preferred to reach an accommodation with the Jin, Yue Fei's successes were something of a mixed blessing.

Almost as self-righteous as Zhu Xi, Yue Fei proved to be a problem for the imperial court through his advocacy of a war to liberate north China. Like Zhu Xi, Yue Fei's Confucian modesty in repeatedly turning down the honors awarded to him was misunderstood, and portrayed by those who favored peace as no more than pride. Aggressive-minded officials backed the actions of Yue Fei, and other loyalists who fought on against the Jin in different parts of the war-ravaged north, with the result that Gaozong was obliged to restrain the war party in Hangzhou. The emperor probably feared that a prolonged campaign would merely induce the Jin to invade south China again. It is impossible now to be sure when the Jin finally realized that this was beyond their strength. There had been abortive peace talks as early as 1132, but they were renewed shortly after the northern drive of Yue Fei in 1140 nearly reached the old imperial capital of Kaifeng. Presumably Gaozong thought the improved military situation was the right time to conclude a peace settlement.

That Yue Fei could advance so far north of the Yangzi is a testimony of his skill as a general. We are told there were "six methods" by which he raised his army to a level of battle effectiveness that frightened the Jin. The first was careful selection: "he stressed quality rather than quantity" and sent home those whom he considered were not of the highest potential. His second method was careful training, a rigorous program in the use of arms coupled with extreme physical fitness. When his soldiers had completed their training, "the people would look on them with awe." The third method was fairness in rewards and punishments. Brave men were immediately rewarded and promoted, while slowness in following orders or carelessness at drill attracted severe punishment. Only the combined pleas of his senior officers converted an order to behead his own eldest son into a caning on the soles of his feet. To the consternation of his father the young man's horse had stumbled and thrown him during an exercise. "What

The Statue of Yue Fei at his Hangzhou memorial temple.

would have happened," Yue Fei asked, "if you were leading men in battle?" Method four was clear orders so that the entire army understood exactly what was required. Strict discipline was number five, so strict, in fact, that when Yue Fei's army was on the march, "there was never the slightest misbehavior such as trampling on people's fields, damaging crops, or inadequate payment for purchases." Decapitation was the immediate punishment for all misdeeds. The sixth and final method was community spirit, the sharing of comfort and discomfort. Yue Fei always shared his soldiers' rations, eating the same things as the lowest ranks, and he always camped in the open with his men. This approach to generalship explains the number of volunteers who flocked to join Yue Fei's army, and the ability of his recruiting sergeants to pick and choose only the best.

Yue Fei wanted to recover not only the territories lost to the Jin on the collapse of the Northern Song but all the lands up to the line of the Great

Wall, nothing less than a restoration of China as it was under the Han and Tang emperors. His fame as a daring leader and successful campaigner meant that in Hangzhou it was not easy for Gaozong to lower popular expectations of re-conquest to a more reasonable level of achievement. The emperor, and many senior officials, doubted whether Southern Song forces were able to hold onto the current re-conquests, let alone the additional ones Yue Fei envisaged. It was a tragedy that Yue Fei's last major campaign happened to coincide with the efforts of the imperial court to come to an understanding with the Jin by surrendering claims to any territory north of the Huai River and submitting to other Jin conditions, one of which was the payment of tribute. In the treaty of 1142, which concluded hostilities, the Southern Song empire was actually termed an "insignificant state."

The Jin withdrew their armies in accordance with the agreement and promised to return the coffin of Gaozong's father, the Northern Song emperor Huizong, who had died seven years earlier. It was therefore vital that the Southern Song troops quit the territories ceded to the Jin, including those occupied by Yue Fei's army. Realizing how exposed his men now were on the withdrawal of other Southern Song forces, Yue Fei reluctantly ordered his army south. He is reported to have commented: "The efforts of ten years are destroyed in a single morning, all the lands regained lost in a single day. The altars of the Empire, its river and mountains, will not be recovered again. The universal order has gone for good." Summoned to Hangzhou with the other generals who had obeyed the imperial order to bring their men southwards, Yue Fei swiftly found himself the sole advocate of continued warfare. His defiant character simply played into the hands of the peace party and he was imprisoned on a charge of treason. Officials sent to interrogate Yue Fei in his cell were unable to establish a case against him, but this did not stop poison being introduced into his food and he died at the age of forty-two.

The elimination of Yue Fei reassured the Jin and made the poisoned general into a national martyr, rather rare for a soldier in the Chinese empire. While the stabilization of their southern frontier encouraged the Jin to settle permanently in north China and in the process turn the empire they had won there into a sinicized state, Gaozong could at least feel that he had fulfilled the duties of filial piety by recovering his father's body and securing the release of his mother. The Jin kept the last Northern Song emperor as a hostage, a welcome decision for Gaozong, whose own position as ruler might have been threatened by the arrival of his older brother. The peace lasted for almost the rest of Gaozong's reign: he abdicated in 1162, once war with the Jin had broken out again.

To rally the armed forces before stepping down, Gaozong admitted his own error in killing Yue Fei, his feeble excuse being the deceit of scheming ministers. Rehabilitating Yue Fei's family, in particular his widow and younger son, was the first step in the promotion of the general as one of China's greatest heroes. By the Ming period there was no doubt that Yue Fei represented the ideal of loyalty: commemorative temples were erected in many cities and at Hangzhou stone sculptures of men and animals were placed besides the general's tomb. In 1513 kneeling figures of his wife and two sons were added. During the Great Proletarian Cultural Revolution Yue Fei's memorial temple was singled out for destruction: the general's terracotta statue was smashed, steles preserving his calligraphy were defaced, and the cast-iron figures stolen. Today the site has been completely restored and the most recent damage quietly acknowledged in a notice that reads: "A major historical relic protected by the state. Destroyed in 1966. Rebuilt in 1979 at the cost of 400,000 yuan."

Less damaged by the Red Guards than Yue Fei's memorial hall and grave is Lingyin, a Buddhist monastery also situated on the northwestern shore of West Lake. Lingyin, "the Soul's Retreat," witnessed the flowering of Chan art. As a popular religion, Buddhism never fully recovered from the suppression of 845, but many individuals discovered in Chan Buddhism, an admixture of Buddhist and Daoist ideas, the perfect solution for a profound unease with the times. Chan's distrust of words was a relief from Zhu Xi's current elaboration of Confucian etiquette into a total way of life. Its emphasis on freeing the mind from such clutter in order to become receptive to flashes of illumination came to many as nothing short of a revelation. To create the right atmosphere for meditative self-cultivation, Chan monks built their monasteries in secluded places of great beauty, similar to the haunts of the Daoist Immortals. West Lake had been recognized as an excellent location long before the Southern Song emperors moved to Hangzhou; Lingyin Monastery in the tenth century already possessed enough buildings to accommodate 3,000 monks.

In seeking to express the moment of shattering insight, a Chan painter relied on the energy of the brush and the subtlety of black ink. This technique was called the "abbreviated stroke" and "splattered ink," and an early master was Shi Ke. *Two Patriarchs Harmonizing Their Minds*, his most famous painting, shows a sage snoozing on an equally relaxed tiger. The weight of the man's arm and head appear to leave the animal undisturbed, even reassured. Such approach was the exact opposite of the refined, meticulous realism that the Southern Song had brought from Kaifeng. A preference for precise detail still influenced court taste in Hangzhou to the

Another view of Hangzhou's West Lake

extent that Liang Kai, a leading landscape and figure painter, gave up a sinecure so as to develop his own style in the peace and quiet of Lingyin Monastery. He refused to accept "the golden belt" awarded by Emperor Ningzong around 1200, thus earning himself the nickname "Madman Liang." His famous portrait of Li Bai reveals how brilliantly he could capture the lofty independence of the Tang poet. In a few strokes he combines the precision of the poet's profile with the casual representation of his shoes and robe. It is the same combination of artful detail and apparent carelessness that typifies the greatest Chan paintings. Not surprising is the number of Liang Kai's works in modern Japan, where Chan Buddhism still flourishes as Zen. Slightly later than Liang Kai, Mu Qi painted works that imply that insight can be triggered by anything, provided the individual is prepared to let it happen. His more simplified style is evident in *Six Persimmons*, thought since the time of its painting to be beyond description. Concrete yet abstract, the fruits suggest one is seeing something as well as nothing at all, which explains why the painting also resides today in a Japanese museum.

Visitors to Lingyin Monastery may notice a story about Su Shi recorded there on a hanging scroll. When he was governor of Hangzhou, Su Shi settled a court case in artistic fashion. The owner of a local fan shop fell deeply into debt because unseasonable cold and rain depressed the sale of fans. For a month he did not sell a single one. With no sign of a change of weather, the shopkeeper faced ruin, even imprisonment for debt. That is until Su Shi told the man to bring him twenty undecorated fans. On each of them the poet-official drew a picture and added a few lines. In the ensuing rush to buy them the shopkeeper earned more than enough to cover his debt. Another decision of Su Shi still remembered with affection is the improvement of West Lake. It had become so overgrown with weeds that a quarter of the lake had been reclaimed as fields. Between 1086 and 1093, Su Shi memorialized the dragon throne asking for funds to restore West Lake to its former glory. "Without it," he wrote, "Hangzhou is like a man lacking eyes and eyebrows. To allow further neglect would be a crime." In consequence, Su Shi was able to employ 200,000 laborers to clear the undergrowth and dig out the mud, using the debris to build the causeway with still spans West Lake from north to south. That Su Shi returned boating on the lake to fashion is clear from Marco Polo's description of the vessels he saw there.

> Boats and barges of all sizes are available for pleasure. These will hold ten, fifteen, twenty or more persons, as they range from fifteen to twenty paces in length and are flat-bottomed and broad in the beam, so as to float without rocking. Anyone who likes to enjoy himself with female company or with his friends hires one of these barges, which are furnished with fine seats and tables, all indeed that is needed for eating and drinking. They are roofed over with decks on which men stand with poles which they thrust into the bottom of the shallow lake, and thus propel the barges where they are told. Inside this roof and the rest of the interior is covered with paintings in bright colors, and all around are windows that can be shut or opened, so that the party at table can enjoy all the beauty and the variety of the prospects on both sides as they go along. For on one side lies the city in all its grandeur and loveliness, its temples, palaces, monasteries, and gardens with their lofty trees, running down to the water's edge. On the lake itself is an endless procession of barges thronged with pleasure-seekers. For the people of this city think of nothing else, once they have finished work, but to spend a part of the day with their womenfolk or hired women in enjoying themselves either in these barges or in riding about the city in carriages.

Marco Polo was impressed, too, by the dining facilities available on the two islands in West Lake. Each boasted a marvelous and magnificent palace, with so many rooms and apartments as to pass belief, so wonderfully built and decorated that it seems like the palace of an emperor. When anyone wishes to celebrate a wedding or hold a party, he comes here. All that is needed for wedding-parties and feasts can be found: everything is ready for a sumptuous banquet. Often a hundred clients hold parties at once, some ordering banquets, others wedding-feasts. Yet they are all accommodated in different rooms and pavilions so effectively that one does not get in the way of another.

Dining out here or on a boat was regarded as the pinnacle of urban luxury. Under the Southern Song emperors these restaurants retained the services of the best chefs, who were able to cook for a sophisticated official class as well as wealthy merchants. These men took full advantage of an acceptance of innovation in order to shape the cuisine we associate with China today. Su Shi himself is credited with the invention of several dishes and his poetry is full of references to eating and drinking. Dongpo pork has remained a favorite of the southern Chinese ever since Su Shi thought of a new way of braising and steaming the meat.

Imperial China never looked upon cookery as women's work. Men and women were both expert in the kitchen and the preparation of the finest dishes virtually became an art form. Su Shi was not the only scholar interested in cookery. In the eighteenth century the distinguished poet Yuan Mei published a cookbook in 1796 in which he boldly stated that a good cook could only produce four successful dishes each day. The undivided attention of such a gastronomic artist alone would be enough to satisfy the informed eater. As an example of an unsatisfactory dinner, prepared by a bevy of kitchen assistants working for a chef, Yuan Mei recounts an expensive meal given by a merchant.

There were three successive sets of dishes and sixteen different sweets. Altogether, more than forty kinds of food were served. My host regarded it all as an enormous success. But when I got home I was so hungry that I ordered a bowl of ordinary rice-gruel. So few of the numerous dishes I had been offered were really fit to eat.

In the mid-820s, when he was governor of Hangzhou like Su Shi, Bai Juyi had faced a severe drought that threatened West Lake. He composed addresses to rain-making dragons on behalf of the hard-pressed peasants who supplied the city with food as well as the shrinking expanse of water that he had come to love. His West Lake poems, written during his governorship and afterwards, established the whole area west of Hangzhou as a poetical paradise. Though he liked to linger under the shade of the willows along the shore of West Lake, Bai Juyi preferred to spend his spare hours at Cold Spring Pavilion, a building in the middle of a stream to the southwest of the Lingyin Monastery. "On summer nights," he wrote, "I take pleasure in the trickling fountain and the chill wind, washing away care and dispersing the smell of wine. With the mountain pines as my roof and the sheer cliffs as my screen, I can sit at ease and dangle my feet in the stream." So clear was the water, according to Bai Juyi, that a glimpse of its purity was enough to cleanse the dust of the world, to remove "the grime from the tongue and heart of either a layman or a monk." Now the pavilion is no longer surrounded by running water, having been moved to another site during the Ming dynasty.

Neither Bai Juyi nor Su Shi was alive when another governor brought the cult of Miao Shan to Hangzhou. An inscription dated to 1104 in the Tianzhu Temple, close to Lingyin Monastery, tells how a girl named Miao Shan assumed "the form of a thousand hands and a thousand eyes and thus appeared to her parents, then once again reverted to her original shape." This image of the Buddhist bodhisattva Guanyin, with a thousand hands each with an eye in its palm, had been introduced to China in the early years of the Tang empire and came to dominate her worship for the next four centuries. But reverence for this particular manifestation of the Goddess of Mercy really took off with Miao Shan.

This upsurge in Buddhism began in the tenth century when China was divided into the Ten Kingdoms. The daughter of a southern king, Miao Shan was a pious girl who spurned marriage and devoted herself completely to Buddhism. She was imprisoned by her father who tried to break her spirit before condemning her to death. But on the execution ground Miao Shan was saved by the spirit of Dragon Mountain. Knowing who she really was, this powerful local deity took her to a tranquil spot where she could fulfill her destiny. For three years she remained on her own, rapt in meditation. Meanwhile her father paid for his cruelty towards Miao Shan by falling terminally ill. Only the arrival of a strange monk seemed to offer a remedy, when he said that the king could be cured by a medicine made from the hands and eyes of a person without anger. Miao Shan provided the ingredients for the medicine in a selfless act of filial piety. When a grateful king and his court went to give thanks for her generosity, they realized who she was at once. Miao Shan then revealed her true identity as the thousand-handed, thousand-eyed Guanyin. After this astonishing transfiguration she resumed her original shape, with eyes and hands intact, before dying cross-legged in meditation.

The popularity of Hangzhou's monasteries and temples as places of pil-grimage ensured that the Miao Shan story spread throughout the Southern Song empire. Her subsequent progress in the Chinese Buddhist pantheon was not unconnected with the rise of goddesses in late imperial China. Not unlike the devotion shown to the Virgin Mary in contemporary Europe, compassion for the sufferings of the world came to be seen as a feminine attribute. In becoming a bodhisattva, Miao Shan seemed to justify the deci-sion of some women not to marry but instead enter a nunnery. As tradition-al Chinese society found such dedicated celibacy difficult to accept, it was not long before a counterbalance appeared in the form of another Guanyin, a goddess who bestowed children on barren wives. Just as statues of the Buddha in China were often decorated with happy children, this new man-ifestation of Guanyin was called "the womb treasury of the world." Duty to the family was too deeply rooted in the Chinese mind for a thousand-hand-ed thousand-eyed bodhisattva to shake.

But there were profound changes in outlook during the Southern Song period. The commercialization of the economy allowed merchants to influ-ence piety through patronage of Buddhist institutions. Their concern for balancing financial investment against spiritual return actually chimed with a growing anxiety over the afterlife. Even Daoism borrowed the idea of sys-tematic punishment for sin, its places of infernal torture being little more than a literal translation of Indian hells. Whereas the Buddhist church in China had at first proposed a purely automatic process that determined the nature of the individual's rebirth according to the merit of the life just com-pleted, now there arose instead a rigorous judgment by an underworld bureaucracy.

This new concept of purgatory soon found expression in painting and sculpture, where the hideous fate awaiting condemned Buddhists could be viewed by all. Though Zhu Xi might disdain such an incredible idea, Daoists were unable to resist this development, if for no other reason than Buddhist hells also drew on indigenous traditions of suffering after death. Old Chinese beliefs in the just deserts awaiting corrupt officials in the underworld combined with Indian concepts of deserved punishment before each rebirth in such a way that Daoist priests were as busy as their Buddhist counterparts in ministering to the dead. Daoist services were intended to help the deceased rid themselves of the consequences of sin in order to gain admission to a paradise. Like Buddhist acts of penance on behalf of souls confined to hell, they reveal a deep concern with death and atonement that may account for the shift of sacrifices to ancestors from the household altar to the grave itself. Zhu Xi deplored this innovation, but he could do nothing to persuade descendants that it was unnecessary to worry so much about a non-existent afterlife. Fervent Buddhists went as far as establishing "grave chapels" with resident monks who were responsible for praying for the deceased as well as the physical upkeep of the tomb.

At Hangzhou the revival of Buddhism had an influence on funerary rights. Opposed to the hotchpotch of contemporary practice to which clung the fear of hungry ghosts, Buddhist monks living there proposed, as an alternative to the presentation of cooked meat, the release of living creatures as well as penitential ceremonies. To make the point, they released fish into West Lake in remembrance of the Buddha. Quite possibly this annual ceremony represented a local adaptation of the Buddhist faith in its suggestion that properly conducted rites brought blessings not only to the less fortunate, but even more to those who sponsored them. That such a view suited an era of rising prosperity meant that before long the focus of Buddhist services was wider than repentance and salvation: they came to include such mundane matters as wealth, longevity, and offspring, objectives close to the heart of those who joined lay congregations devoted to good works. Once the Miao Shan cult arrived, Guanyin carried all before her: Miao Shan's self-multilation was hailed as the ultimate selflessness, a state of grace only attained through unreserved generosity.

How this new emphasis on self-sacrifice related to a merchant's accounts is not hard to see. As the Southern Song faithful began to quantify the burden of sin in an effort to alleviate punishment after death, Buddhist ledgers of merit appeared that prescribed the good work needed to redeem a specific failing. Another method, similar to the European development of indulgences, involved measuring sin in monetary terms and buying redemption through burning purchased "spirit money." Yet it needs to be recalled that Buddhist monks and Daoist priests never performed a role like the clergy in contemporary Europe. They were not parish priests. They served instead as the custodians of shrines and temples, on call in the event of a spiritual emergency. Despite copying much from the Buddhist church, Daoist adepts remained uninterested in evangelism and made no demand for a commitment of faith from those who sought their services. Should they be capable of delivering the required "miracle," they knew that a grateful client would not hesitate to thank the responsible Daoist deity.

After the fall of Kaifeng it was understood that the Southern Song empire should regard the great rivers and the sea as its new Great Wall. Headquarters was set up near modern Shanghai to organize a navy of eleven squadrons and 3,000 men, soon rising to twenty squadrons and over 50,000 men. Some vessels were armored with iron plates; all were capable of discharging gunpowder bombs. So it was that the Chinese become sea-minded for the very first time. Though the immediate cause of this new interest was pressure from the warlike peoples of the northern steppes, the economic and political center of the empire had been shifting for many centuries from the northwest to the southeast, from the great plains of the Yellow River to the Yangzi delta. By the Southern Song period the southern coastal provinces were both the richest and most populated parts of China.

A consequence of the southward movement of the imperial capital, and the loss of northern overland routes for trade, was a remarkable increase in seaborne commerce, an expansion that happened to coincide with a more relaxed official attitude towards merchants. Just how critical the business community had become for government revenue in what was now a money economy can be judged from a comparison of Tang and Song figures. In the eighth century less than 4% of tax was paid in money, but in the eleventh century the amount exceeded 50%. In Kaifeng Wang Anshi's reform program had struggled to control this fundamental change: during the time that Hangzhou was the seat of imperial power officials had no choice other than accept the emergence of banks, credit and shareholders.

Bewildered as they were by these business developments and the vast profits they made, officials turned to merchants for assistance in running government monopolies and enterprises. The status of merchants improved and attention was paid to the need to protect their trading vessels. These great junks deeply impressed Marco Polo. He tells us of the Fujian port of Zaiton, into which come "all the ships from India laden with costly wares and precious stones of great price and big pearls of fine quality. And for one spice ship that goes to Alexandria or elsewhere to pick up pepper for export to Christendom, Zaiton is visited by a hundred." So much of this maritime activity was new to Marco Polo that he felt it necessary to provide shipbuilding details for the benefit of his Venetian compatriots. Rudders had only just arrived in Europe then, multiple masts were still unknown, and the system of adding timbers, or doubling, was centuries away. The bulkhead-built hull, divided into separate waterproof compartments, really caught his attention, since it permitted repairs to be carried out at sea.

Besides the pressing security issue, the imperial bureaucracy gave thought to ways of increasing the volume of trade. A maritime trade commission even fostered contacts overseas by sending officials with gifts of silk to Southeast Asia and encouraging merchants to organize trade missions of their own. These unprecedented efforts soon paid off, as the amount of overseas trade doubled, trebled, and kept on growing to the benefit of both businesses and the imperial exchequer. As it was of benefit also to pirates, calls for protection at sea greatly reinforced the case for a permanent navy. The opening of new ports, the increasing traffic in coastal waters, and the growing wealth of cities close to the sea were bound to stimulate pirate raids. In 1131 the first Southern Song emperor Gaozong sent two squadrons to deal with piracy; their success prompted the officials responsible for coastal security to adopt permanent measures, including regular naval sweeps of rivers and bays and registration of all merchant shipping. Any vessel found without authorization was seized, a measure intended to prevent collusion between private ship owners and pirates. Gaozong's navy initially comprised converted merchantmen, but these were quickly replaced by purpose-built warships. The Huai and Yangzi Rivers provided useful lines of defense, but Gaozong realised that once the Jin acquired warships they could mount coastal attacks whenever they chose.

His foresight saved the Southern Song empire in 1161–2, when the Jin mounted a three-pronged attack. A feint by a cavalry force in the upper reaches of the Yangzi River valley was intended to divert attention from the main crossing lower down at Nanjing and a seaborne assault by 70,000 men aimed at Hangzhou. This armada was intercepted and sunk at sea before it reached south China, while at Nanjing two attempted crossings were foiled by another naval force. The first was met in midstream by a hundred galleys and turned back after hard fighting at close quarters. More disastrous for the Jin was the second attempt because it was received by incendiary weapons, bombs, rockets, and fire-rafts. Still convinced that the Yangzi could be crossed, the Jin commander wanted to try for a third time a month later. But when a Chinese fleet of seventy-four galleys and paddleboats appeared to oppose this third attempt, the dispirited Jin soldiers refused to embark and killed him instead.

After the return of peace with the Jin, the Southern Song emperors were less concerned with the navy, and it remained under-funded until the arrival of the Mongols. These ferocious horsemen had destroyed the Jin empire in 1234, despite the inventiveness of Chinese artisans in Jin employ. During the seige of Kaifeng, the last refuge of the Jin court, both sides used gunpowder as a propellant for projectiles. Against the Mongols, however, the defenders deployed a "flying-fire lance," a prototype gun fastened to a spear. This weapon consisted of a tube filled with a mixture of charcoal, iron filings, powdered porcelain, sulfur, and niter. When ignited by a fuse it threw a flame along with the iron and porcelain for several meters.

It came as a rude shock for the Southern Song when the Mongols penetrated as far south as the Yangzi. Once again merchants had to hand over their larger ships and orders were placed with shipyards for the construction of new warships. The naval revival gave the Southern Song empire a brief respite, but river cities fell one by one as the Mongols added ships to their invasion force. Some of them were captured vessels, others hired from unscrupulous merchants, often ex-pirates or smugglers. A key contest was the five-year siege of Xiangyang on the middle reaches of Yangzi. Its massive fortifications made the city the commanding stronghold of the river basin. To overcome the defenders' stubborn resistance, the Mongolian army needed to perfect its nautical and artillery skills. Kublai Khan was obliged to recruit a multi-ethic force of Mongols, Chinese, Turks, and Persians as soldiers and Koreans and Jin as sailors. For the first three years of the siege Southern Song was able to send supplies and reinforcements to the beleaguered garrison, which refused to contemplate surrender. By 1272 a blockade had isolated Xiangyang and a major bombardment commenced. Two Muslim engineers built catapults of such size and strength that "the machinery went off with a terrific noise, which seemed to shake the earth and the sky, and everything that was hit by the huge stones instantly collapsed."

The surrender of the devastated city in 1273 left south China dangerously exposed. With rivers no longer acting as a Great Wall, Mongol forces were soon able to bring about the surrender of the imperial capital. The boy emperor was taken prisoner but his two brothers escaped from Hangzhou prior to its fall. In turn these children were proclaimed emperor by Song die-hards, who endeavored to prolong resistance to the Mongols amongst the islands off the coast of south China. Their efforts were in vain, for a sea battle near present-day Hong Kong ended in total defeat. Hearing that her last son had perished, we are told that the dowager empress refused to consider

> any plan for continuing the struggle against the Mongols. Her heart was broken, and life had become such a burden to her that she threw herself into the sea and was drowned as well.

Inevitably the Song dynasty was extinguished at sea. For nearly two centuries the Southern Song navy had held off its northern enemies, gaining complete control of the East China Sea. Its successor, the Yuan or Mongol fleet, went on to control the South China Sea as well, while under the native Ming dynasty a resurgent Chinese empire was to make its presence felt in the Indian Ocean as far west as Arabia and Africa. At the beginning of the fifteenth century the Ming admiral Zheng He turned its waters into a Chinese lake.

CHAPTER 9

The Mongol Conquest: Yuan Beijing

Within an inner wall stands the Great Khan's palace, the biggest building that has ever been . . . The main hall is so vast and so wide that a meal might be served there for more than 6,000 people.

THE MONGOL PALACE, MARCO POLO GOES ON TO ASSERT, IS "AT once so immense and so well constructed that no man in the world, granted that he had the power to effect it, could make any improvement in design and execution." The Venetian traveler's amazement at this palatial residence, built in the 1270s by Kublai Khan, was sufficient for him to miss the political significance of its construction on the present-day site of Beijing. In 1272, in the middle of the great building project, Kublai Khan announced that the new city would serve as the imperial capital of a new dynasty within the Chinese succession of dynasties, claiming for himself the heavenly mandate to rule as emperor of China. It was proclaimed that his new dynasty would be called Da Yuan, "the Great Yuan," and his newly built city Dadu, "the Great Capital." Having been awarded north China, the conquered Jin empire, as his personal area of responsibility, this grandson of Genghis Khan decided to move the seat of his government from Karakorum in 1256 to a location in easy reach of China. Kublai Khan chose a site some two hundred kilometers north of Beijing, called in Chinese Shangdu, the Xanadu of Marco Polo. But as early as 1263, when he became the last overlord to be acknowledged by all the Mongols, Kublai Khan was planning to move into China itself. So it was that Dadu came to share with Shangdu the honor of being an imperial Mongol capital: during the winter months Kublai Khan stayed at Dadu, but the heat of a north China summer always drove him back to cooler Shangdu.

How the Mongols changed from nomadic warriors into settled rulers of the Chinese empire is the incredible story behind the building of Kublai Khan's Dadu, the city that would one day become Beijing. In the history of mankind there is nothing remotely comparable to the rise and fall of the Mongols, whose conquests began shortly after 1206, the year the chieftain Temujin was acclaimed leader of all the Mongol tribes with the title Genghis Khan, or "Universal Ruler." The focus of *The Secret History of the Mongols* is Genghis Khan. Commissioned by his successor, Ögedei Khan, this remarkable book relates the greatest clash ever between the nomadic culture of the steppe and the civilization of intensive agriculture.

Genghis Khan encouraged Mongol ferocity. "The greatest joy," he told his men, "is to conquer one's enemies, to pursue them, to seize their belongings, to see their families in tears, to ride their horse, and to possess their wives and daughters." The treatment of the inhabitants of Bukhara in 1220 is representative of the Mongol approach to cities. It was plundered after a short siege and burned to the ground. Although the fire seems to have broken out accidentally, this was of no consequence to the Mongols. If Bukhara had put a stiffer resistance and caused the Mongols heavy losses, then after its capture the male inhabitants would have been massacred, except for craftsmen who, like the women, were always enslaved. As every tribesman was a soldier, the continuous military activity started by Genghis Khan forced the Mongols to rely more and more on servile labor, even in the crucial task of horse-breeding. When necessary both women and children entered the fray and acted as auxiliaries.

At most there were 300,000 Mongol males of fighting age, but this horde had several inestimable advantages over rival armies. Its discipline was perfect and commanders unswervingly loyal. "Their horses," Marco Polo tells us, "are so well-broken-in to quick-change movements, that upon the signal given, they turn instantly in every direction; and by these rapid maneuvers many victories have been obtained." In addition, the Mongol horde proved capable of adopting military technology from other peoples and using non-Mongol troops to deploy the newly acquired weapons. Polish chroniclers relate how at the battle of Wahlstatt in 1241 the Mongols used a smoke-producing device to cause disarray among the combined forces of the Poles and the Teutonic Knights.

Wherever they campaigned the Mongols sought out artisans whose skills had a direct military application. They obtained from West Asia armor for themselves and their horses; from Russia saddles, quivers, and bows; from the Muslim lands catapults for hurling stones and naphtha missiles; and from China guns, bombs, grenades, canons, and nautical expertise. We also know that Genghis Khan was quick to grasp the value of specialized artillerymen. A Southern Song envoy who visited the Mongol court was staggered by the sophistication of the Mongol army. Its siege train included mobile towers for attacking walls, covered moveable passageways for approaching fortifications, and catapults on wheels.

The secret of Genghis Khan's success in creating a steppe empire was organizing a personal following rather than depending on tribal loyalties. Most of the Mongol clans had proved fickle, electing him khan and then showing a marked reluctance to follow his orders. This experience hardened Genghis Khan's heart, making him unwilling to delegate power to his own relatives or other Mongol leaders. This distrust lasted all his life, so that the slightest sign of disobedience, real or imagined, was immediately punished by death. Purges were a regular feature of his rule. Yet Genghis Khan had an ability to attract devotion from his trusted commanders, who mastered the technique of mobile warfare. He also won the respect of his soldiers by seeing that they were well supplied with arms and horses, and that they received a fair share of the plunder. As a result, Genghis Khan lost battles but never a war, and he launched the Mongols on a series of conquests that took them across Central Asia and beyond, into Afghanistan, Pakistan, Iran, the Ukraine, Russia, and Europe. In 1281, at the battle of Homs in Syria, the Muslim rulers of Egypt only just turned back the Mongol onslaught. The engagement was a close contest, its outcome being decided by the inexperience of the Mongol commander.

Even though the Mongol world empire was not really a part of Chinese imperial history, China was very much a part of its history, once the Mongols struck southwards in 1211. By this date Genghis Khan had already collected a group of Qidan, Jin, and Chinese advisers. As the Mongol assault gathered momentum in north China, the number of defectors increased considerably and soon included Qidan and Chinese generals serving the Jin empire. In 1212 the Mongols overran a vast area, but when Genghis Khan was wounded, they abandoned their gains and retired north. The following year saw a more devastating invasion as far south as the Yellow River but, with Genghis Khan needing to fight enemies elsewhere, the Jin empire situated there enjoyed a lull in hostilities. This ended in 1231, when Genghis Khan's third son Ögedei led an all-out invasion and captured the last Jin emperor three years later.

Genghis Khan's struggle to achieve personal supremacy made him determined to hand on his hard-won position to a descendant. A suspicion of illegitimacy prevented him from favoring his eldest son and, as a compromise, Ögedei was chosen instead. Genghis Khan's violent sons accepted

Ögedei, whom they liked, even though they hated each other. Described as a generous person, the new Mongol leader lacked his father's iron will and he made odd decisions when deep in his cups. Once Ögedei Khan learned that a certain Mongol clan had forced its women into what he regarded as unsatisfactory marriages. So he ordered that all its girls over the age of seven and all wives of less than one year be brought to him. Of the 4,000 women thus assembled a number were singled out for his courtiers, who were required to consummate marriage with them on the spot. The rest were split between the khan's harem and his personal attendants. None of these women's relatives present dared to protest.

It was in this strange court that Yelü Chucai made his name as a reformer. A descendant of the Qidan royal family, Yelü Chucai had been an official in the Jin civil service, but he turned to study Chan Buddhism after the Mongol invasion of north China. Taken captive in 1215 on the fall of Yenching, the Jin city near present-day Beijing, he was deeply shocked by the senseless looting and destruction when thousands of people were killed and a great part of the city was burned down in a month of Mongol rampage. Released from captivity after the violence had run its course, Yelü Chucai studied under a Chan Buddhist master who was "well versed in both Confucianism and Buddhism and very thorough in doctrine and expression." That this teacher was also conversant with Daoism indicates he subscribed to the common origin of all three traditions. This idea was very popular then, as we know from Yelü Chucai's later hope for the Mongol regime: he wanted the khans to base heir rule on the teachings of the Three Sages, Laozi, Confucius, and the Buddha.

In 1218 Yelü Chucai was summoned to Karakorum by Genghis Khan. The Mongol leader had already rallied many Qidans to his cause and they had proved faithful allies in his war against the Jin empire. According to Chinese records, the sole source for Yelü Chucai's career, the audience went like this:

> "The Qidans and the Jin," remarked Genghis Khan, "have been enemies for generations. Now I have taken revenge for you." A committed Confucian, Yelü Chucai replied, "My father and my grandfather respectfully served the Jin emperors. How can I, a subject and a son, be so insincere at heart to consider my sovereign and my father as enemies?" Impressed by such directness and the honest look of this fellow steppeman, Genghis Khan gave Yelü Chucai a secretarial appointment at his court. He even gave him a nickname, "Long Beard."

Yelü Chucai's duties were both secretarial and astrological. Like all Mongols, Genghis Khan had an immense fear of unusual natural phenomena, and he would consult his secretary-astrologer whenever the need arose. Yelü Chucai interpreted these occurrences within the Chinese system of omens as indicators of heavenly favor or displeasure. Correctly predicting the death of a determined enemy of Genghis Khan in Central Asia only served to enhance Yelü Chucai's authority at the Mongol court.

Yelü Chucai was above all concerned with mitigating the harshness of Mongol rule in north China, following Ögedei Khan's destruction of the Jin dynasty. Obviously surprised at how ignorant the Mongol leaders were about Chinese culture, he tried to insinuate administrative arrangements suited to a settled population. Had Genghis Khan been aware of the extent of Qidan and Jin sinicization, he might not have welcomed Yelü Chucai so warmly. His standard policy aimed at keeping nomadic culture free from foreign entanglements. The sheer number of Chinese peasant-farmers had always baffled the Mongols. Considered unfit as soldiers and possessing no useful skills, it was proposed to Ögedei Khan that these useless people be exterminated and their fields allowed to revert to pasture. Yelü Chucai argued strongly against this proposal, explaining that if he were permitted to introduce a proper system of taxation and let the peasants work in peace, he could collect enough revenue to support all future Mongol campaigns. As the promised tax flowed to Karakorum talk of genocide ceased.

In spite of ruling a huge empire, Ögedei Khan's outlook remained that of a steppe warrior. He listed his four proudest accomplishments as defeating enemies in battle, creating a post system, digging wells to increase grazing land, and placing garrisons among settled populations. Yet he did grasp that Yelü Chucai was the right man to sort out the problems of administration in north China. His appointment there as chief tax collector, however, displeased some senior Mongols, who feared that the khan's purpose in choosing Yelü Chucai was to assert direct control over revenue collection at the expense of their own interests. Their concern was justified for, about the same time Yelü Chucai was implementing his reforms, Ögedei Khan commissioned a merchant to do something similar in Central Asia. From *Campaigns of the Holy Warrior*, a Chinese chronicle based on a Mongol original, we know that taxation in Ögedei Khan's western lands was reformed between 1229 and 1240. During this period the nomadic pattern of exactions was replaced by a poll tax on adult males paid once a year in cash, and an agricultural tax, collected for the most part in kind. Under Yelü Chucai's tax system the poll tax was assessed in silk yarn. Villagers were also liable for a grain tax, while city-dwellers paid a supplementary levy in silk yarn. In most cases, taxes assessed in silk yarn would be met with a payment of silver.

Ögedei Khan was so pleased with the result that he named Yelü Chucai head of the whole administration of north China, a position that allowed him to push for yet more reform. It is possible that he would have succeeded in this objective had Ögedei Khan not been so prodigal in expenditure. Vast sums were badly invested in merchant enterprises, one wily entrepreneur parting the khan from five hundred ingots of silver, the equivalent of 5 per cent of the annual Chinese tax revenue.

Another measure that Yelü Chucai persuaded Ögedei Khan to back was a restriction on the commercial activities of Buddhist monasteries, since their exemption from tax had encouraged monks to acquire cultivated land and engage in trade. Gradually Yelü Chucai moved taxation back to the Chinese imperial model, but the appointment of civil administrators displeased many Mongols when it was realized that the scholar-officials whom Yelü Chucai recruited were the remnant of the former Jin administration. Once he lost Ögedei Khan's ear, there was nothing Yelü Chucai could do to stop the decision of 1239 to permit tax farming by Muslim businessmen. It was the end of any Chinese influence at the early Mongol court. Yet on the death of Yelü Chucai five years later, Karakorum went into mourning and honored his wish to be buried in the Western Hills near Beijing.

Although Yelü Chucai believed that the Mongol khans possessed the heavenly mandate to rule, he knew that this could only be retained through good administration. That is why his closest friends said he died of a broken heart. Yelü Chucai's insight into Chinese and Mongol attitudes was unique, but prior to the accession of Kublai Khan it was a largely wasted asset at the Mongol court. For all of Yelü Chucai's long and distinguished period of service to two khans, Karakorum remained no more than a steppe encampment, albeit one which controlled a mighty empire.

Following Ögedei Khan's death through excessive drinking in 1241, his second wife Töregene acted as regent. As her husband sank into terminal alcoholism, she had seized power in the Mongol court and blatantly issued orders in his name. According to Mongol custom, when the head of a household died, his widow took charge of his estate until the eldest son came of age. In the face of considerable opposition Töregene managed to have her son Güyüg elected as the Mongol leader, but he died after two years as khan. His successor, Möngke Khan, was a vigorous leader in the mould of his grandfather, Genghis Khan. He ordered his two brothers, Hulegu and Kublai, to extend and consolidate Mongol power in West Asia and East Asia respectively.

To carry out these tasks, they were each given a Mongol army supplemented by locally raised troops. Jin and Chinese conscripts raised the strength of Kublai's forces to over 500,000, although the figure may have been as high as 900,000, to dispatch against the Southern Song. Of the two brothers Kublai was the more ambitious and he exploited the conflict that shattered the unity of the Mongol empire on Möngke Khan's death in 1259. The succession crisis exposed the personal animosities and territorial rivalries of the Mongol nobility. At the end of it Kublai may have become the great khan, but three other khans were now independent rulers. Never again would the Mongols pool their military resources for a joint campaign. The Mongol world empire had fragmented into separate powers with Kublai Khan gaining the lion's share.

From the start of his reign Kublai Khan knew that he had to rely on the resources of China and on his Chinese subjects for support. He admitted as much in a proclamation composed for him in 1260 by the Confucian scholar Wang E. Like Yelü Chucai, this close adviser had been an official under the Jin emperors. Wang E's most outstanding success was a proposal for the compilation of dynastic histories, not only for the Qidans and the Jin, but also the Mongols. He told Kublai Khan that it was a time-honored practice in China to compile historical records so that the merits and faults of former rulers would always be remembered, since an impartial evaluation was only possible in later times. Impressed by this argument, Kublai Khan approved the proposal and accordingly set to work the scholars whom Wang E recommended. Without Wang E's determination to continue a tradition, the history of the Mongol period would be less well known, and that of the Qidans and the Jin not known at all. In his eulogy for the last Jin ruler Aizong, Wang E describes a model ruler.

> When the ministers committed an offense, he punished them leniently with demotion, never killing them . . . He also honored Confucian studies, supervised the appointment of military officials, gave up hunting parks for the benefit of the people, and started court lectures on the principles of government. He encouraged agriculture . . . and the people flourished. Alas, Heaven decreed unification and the Great Mongol dynasty conquered all China.

Heeding these words, Kublai Khan strove to reassure his subjects that he would behave in the manner of a Chinese emperor, and he declared his new southern capital at Dadu the seat of imperial government. With only a short interruption at the end of the fourteenth century, this city, modern-day Beijing, was to remain the capital for the remainder of the Chinese empire.

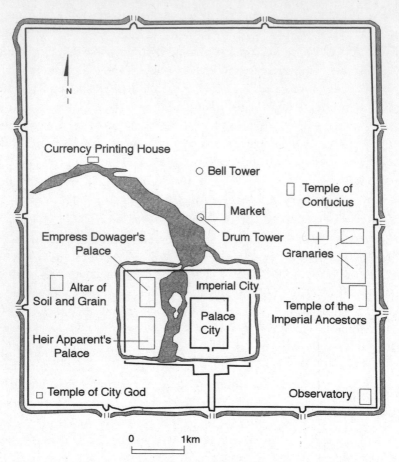

Map of the site of the Mongol capital at Dadu, modern-day Beijing.

Dadu was a double-walled city. The outside wall, built between 1267 and 1268, was nearly 30,000 meters in length. It was rectangular with eleven gates: two at the north, and three at each of the other sides. As in Tang Chang'an, the north-south and east-west avenues ran from one side of the city to the other, except in the south where they met the inner wall of the imperial city, the preserve of the imperial family. Officials could only enter its gates during the hours of daylight, and had to live in the fifty-four wards of the outer city. An unusual feature of the imperial city was its division into an eastern and a western section by an artificial expanse of water, which survives today, to the west of the imperial palace, as three connected lakes. The present buildings dotted on the islands and shores of these lakes mostly date from the Qing dynasty, which the Manchus founded on their occupation of Beijing in 1644. White Pagoda Mountain in the middle of the northern lake, however, has been identified with Kublai Khan who, according to Marco Polo, moved a live forest of trees so as to adorn this man-made eminence. Though his mother was a Nestorian Christian, Kublai Khan had embraced Buddhism under the influence of Tibetan advisors. The palace city, on the site of the present-day Purple Forbidden City, was built for Kublai Khan himself. Within its 3,500 meter-long moated wall there were three compounds: one for imperial audiences, another for the khan's worship, and the last for his private affairs.

Kublai Khan's capital was not the first imperial city to be laid out at Beijing. There the Qidans and the Jin had built capitals from which they ruled north China and other lands. Situated just southwest of Kublai Khan's foundation, the double-walled Jin capital of Yenching had been built on the site of the previous Qidan capital of the Liao kingdom. The Jin captured this smaller city in 1125. A legend about the origins of Kublai Khan's palace begins with a holy mountain. So esteemed was the mountain for its magical powers that the Jin emperors actually transported it from the steppe to Beijing, a circumstance which seems to have led to the mountain's deliberate inclusion in Kublai Khan's palace city. The legend recounts how

Kublai Khan's White Pagoda Mountain at the Dadu capital

geomancers said that the mountain possessed a king-making force that was a danger to the Jin empire, because it was situated within Mongol territory. The Jin and the Mongols were already enemies, but the latter offered no objection to the removal of the mountain. They even laughed at the idea of its removal. So a large force of Jin soldiers was allowed to dig up the mountain and cart it away. At Beijing the mountain was turned into a hill in the middle of a large lake, which was dug to surround it. Flowers and trees were planted and pavilions built for imperial recreation. Not long afterwards the Jin dynasty fell, and Kublai Khan moved his capital to Beijing, and when the walls were raised they enclosed this auspicious hill.

From Jin records it is evident that the pavilions mentioned were in fact a country palace, an imperial residence outside Yenching's walls. It was destroyed when the Mongols overran north China and captured Yenching. What may have remained intact were the rammed-earth terraces on which the Jin palace was erected. If this happened, then their reuse for Kublai Khan's palace city would make sense of the choice of location. Not only was there the pleasant prospect of the mountain in its lake, adorned with trees and flowers, but even more the Mongols would have saved an immense amount of labor in not having to terrace a large area for Kublai Khan's own residence. When the magical associations are taken into account as well, it is possible to appreciate why Kublai Khan was content to spend part of the year in Dadu. He would have pitched his tents at the lakeside and lived in Mongol fashion until his Chinese palace was ready.

Marco Polo visited Kublai Khan's palace around 1275 and its newness strongly influenced his description. Everything he saw filled him with wonder. Here is a condensed version of what appears in *The Travels*.

The palace is completely surrounded by a square outer wall, which is very thick and some ten paces in height. It is whitewashed and battlemented. At the corner of this enclosure stands a large palace of great beauty and splendor, in which the Great Khan keeps his military stores. There are eight palaces, all serving as arsenals. Each is reserved for a particular type of equipment. One contains saddles, bridles, stirrups, and other items of a horse's harness. In another are bows, bow-strings, quivers, arrows, all the items an archer needs. In a third there are pieces of armor such a cuirasses, corselets, and leader-guards. And so with the rest of these palaces.

Within an inner wall stands the Great Khan's palace, the biggest building that has ever been. It has no upper floor, but the terrace on which it is built is raised ten palms above the level of the surrounding earth, and all around the edge of the terrace there is a marble walkway, two paces wide. At the outer edge of the terrace, too, there is a fine gallery with columns, where men meet and talk. On each side of the terrace there are great marble staircases for entry to the palace.

The palace itself has a very high roof. Inside, the walls are all decorated with gold and silver, except where there are pictures of dragons, birds, beasts, horsemen, and scenes of battle. The ceilings are the same. The main hall is so vast and so wide that a meal might be served there for more than 6,000 people. The number of rooms are beyond count. The whole building is at once so immense and so well constructed that no man in the world, granted that he had the power to effect it, could make any improvement in design and execution. The roof is ablaze with color, scarlet and green and blue and yellow, so brilliantly glazed that it glitters like crystal and sparkles in the sunlight, being visible at a great distance. And this roof is strong enough to last for many years. In the rear part of the palace are extensive rooms in which are stored the private possessions of the Great Khan. Here is his treasure: gold, silver, gems, pearls, and vessels made from silver and gold. Here live his ladies and his concubines in great comfort and convenience. No outsiders may enter these private rooms.

Between the inner and outer walls are stretches of park-land with tall trees. The grass is lush and the raised paths are never muddy or covered in puddles. . . . Here is a great variety of game, such white harts, musk-deer, roebuck, stags, and other splendid animals. These animals roam about, but keep away from the paths that people walk on. In the northwestern corner of the grounds is a great lake, from which the earth was removed to raise a hill. The lake is fed by a fair-sized stream so as to form a convenient source of water for the animals. The stream flows out through a channel near the hill and then fills another lake.... At the farther end of this second lake there is an outlet for the stream, through which it flows away. There are gratings of iron and copper to stop the fish escaping. Swans and other waterfowl live on the lakes.

On the northern side of the palace, at the distance of a bow-shot but still within the walls, the Great Khan has raised a hill fully one hundred paces in height and well over a kilometer in circumference. This hill is covered with a dense growth of trees, all evergreens that never shed their leaves. Whenever the Great Khan hears about a particularly fine tree, he has it pulled up, roots and all with a quantity of earth, and brought here by elephants. No matter how large the tree may be, he does not hesitate to transplant it. In this way he has assembled the finest trees in the world.

In addition, he has covered the hill with green rocks, so that people call it
the Green Mound. On the top, at the center, is a large and handsome
palace, which is green as well. So striking is the hill, with its trees, rocks
and palace, that it delights all who gaze upon its beauty. Thus the Great
Khan arranged this for his own refreshment and pleasure.

Clear from this first-hand account of Kublai Khan's palace is how much it
conformed to the Chinese imperial model. That Chinese cosmological
expectations were fully met in the layout of his capital is apparent from the
Ming attitude towards Beijing, for its native emperors retained the scope
and style of Kublai Khan's city to the extent that many of the Ming buildings were near replicas of those that the first Mongol emperor had accepted as necessary for a foreign Son of Heaven to rule China.

The exact location of the Green Mound is still disputed. It is quite possible that White Pagoda Mountain and the artificial hill Marco Polo
described are one and the same. If they are not, then the Green Mound may
have been situated at some distance from the lake and north of the palace
enclosure. In this case it could have been altered on the construction of
Ming Beijing, when five hills were made, using unwanted earth from the
moat around the imperial city. They could have been raised next to the
Green Mound.

Influential in Kublai Khan's patronage of Buddhism was his second wife,
Chabi. She was an ardent Buddhist and leaned towards the Tibetan form of
the faith. Her eldest son was given a Tibetan name, Dorji, but he died before
Kublai Khan and so her second son was designated as heir apparent. When
this prince also died in 1285 Kublai Khan was heart-broken. He had lost
Chabi four years earlier. The desolation Kublai Khan felt at the close of his
reign had much to do with the death of this astute woman. She had opposed
the idea that the area around Beijing be turned into pasture and pointed out
the need for intensive agriculture to supply the imperial capital with food. In
the dynastic history we are told of her intervention.

Mongol officers persuaded Kublai Khan to let the imperial suburbs be
grazed by horses. Before she argued against the decision, Chabi repri-
manded one of the Khan's principal advisers for not speaking up, saying:
"You Chinese are intelligent. When you speak the Emperor listens. Why
have you not remonstrated with him?" Then she said to her husband,
"This is a departure from our usual practice here. Why should land be
confiscated now?" Kublai Khan was silent, but the proposal was quietly
dropped.

Because Chabi embodied so many wifely virtues Kublai Khan always listened to her opinions. After he stopped her taking silk from the palace military stores, she personally took charge of making clothes for his women. "She collected discarded silk bow-strings, softened them by boiling, and twisted them into thread, which could then be woven into cloth." As for heavier material, "she used old sheep skins, sewing them together in order to make rugs. She was never wasteful in making clothes or furnishings." Her frugality was matched by a practical approach to fashion. Kublai Khan was concerned that Mongol hats gave no protection from the sun and so Chabi designed a hat with a rim, which became the standard headwear. Later she designed sleeveless garments that could be worn in combat. The dynastic history reminds us how clever Chabi really was. Not only did "she understand matters of the moment," but she also appreciated how "her husband needed to identify himself with the greatest Chinese emperors of the past." Chabi always encouraged a comparison between Kublai Khan and Li Shimin, the second Tang emperor: both rulers had come to power by force of arms and both were well served by advisors.

At the outset of his reign, Kublai Khan's Chinese advisors took advantage of the support they received from Chabi to try to turn Mongol domination into a Chinese-style government. Above all else they advocated that the ruler should be open in his dealings with others, should consult when making decisions, and should be consistent in his policies. They recommended that the empire be ruled from north China because it was the traditional place of residence for emperors: only a subsidiary administration was to be maintained at Karakorum to keep an eye on the steppes. But sympathetic though Kublai Khan was to many of the ideas that his Chinese advisors proposed, the first Mongol emperor was more interested in attracting Chinese support for his regime than becoming an out-and-out Chinese ruler. He was very reluctant to hand over his authority to subordinates and he was uninterested in possessing bureaucracy recruited by examination. To help him run his administration he preferred a mixture of peoples, including European adventurers like Marco Polo. Kublai Khan never totally trusted his Chinese subjects, who outnumbered the Mongols in China by 300 to 1. Given this disparity, the Mongols had to retain control of the leading positions in government if they were to survive and avoid being overwhelmed by the Chinese. Of all this state of affairs Marco Polo had only an inkling when he came to Dadu, which *The Travels* tells us was

enclosed by earthen ramparts, twenty paces high and ten paces wide at the base. At the top of the width is only three paces because the sides of the

212 ● THE IMPERIAL CAPITALS OF CHINA

ramparts slope. They are all whitewashed and battlemented. There are eleven gates, each with a fine pavilion. The streets are so broad and so straight that from the top of one gate you can see along the whole length of the road to the gate in the opposite rampart. The city is full of fine mansions, inns, and houses. All the way down the sides of every main street there are stalls and shops of every sort. All the land inside the city is divided into squares, carefully measured by rule. In them stand large houses with ample courtyards and gardens. Each of these blocks, or squares, are surrounded by excellent roads, so that the whole city is laid out in squares like a chessboard with such masterly precision that no description can do justice to the arrangement.

In this city are very many houses and very many people, both inside and outside the walls. There are indeed more people living outside the walls in the suburbs than in the city itself. Next to each gate is a suburb… and at a kilometer's distance from the city are to be found in them fine hostels that provide lodgings for traveling merchants. Each hostel is assigned to a particular people. Merchants and others come here on business in great numbers, both because it is the Khan's residence and because it affords a profitable market. And the suburbs have as fine mansions and houses as the city, except of course for the imperial palace.

No one who dies is buried in the city. If someone dies, the body is taken to the place of cremation, which lies beyond the suburbs. Otherwise they are buried at a distance from the city. Executions are never carried out in the city. And no prostitute dares to dwell there, except in secret. Ladies of the town all live in the suburbs, where as many as 20,000 of them serve men for money. They have a head because whenever ambassadors come to the Great Khan, they are entertained on a lavish scale, and the head of the prostitutes is called upon to provide one of these women every night for the ambassador and one for each of his attendants. They are changed every night and receive no payment, for this is the service they owe to the Great Khan.

In the center of the city stands a huge palace in which there is a great bell. Each evening this bell sounds. Once it peals three times no one may venture abroad. Every night there are guards riding about in troops of thirty or forty, to apprehend those who ignore the curfew. If caught, they are arrested and imprisoned. Next morning an official examines each case. The guilty are punished with heavy rod, which sometimes can result in death. This form of punishment is preferred for the reason that killing felons is believed to be wrong. Every gate is guarded by a thousand soldiers. They are responsible for maintaining order, since the Great Khan harbors suspicions of his subjects. To protect his own person, he has a bodyguard of twelve thousand men. A quarter of them in turn reside in his palace for three days and three nights, and at the end of that time another quarter of the bodyguard take over.

How well Marco Polo knew Kublai Khan is a matter of conjecture. The Venetian asserts that they often talked together, and he calls the Mongol emperor "the greatest lord that ever was born." According to the description in The Travels, Kublai Khan was "neither too small nor too large" and boasted a "well made nose." He was white faced, though after a drink his cheeks were red, something his Chinese advisors would have been pleased to note since ruddy cheeks were associated with a grateful disposition.

Kublai Khan seems to have taken to young Marco Polo, whose facility with languages impressed all he met. What the Mongol ruler wanted was as many non-Chinese officials as he could recruit to administer his empire. From Marco Polo's account of the Mongol court it is obvious that he was very familiar with its workings:

> Seating at banquets is arranged like this: the Great Khan sits at a high table at the north end of the hall, with his principal wife seated on his left. On his right, at a somewhat lower level, sit his sons in order of age, and his grandsons and close relations. They are so placed that their heads are on a level with the Great Khan's feet. Next to them are seated other noblemen at other tables lower down again. The seating arrangement for the ladies is the same. All the wives of the khan's sons and grandsons and close relations are seated on his left at a lower level, and next to them the wives of his nobles lower down still. The tables are placed in such a way that the Great Khan can observe everything. But do not assume all are seated at tables, for most of those in attendance sit on carpets. Outside the hall another 40,000 are also entertained. For they include many visitors bearing costly gifts, men from strange countries with strange presents, and some who have held high office and seek further advancement. Such are the guests who come to banquets whenever the Great Khan is holding court or celebrating a wedding.
>
> In the center of the hall where the Great Khan has his table is a very fine piece of furniture of great size and splendor in the form of a great chest, each side being three paces in length, elaborately decorated with golden animals. Inside is a huge golden vessel filled with wine, plus others containing mares' milk, camels' milk, and other alcoholic beverages. On the top of the chest are the Khan's own cups, in which drink is served to

him. From the chest the different drinks are drawn off in golden containers, each of which contains enough to satisfy eight to ten men. One of these is set between every two men seated. There are many musicians in the hall, of every kind, and when the Great Khan is about to drink they play. As soon as the cup-bearer has handed him his cup, he steps back three paces and kneels down, at which signal all the guests go down on their knees and make a show of great humility. Then the Great Khan drinks. When the food is finished, the tables are removed to let jugglers, acrobats, and other entertainers come into the hall and perform their tricks. They afford great amusement in the Great Khan's presence, and the guests show their enjoyment by peals of laughter. When all is over, the guests take their leave and return each to their own lodging or house.

In spite of gifts and tribute, Marco Polo thought that Kublai Khan's riches rested primarily on the printing of paper money. "His mint," he claims, "is so organized that you might well say that he has mastered the art of alchemy." *The Travels* never mentions the inflationary pressures caused by the printing of too many notes. It was something the Mongols never managed to control, the collapse in the value of the currency in the 1330s being a critical factor in the overthrow of their dynasty. Another wonder that Marco Polo discovered was coal, "a sort of black stone which is dug out of veins in the hillsides and burns like logs. These stones keep a fire going better than wood, and being plentiful and very cheap, they effect a great saving of trees."

The most pressing problem to confront Kublai Khan at Dadu was not fuel but, as Chabi foresaw, the food supply. Transportation of grain from the Yangzi valley was slow and arduous, since the canal system had suffered through war and a change in the course of the Yellow River. As a result a sea transport service was started from the Yangzi delta. It succeeded admirably until, in 1286, a typhoon struck the northward-bound rice fleet off the Shandong peninsular and sank a quarter of the ships. At another time perhaps this disaster would have had less impact, but that year the harvest in north China was bad, the worst on record, and the Yellow River burst its banks at Kaifeng, flooding vast areas of cultivated land.

To deal with this crisis Kublai Khan turned to a Uighur Turk by the name of Sangha, who claimed that he could solve the all the difficulties facing the Chinese empire. This ruthless minister did curb inflation for a while by restricting the issue of paper money and he pleased Kublai Khan by increasing state income from taxation as well as government enterprises, but Sangha overplayed his hand and mortally offended Chinese officials through the pillage of Song dynasty tombs. Over a hundred belonging to members of the imperial family were ransacked in a search for gold, silver, jade, gems, and other precious grave goods. His tomb robber was a Tibetan monk who used the loot to repair Buddhist foundations and covert Confucian and Daoist temples to Buddhist use. Throughout the 1280s the Buddhist church acquired more and more wealth, land and power: a census reveals that there were 213,148 monks and nuns residing in 42,318 temples and monasteries. Even though the rising chorus of complaint against the Buddhist abuses compelled Kublai Khan to demote Sangha in 1291, the ex-minister's trial and execution the same year upset him.

The basic difficulty for the Mongols was that their expenditure grew faster than they could raise money from China. One non-Chinese minister after another claimed to know how to solve the financial deficit, and for a brief period ran the Chinese empire; then each of them was challenged, accused of misdeeds, and finally executed. Lonely and out of touch, Kublai Khan could do no more than watch his imperial dream fade. Abortive expeditions to Japan, Vietnam, and Java outstretched his military resources, while stiffer taxes spread unrest among his Chinese subjects. In the early fourteenth century the strain was clearly evident in the differences between the Mongol tribes, which in twenty-five years raised nine candidates to the dragon throne. The conflict opened the way to a partial recovery of influence by Chinese officials, but the restarting of the examination system in 1315 came too late to rally lasting support to the Mongols, against whom popular rebellions steadily increased in number and extent.

Following the death of Kublai Khan, the Mongol dynasty was plagued by severe factionalism at the imperial court. Rival princes brought the political violence of the steppe to China and inaugurated a series of coups, murders, poisonings, and purges. Kublai Khan's successor, Timur, did not ascend the dragon throne without opposition and he struggled to impose his will on the Mongols, not to say his other subjects. Drunkenness may have been a cause of the problems he encountered. His grandfather Kublai Khan had reservations about his suitability as a ruler but, without a better candidate in sight, Timur Khan took up residence in the splendid imperial palace at Dadu and soon fell under the domination of his wife Bulugan, whose abiding aim was the advancement of her son. He was appointed as the heir apparent, and to ensure a smooth succession all potential rivals were sent away. But Bulugan was thwarted by the unexpected death of her son in 1306, the year before Timur Khan himself died from the effects of heavy drinking at the age of forty-one.

The dynastic history records the intense power struggle that erupted in the absence of a designated successor. Prince Ayurbarwada, Timur Khan's nephew, stormed the imperial palace at Dadu, killing the chief minister, Akhutai, during the assault and arresting Prince Ananta, who had been favored to succeed, and Empress Bulugan afterwards. Although Ayurbarwada enjoyed the advantage of having Beijing under his control, his brother, Khayishan, was not only older but also commander of larger forces. At the suggestion of their mother, the brothers reached a compromise whereby Khayishan promised that he would make Ayurbarwada the heir apparent after his own enthronement.

During Khayishan's brief reign as Külüg Khan, the example Kublai Khan had set as the Son of Heaven was forgotten, as the new emperor relied on the personal retainers he had brought with him from Mongolia. No attempt was made to run anything like a Chinese-style administration, and Külüg Khan handed out official posts as his mood dictated. Local butchers, priests, and actors found themselves in the imperial government, while hangers-on enormously increased its running costs. A Chinese official submitted a memorial bluntly pointing out Külüg Khan's total disregard for tradition, but it failed to bring the third Mongol emperor to his senses. A mounting financial crisis obliged him to issue new currency notes, whose inflated value only further undermined confidence in "the Great Yuan Treasury." Copper coins became the trusted form of exchange, although thousands of these coins were supposed to equal one of the new "silver notes" which the Beijing printers turned out in vast quantities.

Despite all this uncertainty and confusion, in 1311 Ayurbarwada quietly succeeded his brother in what was the most peaceful of all Mongol successions. One of Ayurbarwada Khan's first acts was to order that the *Classic of Filial Piety* should be translated into the Mongolian language, and copies given to members of his family, in the probably forlorn hope that its Confucian message might encourage cordial relations. As Ayurbarwada Khan was able to read and write Chinese with ease, he understood the need to return to Kublai Khan's method of imperial rule, although it did not stop him from using drastic measures of his own in order to speed up this process. Three days after becoming ruler, Ayurbarwada Khan executed his brother's ministers. By allowing Chinese scholars a greater role in the imperial administration, he undoubtedly improved its performance, but these officials were never able to challenge Mongol supremacy in Dadu. Ultimately Mongol-Chinese co-operation failed because of the power of the Mongol princes, tribal leaders who were unwilling to forfeit any of their authority in order to strengthen a centralized administration. When Ayurbarwada died in 1320, at the age of thirty-five, there were Chinese officials who still believed in the evolution of the Mongol empire into a

Chinese-style state. They were to be disappointed as Ayurbarwada Khan's son was deposed three years later. After overwhelming his temporary encampment halfway between Shangdu and Dadu, the young ruler was murdered by a group of conspirators that included five princes.

These Mongol princes joined the conspiracy because their annual grants had been twice stopped because of financial stringency. A new Mongol ruler would restore their fortunes, and in Yesün Temür Khan they hoped that they had found their man. Most likely a fellow conspirator, Yesün Temür Khan at first appeared as a savior but, once firmly established in power, he executed the conspirators with the exception of the five princes, who were exiled to distant lands. A complete stranger to China, the new Mongol emperor had no sympathy at all for its traditions and filled his government with Mongols and Central Asian Muslims. Fearing to be branded as a regicide, Yesün Temür Khan invited friend and foe alike to Dadu, where the imperial court came to look like a Mongol camp. Annual grants were restored in full and special gifts went to all supported Yesün Temür Khan, even if they had committed serious crimes. His personal security came at more than a financial price, however, for he had to relax control over the princes as well. When he died at Shangdu in 1328, the bloodiest succession struggle ever in Mongol history swiftly ensued. While Yesün Temür Khan's nine-year-old son was enthroned at Shangdu, another prince was elevated in Dadu. According to the dynastic history,

> the chief minister in Dadu saw the enthronement of a boy as an opportunity for advancing his own fortunes. So he seized the supporters of the young emperor at the imperial capital, confining them to prison, and then sent for Tugh Temür, who was in Nanjing, and offered him the dragon throne. Arriving at Dadu, Tugh Temür killed those who dared to oppose his coup in the imperial court. Then he sent a force to Shangdu in order to seize Yesün Temür Khan's son. The city was soon taken and the hapless ruler never to be seen again. The chief minister now urged Tugh Temür to become the ruler, but at first he refused. He wished to await the arrival of his elder brother and, as Mongol custom dictated, hand over the reins of power to him. When he was told that any delay was dangerous, and the chance of ruling China might slip away from his family, he finally consented to the chief minister's proposal, and became Emperor Wenzong. But hearing the news of this, his elder brother was so displeased that his rights had been usurped that he refused to come to Dadu. Coaxing eventually got him set out for Shangdu, near which city the brothers met and were apparently reconciled. They treated each other with every sign of affec-

tion, and for three days they spent the time in feasting and drinking. But on the last day the elder brother was found dead in his tent, shortly after Tugh Temür Khan had left it.

The disappearance of Yesün Temür Khan's young son at Shangdu, and the murder of the elder brother nearby, left Tugh Temür, or Jayaatu Khan, as he became, free to rule as the ninth Mongol emperor of China. In a nod to Mongol custom the murdered brother was posthumously declared the eighth emperor. Yet Jayaatu Khan's brief reign was no reign of terror because he was happy to leave the government entirely in the hands of his ministers, as indeed the scheming chief minister expected him to do. His imperial title Wenzong means "Cultivated Ancestor," a backhand compliment about the ruler's preference for Chinese poetry and painting rather than affairs of state.

Plots against Jayaatu Khan reflected the continued discontent of the Mongol princes and further undermined political stability, already under pressure from natural calamities and popular uprisings. During the reign of Ukhaatu Khan, the last Mongol emperor, rebellion was so frequent and so widespread that Dadu became increasingly irrelevant to the government of China. In part this was due to Ukhaatu Khan's indifference to the world outside the imperial palace. "He was only concerned with his pleasures," we are told, "because he issued an imperial edict that no girl over sixteen should be allowed to marry until his agents had looked at her." By this device he intended to maintain the quality of his very large harem.

In the 1350s China was rent by violence on a scale that had not been witnessed for centuries. With the breakdown of central government, powerful regional movements developed, whose aims differed according to their origin and location. Some of these rebellions aimed to protect local interests, others had a national aim in bringing down the Mongol administration. The largest group of rebels belonged to the White Lotus, a secret society whose doctrines were an amalgam of Buddhist and Daoist ideas. It was believed that the disorder into which the Chinese empire had fallen was proof that the future Buddha, Maitreya, would soon appear and relieve the sufferings of mankind by establishing an earthly paradise. White Lotus teachers appeared right across China, spreading the message of rebellion and renewal.

Zhu Yuanzhang, the future Ming emperor Hongwu, was the peasant leader of northernmost concentration of rebels but, in 1356, he was obliged to move south, cross the Yangzi River and make the city of Nanjing his base for future operations. From there Zhu Yuanzhang gradually extended his authority over all of south China. On his arrival in Nanjing:

a deputation, headed by an elderly scholar, came to congratulate him. For it was clear that Zhu Yuanzhang was not like the other adventurers that were now striving for mastery of the empire. Most of them were bandits on a large scale, and only sought to enrich themselves at the expense of the places they occupied. Zhu Yuanzhang was different, and did not desire to rise to power through the misery of the people. He also made it obvious that he intended to restore peace throughout the empire.

Zhu Yuanzhang was impressed by the advice the Confucian scholar gave him. The deputation's leader said, "Fortify Nanjing, store grain in the city, and proclaim yourself as ruler slowly." So it was that Zhu Yuanzhang did not declare his new dynasty of the Ming until, in 1368, he was ready to march on Beijing, at which point the Mongols retreated to a nomadic existence in the steppes. In breaking with the time-honored custom of taking as the dynastic title an ancient name of a locality associated with the imperial house, and choosing instead the epithet Ming, meaning "bright," he was making the point that the Chinese empire desperately needed to be restored to its former brightness.

PART FOUR

THE LATE EMPIRE
1368–1912

A Qing seal

CHAPTER 10

The Chinese Revival:
Ming Nanjing and Beijing

A certain man went to Beijing, and when he came back he praised everything in Beijing. Once he was walking in the moonlight with his father, and met a friend who said, "What a fine moon tonight!" He quickly replied, "This moon is nothing. You should see the moon in Beijing. It's far, far better." His father was angry and said, "The moon is the same everywhere. Why say that the moon in Beijing is superior?" and, clenching his fist, he gave him a good box round the ears. Through his tears his son said, "Your fist is nothing wonderful. You should feel the fists in Beijing!"

THE DECISION OF ZHU YUANZHANG TO RULE FROM NANJING instead of Kublai Khan's great northern capital at Dadu meant that the excessive admiration mocked in this story was still some years away. Yet Beijing would come to be seen as the quintessence of China down to the end of the empire itself. Every scholar wished to visit this imperial capital once in his lifetime.

Previously Nanjing had served as the capital of all the southern dynasties during the partition of the Chinese empire from 317 to 588. Standing there today are the city walls that Zhu Yuanzhang was advised to strengthen. At thirty-three kilometers they are the longest in China and indeed in the world. What the first Ming emperor did was to treble the size of Nanjing by enclosing a greater area for habitation with his strong new walls. The work took twenty years to complete. Except for Southern Song Hangzhou, the layout was the most irregular of all imperial capitals, with the palace itself situated in an eastern extension of Nanjing. The need to ensure security after the Mongol conquest explains the twisting path of the city wall, which seeks to take full advantage of the uneven terrain. A similar concern is evident in the two surviving gateways; they acted as powerful defensive strongholds, having three gates set inside vaulted tunnels.

As Zhu Yuanzhang's city wall enclosed an area of more than forty-one square kilometers, it seems unlikely that all the ground within the defenses was occupied, because the population of Nanjing was still under half a million. Originally this imperial capital had a total of thirteen gateways: three on the southern, five on the western, four on the northern, and one on the eastern walls. The single gateway facing east gave almost immediate access to the imperial city and its palace. The wall surrounding the palace itself measured half a kilometer on each side.

Zhu Yuanzhang favored traditional Chinese architecture for a residence of the Son of Heaven, a ceremonial center fit for imperial audiences and ritual. Completed in 1372, the Nanjing palace was praised for an elegance and beauty similar to that of the present-day palace at Beijing, with which it shared many features, including a series of marble bridges spanning a stream. Badly damaged in the civil war following Zhu Yuanzhang's death in 1398, the repaired buildings were initially used by the third Ming emperor Yongle. Only briefly in the 1640s was the Nanjing palace again an imperial residence, when an effort to revive the Ming dynasty there failed. A relative of the last Ming emperor was driven from the palace by Manchu troops, who went on to subdue all of south China in the name of the Qing dynasty. Now there are merely column bases to show where Zhu Yuanzhang's great palace once stood, but we can obtain an idea of its appearance from the drum tower he built in 1382 at the center of the city. It contained drums and bells as well as bamboo horns and other musical instruments, which were sounded to welcome important visitors to the imperial capital. Another surviving lookout tower is the one Yongle built for the examination compound. As concerned about his image as a Confucian ruler as he was about his legitimacy, this usurper-emperor placed considerable emphasis on orthodoxy and especially the interpretations of Zhu Xi, the Song commentator on the classics. To establish his position as an enlightened ruler, in 1409 Yongle published a work he had written on the duties of subjects and descendants.

The thoughts of the emperor on social conduct would of course have influenced the grades given by examiners to candidates in the civil service examinations. Would-be officials were expected to be aware of Yongle's preferences, not least after he authorized a compendium of Confucian learning as a kind of shortcut to proficiency in accepted dogma. But it was the gigantic *Yongle Encyclopedia* that really typifies the Chinese recovery

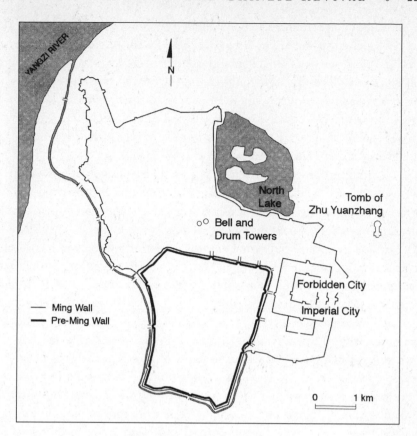

Map of the site of Ming Nanjing

under the Ming emperors. On completion in 1407, its 11,095 volumes were judged too numerous for a printed edition, a misfortune because the main collection perished when British and French troops sacked the Summer Palace at Beijing in 1860. Sections from books all over the empire were copied into the encyclopedia. This antiquarian approach led directly onto the new disciplines of philology and phonetics, with a consequent reassessment of the authenticity of many ancient texts. The Chinese intellectual revival contrasts with the scientific aspects of the European Renaissance, and appears strangely anti-scientific in the context of the previous millennium of technological advance pioneered in China.

"Encouragement of learning," the dynastic history tells us, "was a key policy . . . and the imperial university received special attention, its graduates gaining honors and privileges which inspired scholars everywhere to aim at becoming members of it." Two avenues were soon fixed as the routes to officialdom: the examinations conducted by the imperial university and the civil service examinations themselves. Entry to the imperial university was limited to the sons of officials whose performance was outstanding at school. The civil service examinations, on the other hand, were open to all those who had passed qualifying examinations in the provinces. Both graduates of the imperial university and successful candidates in the civil service examinations, which were held regularly in Nanjing, could take the palace examinations, the final arbiter of merit.

According to the grades awarded in the palace examinations, scholars received appointment as officials in the metropolitan or provincial administration. As in earlier times, a leading minister could expect to marry into the imperial family. The strictest precautions were taken at every stage of the examination process in order to ensure fair and honest results, though cheating was never entirely stopped. In Nanjing the examination compound, subdivided within and isolated from the outside world by a high wall, contained thousands of cells. These tiny brick compartments were about 1.1 meters deep, 1 meter wide and 1.7 meters high. They possessed two stone ledges, one serving as a table, the other a seat. During the two days an examination lasted the candidates were observed by soldiers stationed in the lookout tower. Since a soldier who discovered a book or any piece of paper with writing on it was rewarded with silver, the scrutiny remained very stringent day and night. The only movement allowed was the passage of servants replenishing food and water supplies, or removing human waste. When a candidate became tired, he could lay out his bedding and take a cramped rest. But a bright light in a neighboring cell would probably compel him to take up his brush again, in an attempt to answer the complicated literary questions set.

It is quite possible that each candidate would have learned by heart the 431,286 characters in the Confucian canon and the classics. Overwrought and exhausted, as well as conscious of the sacrifice his family had already made for such detailed preparation, many a candidate was subject to nightmares and daydreams. There are records of candidates going completely insane under the pressure. A contributing cause must have been the belief that the examination compound was a place where the ghosts of wronged people could seek revenge. Scholars who had disastrously dabbled with the affections of servant girls or married women were often removed screaming from their cells. Above all else, the straitjacket of the curriculum brought about a conformity of thought and led to an almost unquestioning acceptance of the will of the Ming emperors.

For those who failed to become an official, the most lucrative as well as the most honorable career available, there was a lasting sense of inadequacy. One Nanjing candidate is supposed to have accidentally let ink fall on his essay. Seeing that there was not enough time to re-write the essay and pass the examination, he rushed out of the compound and committed suicide by plunging head first into a well. Had he died inside the examination compound, his body would have been passed over the wall, as it was considered bad luck to have a corpse pass through the door. In 1469 there were only 100,000 civil and 80,000 military officials in the imperial service. During the Ming and Qing dynasties competition became steadily worse with the passage of time, in the late eighteenth century the odds against succeeding in the palace examinations become as high as 3,000 to 1.

Humble though his own background was, Zhu Yuanzhang appreciated the role that education would need to play in the recovery of the Chinese empire. He assigned some of the best Confucian scholars as teachers to his eldest son, the heir apparent. The concern of the first Ming emperor for renewal is apparent in the inscription he had engraved on a great stone near his tomb: its characters command his descendants to "Rule like the Tang and the Song." One of the sights of present-day Nanjing, Zhu Yuanzhang's mausoleum, situated in the hills to the east of the city, is approached by an avenue lined with splendid yet daunting statues of animals and men—elephants, camels, lions, as well as officials from both the civil and military arms of government.

As China had been racked by warfare for over thirty years, Zhu Yuanzhang understood on his accession in 1368 that reconstruction was essential. "We should not pluck the feathers of an infant bird," he said, "nor should we shake a newly planted tree." Considerate as Zhu Yuanzhang was to the sufferings of the Chinese people, he had no sympathy for ministers who found reason to oppose his decisions. In 1380 he reacted violently to the alleged sedition of a high official, striking down the minister's family and friends; the total number of people directly or indirectly implicated came to over 30,000, all of whom were executed. Few of those who helped Zhu Yuanzhang in founding the Ming dynasty died naturally, in contrast to the peaceful accommodation the first Song emperor reached with the field commanders responsible for his coup.

To strengthen the power of the dragon throne, Zhu Yuanzhang abolished many senior posts, thus bringing the heads of bureaux and the armed forces into direct relation with the emperor. This move towards despotism, which was to be the major trend in Chinese politics until the beginning of the twentieth century, had real dangers for the stability of the empire, particularly at times when children or ineffective individuals were seated on the dragon throne. The unusual position of scholar-bureaucrats at the imperial court can be glimpsed in the introduction of corporal punishment for maladministration and impropriety. Zhu Yuanzhang's intolerance of opposition tended to manifest itself in cruelty.

In order to perpetuate the imperial house, the first Ming emperor appointed his relations to fiefs scattered throughout the empire. These holdings were kept small and separate from the civil administration, but the military unit each was allowed to maintain could be summoned to Nanjing in an emergency. A fierce struggle between the fief-holders erupted when Zhu Yuanzhang successor, Huidi, tried to curtail the system. The civil war ended in 1402 with the capture of Nanjing by Huidi's uncle, who declared himself to be the third Ming emperor Yongle, meaning "Perpetual Happiness." At the time it was believed that Huidi had been burned alive in the firing of the imperial palace, but it later transpired that the twenty-year-old emperor, disguised as a Buddhist monk, had escaped into the countryside, where he lived a wandering life for years. Apprehended at last in 1441, after the death of the usurping uncle, he was allowed to spend the rest of his life in quiet seclusion.

The accession of Yongle was a very violent start to an otherwise successful reign. His execution of those who were loyal to his unfortunate nephew showed that he had clearly inherited his father's violent temper but, once secure in power, the third Ming emperor exhibited none of the paranoia at opposition that marred the reign of Zhu Yuanzhang. For Yongle was a most conscientious ruler and rose at 4 o'clock every morning in order

> to ponder over all the matters from the four corners of the Empire. He prioritized issues and made big as well as small decisions and then sent them out to the appropriate ministries and bureaux for action. After the audience with his chief officials, he never went straight to his private quarters. Instead, he read every memorandum and report from the four quarters.

Yongle was a strong ruler reminiscent of Qin Shi Huang Di. He had been so fiercely independent as a child that once Zhu Yuanzhang confined him in a remote country cottage as a punishment. Had his mother not secretly dispatched servants with food and drink to the ten-year-old prisoner, Yongle would have in all probability died. This early experience seems to have confirmed his own belief in the correctness of his actions, another trait that Qin Shi Huang Di possessed in abundance. While Yongle would have loved his subjects to associate him with the Confucian ideal of the wise ruler who listened to his advisors, he always kept his officials on a short and tight leash.

A mixture of ruthless brutality and moral idealism made Yongle the perfect absolutist ruler. Of his competence there was never any doubt. Even before he usurped the throne, his swift action in 1396 had foiled a Mongol counter-attack, when he marched beyond the Great Wall and caught the enemy before a full concentration of tribesmen could take place. Possibly his awareness of continued danger from the steppe, which he gained from living in his northeastern fief, was one reason for Yongle's decision to abandon Nanjing in favor of Beijing. The spoiling blow delivered in 1396 had slowed down the Mongol military recovery, but other campaigns were necessary before the northern frontier was properly secure. Foreign affairs were given serious attention during the time Yongle remained at Nanjing. Already Chinese influence had been restored over Vietnam, and action taken against Japanese pirates. Unrest in Japan eventually led to a falling away of raids, but the impression was left in the Chinese mind that all foreigners who arrived by ship were both unreliable and pugnacious, a belief soon confirmed by the advent of European buccaneers.

The threat from the sea was never more than an annoyance. At the same time as imperial armies consolidated the empire's frontiers, Yongle dispatched a great fleet under the command of the grand eunuch Zheng He to cruise in the southern seas. Brought up in the Muslim faith, Zheng He was appointed to oversee the construction of a fleet in the Nanjing shipyards and then sail it as far as India, Africa, and Australia. Between 1405 and 1433 there were seven major seaborne expeditions that caused more foreign rulers than ever before to acknowledge the power of the Son of Heaven— even distant Egypt sent an ambassador. In 1415 the sultan of Malindi (in modern Kenya) sent an embassy to China with exotic gifts, among them a giraffe for the imperial park. At the gateway of the imperial palace in Nanjing Yongle personally received the animal, together with a "celestial horse" and a "celestial stag." The giraffe was regarded as "a symbol of perfect virtue, perfect government, and perfect harmony in the Empire and the Universe." To mark the emperor's appreciation the ambassadors were conducted all the way home to East Africa on the fifth voyage of 1417-19.

The Ming seaborne expeditions were very different in character from those of the Portuguese, the first Europeans to sail into eastern waters. Instead of spreading terror, slaving, and planting fortresses, the Chinese engaged in diplomatic missions, exchanging gifts with distant rulers from whom they were content to accept merely formal recognition of the Son of Heaven. No greater contrast could be drawn between the peaceful trading of Zheng He at the great city of Calicut in southwest India, and the atrocities practiced there in 1502 by Vasco da Gama. There was no Chinese equivalent of the Portuguese habit of entering an Indian port with corpses hanging from the yards.

Archaeological testimony for Zheng He's pacific diplomacy comes from Sri Lanka, where a stele, dated 5 February 1409, has been found with a trilingual inscription. The Chinese text relates how the voyages were intended to announce the mandate of the Ming dynasty to foreign powers, the inscription ending with a list of presents offered to the Buddha: gold, silver, silk, porcelain, and so on. Here we have a Muslim ambassador from China dedicating in a Buddhist monastery situated in South Asia gifts from the Son of Heaven, the One Man of Confucian philosophy. More fascinating still is that the other two inscriptions do not translate the Chinese one. The Tamil text praises an incarnation of Vishnu while the Persian invokes Allah. Such urbanity has nothing in common with the religious fanaticism of the Portuguese.

On the death of Yongle in 1424 voyages were suspended, and in spite of the seventh expedition of 1431–33, the era of maritime exploration and diplomacy came to an end. Shortly after its return, Zheng He died at the age of sixty-five. The passing of the great admiral coincided with a gradual turning away from the sea, for by 1525 it was an offense to own or build a vessel with two or more masts. Not all the reasons are apparent for this momentous alteration of imperial policy, which the Indian Ocean a power vacuum into which Vasco da Gama unwittingly sailed. Had the Portuguese explorer rounded the Cape of Good Hope seventy years earlier, he would have found his own vessels of 300 tons sailing alongside a Chinese fleet with ships of 1,500 tons. All that remains in modern Nanjing to recall Zheng He's achievements is an inscription set up by Yongle as a thanks-offering to Tian Fei, goddess of the sea. It once stood in a temple dedicated to this controller of "the wind, rain, thunder, lightning, and waves."

Even more significant than Zheng He's ocean voyages was the relocation of the imperial capital from Nanjing to Beijing. As it was to stay there for the next half millennium, the northern location might well have been a factor in the decline of China's interest in seafaring, because the Great Wall some fifty kilometers distant became the focus of attention. In 1417 over 200,000 men repaired Beijing's moats, walls, and bridges while a new imperial palace was under construction on the site of Kublai Khan's residence. By 1420 enough building work was completed for Beijing to assume its role as China's greatest city. Not all the officials were as pleased with the new imperial capital as Yongle and, when three of the new palatial buildings were damaged by violent storms and lightning, one of them addressed a memorial to the emperor which was critical of the huge expenditure involved in the transfer of the capital northwards. Suggesting that the damage was a divine warning about this extravagance, the official wrote:

> For over twenty years Your Majesty has been engrossed with the construction of Beijing. But from the start of the project, the costs have been staggering, and the staff in charge have not correctly fulfilled their duties. The people, who were forced to provide the labor, have been separated from their families and could not farm their land, while the demand for materials has increased day by day. When green and blue paint was required, hundreds of thousands of people were ordered to find what was needed. If they were unable to provide what the officials demanded, they had to pay money instead, some of which was pocketed by them. Now the capital is truly the foundation of the world, but the people are the true foundation of the capital. If the people feel secure, then the capital will be secure, and if the capital is secure, the foundation of the Empire is strong, and the world will be at peace. But since the very beginning of building work, carpenters and masons have used your name to force people to move out of their homes, thereby creating a new army of homeless people. At present many eat nothing but tree bark, grass, and whatever else they can find. In contrast, tens of thousands of Buddhist monks and Daoist priests, who were brought here to pray in the various temples, daily consume mountains of rice. Since the Hall of Supreme Harmony, the place where the Dragon Throne itself is situated, was struck by lightning, it is the moment to reflect and reform. Your Majesty should send all the poor workers home so as to placate Heaven. I for one would gladly accompany you if you decide to return to Nanjing and to report the natural calamities at the tomb of your father, the founder-emperor of the dynasty.

Even though Yongle was unsettled by the natural disaster, he could not disguise his fury at this remonstrance and had its author imprisoned. This alarmed the officials and they fell silent.

Yongle's Beijing was slightly smaller than it had been under the Mongol emperors. It was shorter from north to south, and the number of city gates was reduced from eleven to nine. The Ming imperial capital represents, nonetheless, the final stage in the development of traditional Chinese architecture. Despite extensive rebuilding during the twentieth century, the chessboard pattern of the streets in Beijing is still apparent, with the division of the great city into distinct quarters. At the center is the imperial palace, the so-called Purple Forbidden City, a literary allusion to the Pole Star at the center of the celestial world. Arranged in accordance with this

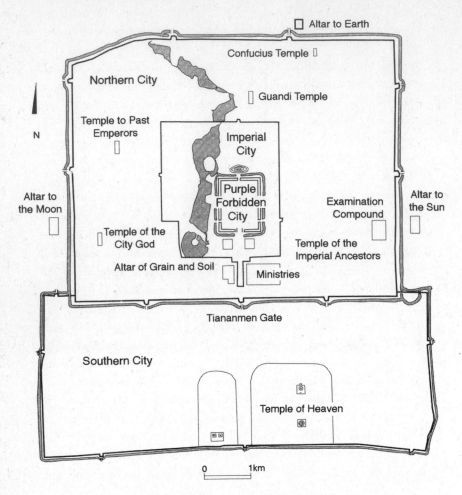

Map of the site of Ming Beijing

cosmic dimension, the Purple Forbidden City has the usual north-south orientation, all its principal terraces and openings facing south. The middle of its three sections was the most important because it contains the great ceremonial buildings of the state.

Enclosed by a moat and a high wall, not quite a kilometer square, and divided internally into numerous compounds and courtyards by lesser walls and buildings, the Purple Forbidden City has its official place of entry in the Meridian Gate, thought by some to be the finest architectural unit in all China. Erected in 1420, re-erected in 1647 and restored in 1801, this monumental gateway comprises an open rectangle, the sides projecting 92 meters towards the south and forming both ends of a kind of bastion upon which pavilions are placed. The central building, 126 meters in length and 20 meters in height, is crowned by a double roof and pierced by five vaulted tunnels. The impression of grandeur and solidity is strengthened by the use of gorgeous colors. The walls are built of brick coated with red plaster; the wooden pillars of the pavilions are covered with thick lacquer and painted bright vermillion; the roofs are laid out with glazed yellow titles; and the staircases and balustrades are of white marble. As Oswald Siren shrewdly wrote in the 1920s:

> The splendor of the palaces depends mainly on their very clear and natural wooden construction, their perfect balance and symmetrical arrangement, their striking contrasts of color, their position on high terraces, their unity of style and artistic purpose. They are all elements in the same composition; the whole labyrinth of walls and courts and colonnades and roofs is one great work of art, not an individual creation but the result of a gradual growth (and decay) in accordance with the architectural principles and the ancient traditions of might and splendor, which have prevailed in the construction of all the great Imperial Palaces of China.

The Gate of Supreme Harmony in modern Beijing

The approach to the Meridian Gate was via a walled avenue, approximately a third of a kilometer in length. Access to this rectangular enclosure was gained through the Tiananmen, the "Gate of Heavenly Peace." The Meridian Gate itself gives access to a vast flagged court across which in a wide curve from east to west flows Golden Water River, spanned by five marble bridges with carved balustrades.

Straight ahead is the Gate of Supreme Harmony, a pavilion with tall columns, whose middle doors, like those in all the gates, were only opened for the Son of Heaven, while his officials passed through the side entrances. The imperial pathway can be traced in the decorative marble slabs carved with dragons and other symbolic animals that comprise the central sections of the gently sloping stairways leading to and from the terraced gateways, halls, and temples. Standing before the Gate of Supreme Harmony are two enormous bronze lions and two marble ornaments representing the emperor's authority; on a large scale are sculptured the box in which petitions to the dragon throne were placed and the box in which the imperial seals were kept.

Nearby 200 meters beyond the Gate of Supreme Harmony, at the northern side of an empty court, stands the Hall of Supreme Harmony,

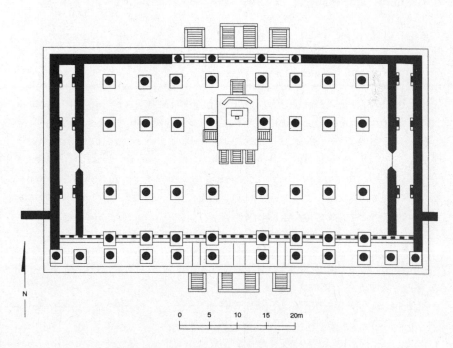

N

0   5   10   15   20m

Above: the map of Hall of Supreme Harmony

Opposite: One of the two bronze guardian lions standing before the Gate of Supreme Harmony

Middle Harmony Hall

one of the three big ceremonial buildings of the palace. Here were held the rites and formalities connected with the great occasions of the year, the winter solstice, the New Year, the emperor's birthday. On a high dais, approached by three flights of steps, is the dragon throne itself. The interior of the Hall of Supreme Harmony measures 52 by 30 meters, and is divided by three rows of columns. Several reconstructions have taken place, the most significant being the one in 1645 when the present name was adopted. Prior to the rebuilding, it was known as the Hall of the Supreme Ruler. Repairs were again required a century later, and a final face-lift was ordered by Yuan Shikai in late 1915, just before this ambitious general made an abortive bid to found a new dynasty of his own.

Immediately behind the Hall of the Supreme Harmony on the same high terrace are the Middle Harmony Hall and the Protecting Harmony Hall. A small building 16 meters square, the Middle Harmony Hall served as a tiring room for the emperor before he participated in the ceremonies and audiences held in the Hall of Supreme Harmony. It was here that mes-

sages to be read at the memorial services for imperial ancestors were prepared and, each spring, the emperor inspected an array of agriculture
implements and seeds. In 1890 this pyramidal hall was entirely rebuilt as an
exact copy of the original, which had fallen into a state of extreme disrepair.
The Protecting Harmony Hall, the final ceremonial building, is much larger, the outside measurements being 49 by 23 meters, and under its double
roof the most successful candidates in the palace examinations were personally received by the emperor.

The terrace on which the Hall of Protecting Harmony stands ends in
a triple staircase of the same type as the one in front of the Hall of Supreme
Harmony, the throne room. At the bottom of this staircase is the southern
gateway of the inner court of the palace, which contained the emperor's private quarters. At the Gate of Heavenly Purity, the main entrance to the
inner court, it was customary for Ming emperors to hear reports from min-

The Grand Staircase approaching the Hall of Protecting Harmony.

isters and other senior officials. The palaces here all date from Yongle's reign, although fires necessitated considerable restoration work in the late eighteenth century. The imperial family and members of the imperial harem lived in this secluded section of the Purple Forbidden City, attended solely by eunuchs. Other buildings, to each side of the great ceremonial halls already described, include libraries, lecture halls, small residences, kitchens, and storage rooms.

Close to the Purple Forbidden City were areas reserved for imperial use, including Coal Hill, so named according to tradition because an emergency supply of coal was stored there by one of the Mongol emperors, and the islands and shores of three large lakes. It was on the lakeshore here that Kublai Khan had pitched his tent while his capital city of Dadu was being completed. It has even been suggested that Yongle's new residence was little more than a replica of Kublai Khan's residence. This seems improbable, for nowhere in the Ming palace is there any trace of the great dining hall that so impressed Marco Polo. Most of the present-day structures around the lakes are the handiwork of the Manchus, the last northern people to take control of the Chinese empire. More attractive than any part of the Purple Forbidden City are the Sea Palaces that they built here. These consist of temples, theatres, libraries, studios, residential quarters, reception halls, offices, open galleries for the enjoyment of the scenery, pavilions for quiet meditation or poetical composition, boat-houses, towers, gateways, and bridges, besides all the rockeries, terraces, and picturesque walls which enclose the gardens.

One of the distinguishing features of Beijing during the late Chinese empire was the large number of religious establishments it possessed. Twenty-four major altars or temples played a significant part in the life of the imperial capital. To the south of the Meridian Gate, on each side of the north-south avenue that bisected Beijing, were situated the Altar to Soil and Grain and the Imperial Ancestral Temple. The site of the Altar of Heaven farther south, a circular three-tier terrace nearly five meters in height, and the famous Temple of Heaven, a circular edifice with a triple roof of blue tiles, now acts as an enormous public park. Nearby was the Altar of Agriculture, whose sacrifices were connected with the spring plowing and were directed at securing good harvest. Today it is occupied by a sports ground with a stadium and a swimming pool.

Another important building within the city walls was the temple dedicated to Confucius, whose quiet and spacious grounds were close to the north wall. It once housed the steles on which were carved the names of scholars who had been successful in the palace examinations. The actual examination compound, which Yongle constructed, was some distance to the south. Old plans reveal the 8,500 examination cells it once contained. Carp Street nearby was the location of a travel agency that sold tickets to candidates who were traveling home to south China by boat. The red dot on a carp's forehead was said to be the mark of those who had failed: the fish acquired the mark in an abortive attempt to leap the rapids on the Yellow River and become a dragon. The greatest honors went to the candidates who were judged to have come in first, second, and third. After presentation to the emperor, they were allowed the rare privilege of leaving the Purple Forbidden City through the middle arch of the Meridian Gate, following an official who carried the ranked list of graduates. In a great parade, the three men then circled the palace city before returning to the lodgings of friends and relatives for private celebrations. Later the Emperor threw a banquet for all successful candidates.

Other religious sites included the Temple of the City God, a feature of every Chinese city, the Temple of Past Emperors, a kind of collective ancestral temple, the Temple of the Fire God, and the Guandi Temple. Based on the historical Guan Di, a prominent general during the period immediately after the fall of the Later Han dynasty, his worship as a deity of war was peculiarly Chinese in character, since he was believed to prevent conflict. No bloodthirsty Mars, Guan Di was concerned with martial valor rather than gathering spoils. The popularity of tales about him, both on stage and in fiction, made the war god the most worshipped deity in Beijing. Only the Buddhist goddess of mercy, Guanyin herself, came close as a rival.

As the grave of Beijing's founder was never located, Kublai Khan took his place along with the founding emperors of the Han, Tang, and Song dynasties in the newly constructed Temple of Past Emperors. It was at Kublai Khan's court that the theatre first became fashionable. The prolific Beijing dramatist Guan Hanqing had his plays regularly performed there. In his *Snow in Midsummer* a girl is executed as the result of official corruption. As she laments just before her beheading,

> Because officials here have no conscience,
> Ordinary people dare not tell the truth.

Whether the Mongol court was sympathetic to this message we do not know, but drama did form a large part of its entertainment. Plays about the exploits of Guan Di were well received, as was the knockabout humor associated with Xuanzang's pilgrimage to India in search of Buddhist scriptures. His protector Sun Wukong, the Chinese version of the Indian monkey god

Hanuman, is an intensely human figure despite of the havoc he causes to those who oppose the pilgrim's progress. In *Journey to the West* Wu Cheng'en turned these well-known stories into one of China's greatest novels. Though its Rabelaisian humor may surprise Western readers, the wisdom of honest laughter was appreciated by the Chinese as a potent weapon to deploy against fanaticism. Mao Zedong, who was never above an earthy joke if it hit the target, preferred the earlier Ming novel *Outlaws of the Marsh*. This account of the heroic actions of a peasant army during the Northern Song era is believed in the People's Republic of China to "have enthused the masses and angered the ruling class." Its author remains a mystery.

From the fifteenth century onwards the novel became China's leading literary form. Luo Guanzhong's *Romance of the Three Kingdoms* had an immense influence on other authors. An early Ming novel like *Outlaws of the Marsh*, it used popular material and especially the tales about Guan Di and his troubled life. On a scale akin to Tolstoy's *War and Peace*, this narrative confirmed the honesty of the general as the exact opposite of Cao Cao, the warlord who was prepared to betray everything for his own advantage. Yet it is in the humor of Wu Chengen, rather than in the conflicts of either *Outlaws of the Marsh* or *Romance of the Three Kingdoms*, that we find the authentic voice of the Ming empire: a worldliness that is still able to relish the quirks of human existence. It is especially clear in the humorous stories collected at this time. Not untypical is this tale of the poetical flourishes of an admirably opportunist scholar, ready to use his education in an emergency.

A distinguished official died and found himself standing before the King of the Underworld. When this fearsome ruler accidentally farted, the scholar sang a eulogy of the fart in endless verses. At one point he declaimed:

> Let regal steam free passage find
> From golden buttocks raised behind,
> As when such sounds of music soft
> Of organ pipes and strings do waft;
> Such fragrance is not held a stain
> Though quivering scent the nostrils strain;
> While rapt in thrall thy servant low
> Exults, o'erwhelmed by massy blow.

So pleased was the King of the Underworld with the poem that he extended the scholar's life for ten years. The scholar returned to the world of the living and at length the time came for him to leave again. When on his

second arrival the King of the Underworld asked the scholar who he was,
one of the little devils answered, "He is the Crap Poet!"

Hopefully the pseudo-Miltonics catch something of the original, a wonderful parody of the celebratory verse an official was expected to be able to
extemporize on great occasions. The imperturbability of the scholar in
front of the black-faced ruler of the dead is remarkable in suggesting that
learning is a protection for the individual everywhere. When the legendary
Yellow Emperor's chief minister first devised the original Chinese characters, all the spirits were supposed to have cried in agony, as the innermost
secrets of the world could thereafter be recorded. Such was the respect
accorded to literacy in China that Confucian temples had special ovens for
the ritual disposal of unwanted paper with writing on it.

On Yongle's death in 1424, his son decided to return the imperial capital to Nanjing, but this emperor's early death left the matter unresolved. So
it was not until 1441 that Beijing finally became the Chinese empire's last
capital city. Yongle's entry into the spirit world, his interment in a grand
tomb some forty-five kilometers northwest of the imperial capital, was also
not without its complications. Though his father, Zhu Yuanzhang, had
already established an imperial cemetery at Nanjing, Yongle gave orders
that a propitious place be found for a new cemetery. The question of the
site was critical because, if it was wrongly placed, the spirits of deceased
emperors would be displeased and the future of the dynasty endangered.
Once he was satisfied that his father's tomb at Nanjing was worthy of a
founding emperor, Yongle settled on a site for himself near Beijing.

All his successors followed his lead except one, the seventh Ming
emperor Zhu Qiyu, who was dethroned. He was buried in a modest tomb
much closer to the imperial capital. Zhu Qiyu had been elevated to the
dragon throne in 1449 after his elder brother, Zhu Qizhen, was captured by
the Mongols at Tumubao, an unnecessary battle in an unnecessary campaign. The young emperor Zhu Qizhen was so dominated by the eunuchs
that he appointed one of them, Wang Zhen, as commander-in-chief and
then accompanied him on the ill-fated expedition. Wang Zhen seems to
have been more concerned with entertaining the ruler in his native village,
close to the northern frontier, than with either a success against the
Mongols or the safety of the army. Ignoring the advice of regular officers
who had long experience fighting the Mongols, Wang Zhen exposed his
soldiers to attack in a situation where they lacked even water. After their
defeat and the capture of the emperor, it was decided to place Zhu Qiyu,
Zhu Qizhen's brother, on the dragon throne instead. Some officials advised

an immediate withdrawal to Nanjing, others were all for remaining in the new imperial capital. The second viewpoint prevailed and, after a tremendous battle in the suburbs, the Mongols gave up the investment of Beijing and returned to the steppe.

Resoluteness on the part of officials who opposed the abandonment of Yongle's foundation was not, however, rewarded by increased influence in the imperial court, since emperors soon forgot that Zhu Qizhen's humiliation had been brought about by a eunuch. A year later the Mongols released Zhu Qizhen, who returned to Beijing and found Zhu Qiyu, now Emperor Jingdi, enthroned in his stead. As a result, he was confined for seven years, comfortably looked after but entirely cut off from the outside world. When in 1457 Jingdi fell ill, the eunuchs hid the seriousness of his condition for as long as it took to restore Zhu Qizhen as emperor. An astonished Zhu Qizhen was raised to the dragon throne again as Emperor Tianshun while a eunuch strangled his younger brother on his sickbed.

Today the imperial Ming tombs are approached through an enormous white marble archway richly decorated with animal sculpture. Then comes the Great Red Gate, a three-arched gateway that marks the beginning of

Opposite and below: ceremonial sculptures of Yongle's tomb in Beijing

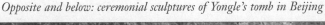

the official road up to the tombs. Half a kilometer farther on stands a large square pavilion with arches opening to the four sides: it contains the largest memorial stele in China, cut from a single block of stone ten meters high. All the imperial tombs have individual steles as well. One indicates the path to the grave, while the other is placed in a pavilion at the entrance of the grave itself. Beyond the stele pavilion is the so-called Spirit Road, an avenue flanked by twenty-four stone animals and twelve stone men, symmetrically placed in pairs and facing each other. The figures of the men are all standing because it was forbidden for a man to sit in the presence of an emperor, dead or alive. The curves in the Spirit Road, and indeed the pathways to the different tombs, were introduced to keep evil influences at bay, as bad spirits have always been thought by the Chinese to move in straight lines. The pathway to each imperial tomb is replete with its own stone guardians.

Yongle's tomb has now been restored to the condition it was on his burial. A triple gateway leads into a spacious and planted courtyard on the far side of which is situated the Gate of Heavenly Favors, really a large entrance hall with a double roof. This brightly decorated hall served as a reception room for members of the imperial clan who came to pay their respects to Yongle's spirit. Here they would have checked that their robes were in order, and perhaps received a cup of tea. Beyond the Gate of Heavenly Favors is the main courtyard in which stands the place of sacrifice, the Hall of Heavenly Favors. Two small ovens, faced with green and yellow tiles, were used to burn sacrificial offerings. They are between the Hall of Heavenly Favors and an ornamental gateway that gives access to the front of the tomb mound. The stele tower and pavilion rise majestically above the visitor, a reminder of the power once possessed by the Ming. As the Manchu emperors were keen to demonstrate that they had become the rulers of the Chinese empire in the traditional manner and not as foreign interlopers, they were punctilious in showing respect to the Ming tombs, several of which had been damaged by the followers of rebel leader Li Zicheng, who captured Beijing just before Manchu takeover in 1664.

The repairs that concerned Yongle most were those to the Great Wall, which assumed its final form under the Ming emperors. Even before the disaster at Tumubao, the security of the northern frontier had become a subject of heated debate between the advocates of offensive and defensive strategies. While Yongle mounted campaigns against the Mongols on the steppe, he also ordered the building of stone forts in key passes and the

*Opposite: a section of the Great Wall north of Beijing.
These ramparts were newly fortified by the Ming dynasty
in an offort to keep out the Mongols.*

renewal of rammed-earth walls elsewhere. Long walls are not mentioned in the dynastic history until the year 1429, by which date the Chinese hold on the steppe had weakened considerably.

Instrumental in strengthening the Great Wall was Qiujun, an official who hailed from the southern island of Hainan. In 1487 he presented at the imperial court a treatise outlining his approach to statecraft, including new ways of handling border problems. Qiujun argued that unless the Chinese controlled the Ordos, the expanse of semi-desert enclosed by the great northern loop of the Yellow River, the nomads had a perfect starting-point for attacks in a number of directions. New ramparts and strongholds were eventually built across the southern part of the Ordos, their line in the early sixteenth century being extended eastwards across the mountainous country north of Beijing, until they reached the coast at Shanhaiguan. Its great fortress, constructed astride the main route between China and Manchuria, was famous for the inscription carved above the outer gate: First Gate to All under Heaven.

Unable to crush the Mongols, there was no choice but to exclude these troublesome nomads by building walls. The impressive section of the Great Wall north of Beijing today dates from the sixteenth century. Then it was not referred to as the Great Wall; instead the whole defensive system went by the name of the Nine Border Garrisons. To create a really strong frontier the materials used for construction changed: a rammed earth core was now faced with brick and stone. Although work was still proceeding on the Great Wall when the Ming dynasty fell, this fixed defense, like the Maginot Line, turned out to be of little use when the real threat appeared. In the Ming case, the threat came from the Manchus, a northern people settled beyond the gate at Shanhaiguan. Let through this fortress as allies in a civil war, the Manchus occupied Beijing.

The Ming emperors were struggling to hold onto power well before the arrival of the Manchus. Popular rebellion and falling tax returns coupled with increased expenditure left the imperial administration in a perilous position. It was not helped by the grip that the eunuchs exercised over state policy. The dynastic history reveals the unique position attained by the eunuchs when it singles out Liu Jin,

> an ambitious and cunning eunuch, who with seven others, the attendants of the young Emperor when he was heir apparent, came to dominate Beijing. They gratified the tastes of the Son of Heaven to such an extent that matters of state were neglected. The emperor was beguiled with dancing, music, wrestling matches, and a menagerie of exotic animals. He was even persuaded to roam the streets of the imperial capital in disguise, on the lookout for pleasure.

The ruler mentioned in this extract is Wuzong, the tenth Ming emperor. In 1506, a year after his enthronement, he gave Liu Jin permission to collect taxes, after the eunuch told him that the decline of revenue was the result of official inefficiency and corruption. While Wuzong was kept distracted, Liu Jin set about the task of consolidating his own authority. The fourteen-year-old emperor was warned of Liu Jin's immense ambition by officials as well as others eunuchs fearful of his growing power, but Liu Jin was able to persuade Wuzong that the warning was no more than palace intrigue. Afterwards Liu Jin issued an imperial edict that gave eunuchs loyal to him an authority equal to that of the highest civil servants.

Eunuch power now seemed irresistible. Liu Jin spent money faster than he collected taxes, and tried to cover a growing deficit by the sale of official positions, heavy fines, and arbitrary levies. So bad did the situation become that an anonymous memorial, outlining Liu Jin's misdeeds, came to the emperor's attention. It had been dropped on the pathway reserved for the Son of Heaven. Once again the wily eunuch escaped punishment. Liu Jin's other exploits included obliging senior officials to kneel before him for hours in the main courtyard of the Purple Forbidden City. As it was a very hot day, some of these distinguished men collapsed, only to be rudely dragged away. Those who dared to object at this degrading treatment were at once imprisoned.

But Liu Jin's luck did not last and he was implicated in a plot to replace Wuzong with a relation of his own. The drunken emperor was not convinced at first that his favorite intended to betray him. Only when Wuzong had seen with his own eyes the hoard of gold and silver that Liu Jin had collected, along with armor, weapons, and passes to the imperial palace, was he disposed to act. Liu Jin was questioned at the Meridian Gate, the main entrance to the Purple Forbidden City. When the eunuch appeared, no official spoke and it looked as if Liu Jin would survive once more. Then an imperial consort asked why he had so many arms hidden in his residence. As Liu Jin could not answer the question, he was condemned to the lingering death, which lasted for three terrible days. Whether Liu Jin actually intended to assassinate Wuzong in 1510 remains uncertain. He never admitted his guilt and his death sentence was carried out with unusual dispatch, notwithstanding the deliberately prolonged period of pain.

Four years later the first Portuguese ships put into Guangzhou, known to most foreign visitors as Canton. The violent and ungovernable behavior of the Portuguese sailors soon led to bloody clashes, which were not contained until nearby Macao was leased in 1557 as a trading base. Its rapid growth soon caused the local Ming authorities some uneasiness, and they constructed a wall right across the isthmus connecting Macao with the mainland, posting soldiers to guard a single gateway, above which was written: "Fear our greatness, respect our virtue." Movement through the gate was henceforth denied to foreigners lacking official Chinese passes. From this tiny territory, however, merchants conducted the most lucrative of all Portuguese trading ventures, because they had stumbled upon a great illicit market.

Pirate raids had led to the prohibition on direct trade with Japan, a gap the Portuguese happily filled until the arrival of the Dutch. In 1622 the Dutch attacked Macao and then turned their attention to other parts of the Chinese coast, repeating the initial outrages of the Portuguese. To the dismay of the Chinese, English vessels soon appeared and behaved in a similar manner, although one of the Cornish adventurers who bombarded Guangzhou in 1637 was sufficiently impressed by what he saw to keep an illustrated diary. "This Countrie," he wrote, "May bee said to excell in these particulers: antiquity, largenesse, Richenesse, healthynesse, Plentiffulnesse. For the Art and manner of government I thinck no Kingdom in the world Comparable to it. Considered altogether."

A foreign visitor who made a favorable impression on a number of senior officials was the Jesuit missionary Matteo Ricci. Once he realized that in China priests did not enjoy the degree of respect bestowed on them in Europe, Ricci abandoned the robes of a Buddhist monk for those of a scholar. That he was prepared to tolerate the rituals of ancestor worship further endeared him to those brought up to believe in the teachings of Confucius. It was from Jesuit descriptions of the Chinese empire, including the extensive diary kept by Ricci himself, that influential writers in the West like Leibniz and Voltaire obtained a tantalizing glimpse of an alternative civilization. They thought that China had a model form of government because of the absence of hereditary privilege and a powerful clergy, unlike Europe in the seventeenth and eighteenth centuries. Ricci lived the last years of his life in Beijing, dying in 1610.

By 1515 Wuzong, now in his mid-twenties, was so bored with life in Beijing and irritated by the constant criticism of his officials that he developed an interest in warfare with the encouragement of an officer named Jiang Bin. When Wuzong decided to take up residence near the Great Wall in order to witness actual fighting, he found that the gate in a pass north of the imperial capital barred against him. The official in charge of the pass refused to open the gate until he had received an order bearing the seals of the emperor's wife and mother. Unable to get beyond the pass, the emperor was forced to return to the Purple Forbidden City. A second attempt was successful because the Son of Heaven went northwards in disguise. When he reached a town close to the northern frontier, Wuzong appointed himself as the commanding general, and issued orders for requisitions with a military seal. Quickly bored, he forcibly removed local women from their homes and added them to his harem. Now the all-powerful Jiang Bin persuaded the emperor to indulge his military fantasies with campaigns in the southern provinces, the scene of several uprisings. Almost always drunk, Wuzong moved to Nanjing and took the credit for victories over the rebels. On his entry to Beijing in 1521 thousands of bound captives lined both sides of the great avenue that ended at the Meridian Gate. In full military uniform Wuzong rode through these captives and into the Purple Forbidden City. It was his last imaginary triumph, for three days later he collapsed while sacrificing at the Altar to Heaven and had to be carried back to the imperial palace. On his deathbed the twenty-nine-year-old emperor is reported to have said,

> Whatever happens, tell the Dowager Empress that she must decide pressing matters of state with the aid of the Grand Secretaries. This is critical. None of my eunuch attendants is at fault. I am the one who ruined the affairs of the Empire.

As no successor had been designated by Wuzong, the emperor's younger cousin was chosen as the next emperor with the approval of the empress dowager. So a thirteen-year-old boy was declared Shizong, the eleventh Ming emperor.

At once Jian Bin was beheaded and the worst of Wuzong's eunuchs were dismissed. But another eunuch-led administration formed because Shizong filled key appointments with his own eunuchs and hardly bothered to meet his officials. This reluctance to be engaged with the day-to-day affairs of the empire increased dramatically after the attempt on his life by harem ladies. One night in 1542 they tried to strangle him while stabbing his groin with their hairpins. Shizong only just survived and spent the rest of his reign living at a safe distance in the palace gardens, where he saw only the smallest possible group of advisors. Most of his successors followed this example of imperial detachment, which allowed senior officials to regain some of the ground they had lost since Yongle's reign. It meant cooperation with the eunuchs, something neither officials nor eunuchs enjoyed, but at least the running of the Chinese empire was freed from the whims of an emperor.

In 1644 the dynasty fell almost by accident. The Manchus did not conquer China on their own: it was conquered for them by the complicated civil war which followed the usurpation of the dragon throne by Li Zicheng, whose rebel army was strong enough to take Luoyang in 1643 and Beijing a year later. The sixteenth and last Ming ruler Sizong hanged himself in a pavilion on Coal Hill. Li Zicheng, a man of the people, might have established another Chinese dynasty. Li Zicheng, however, failed to take into account the general in charge of the Great Wall immediately north of Beijing. This infamous soldier, Wu Sangui, had a grudge against Li Zicheng, since his favorite concubine was forcibly enrolled in the rebel leader's harem. Seeing that other frontier commanders were getting ready to oust Li Zicheng, Wu Sangui reached an agreement with the Manchus and opened the First Gate to All under Heaven at Shanhaiguan. Whatever he might have hoped to gain from this pact, the abandonment of the main route between Manchuria and China was a fatal error, for upon it hinged the whole system of northern defense.

Fearing that Wu Sangui would defy him but unaware of the alliance the general had made with the Manchus, Li Zicheng marched to Shanhaiguan so as to overcome what he thought was his last opponent. The dynastic history recounts that to "strengthen his position Li Zicheng took with him the father of Wu Sangui and the son of the last Ming emperor." The former was led in front of the frontier fortress, where he implored his son to surrender and save his life. When Wu Sangui declared that he was a loyal supporter of the Ming, his father was beheaded before his eyes, an action which made him become more than ever determined to defeat the rebels. In the ensuing battle, which occurred during a fierce storm, we know that the decisive moment came when "20,000 iron breast-plated Manchu horses galloped into the rebel host." Unnerved by the unexpected attack, the rebels broke ranks and fled, following their leader's example. While Wu Sangui pursued Li Zicheng westwards, the Manchus quietly occupied Beijing and installed their king as the first Qing emperor.

CHAPTER 11

The Last Imperial Capital: Qing Beijing

The imperial capital stands on at least a third less ground than London, including Westminster and Southwark, but it is still one of the largest cities in the world, and justly to be admired for its walls and gates, the distribution of the quarters, the width and allineation of its streets, the grandeur of its triumphal arches and the number and magnificence of its palaces.

IN 1644 FEW CHINESE PEOPLE COULD HAVE ANTICIPATED THAT THE Manchus would rule for so long. None of them could have realized that their dynasty, the Qing, was to be China's last imperial house. For the residents of Beijing, the consequences of the change of dynasty were particularly dramatic, since it was here that the Manchus first established themselves. Manchu soldiers and their families were ordered to move into the imperial capital. In order to accommodate them, Chinese residents were moved from their homes: the southern area of the city became the residence of the relocated Chinese. The northern residential area was actually settled according to membership of the eight Banners, the main units of the Manchu army; their names were Bordered Blue, Plain Blue, Bordered Red, Plain Red, Bordered Yellow, Plain Yellow, Bordered White, and Plain White. From the outset therefore a distinction was made between the Manchu followers of the new Qing emperor and his Chinese subjects, who were visually identified by the queue, which they were forced to wear in order to demonstrate their acceptance of Manchu rule. Every Chinese man was required to shave his forehead and braid his hair into what Europeans soon called a pigtail. Failure to do so was punishable by death.

The Manchu rulers had already claimed Yongle's palace as their own place of residence. They kept to the original layout, although most of the

Side-by-side Chinese and Manchu writing

halls were refurbished or repaired at intervals. Because the Manchus singled out the eunuchs as the cause of the Ming collapse, management of imperial household passed into the hands of the Qing emperor's own kinsmen. Chinese officials were so pleased with the return of the eunuchs to their traditional role in the imperial harem that they made no adverse comment on the imperial court's interest in religion. Qianlong, the fourth Manchu ruler, installed both Tibetan deities and eunuch-lamas in 1720 when this remote country was for the first time incorporated into the Chinese empire. Qing expansion westwards into Turkestan proved a lasting strategic benefit to China because it ended the menace of nomad raiders, although this extension of borders was to cause conflicts in the nineteenth century with the Russians who were simultaneously occupying other parts of Central Asia as well as Siberia. The conquest of Tibet seems to have been specially significant for the Manchus, whose emperors were attracted to Jam-dpal, the Tibetan version of the bodhisattva Manjusri. Believed to have been a disciple of the Buddha, even his spiritual son, Manjusri was always regarded as the fount of compassion. One legend says that the Buddha miraculously created the bodhisattva as a means of enlightening China, where he was called Wenshu.

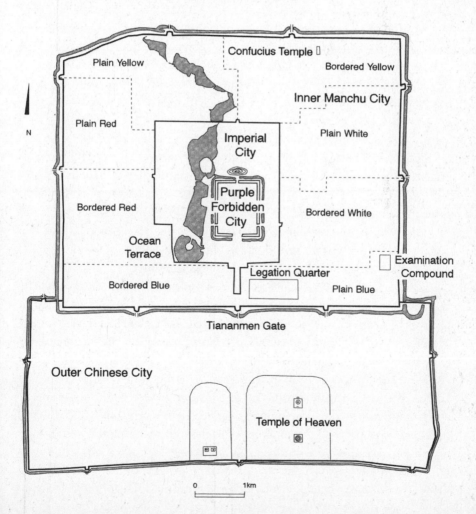

Site map of Qing Beijing

Perhaps the uncertainty of the early years of Qing rule encouraged its emperors to espouse Tibetan deities. While the ex-Ming general Wu Sangui pursued the rebel army of Li Zicheng into the provinces, the Manchus secured their hold on north China and waited upon events elsewhere. In 1644 they possessed neither the manpower nor the firearms necessary to subdue the whole Chinese empire. Their eventual takeover depended upon the Chinese themselves, who were slow to rally against them. Shortly after Li Zicheng had entered Beijing and the last Ming emperor committed suicide, an imperial cousin was persuaded in Nanjing to declare himself the emperor of the Southern Ming. This regime proved to be no Southern Song dynasty, for its inability to agree on how to deal with the Manchus left it vulnerable to attack. Discord among the commanders sent to oppose any Manchu move southwards soon led to disaster, while an uncoordinated defense allowed the Manchus to reach Nanjing, where in pouring rain, high-ranking civil and military officials surrendered outside the city walls. After these men had acknowledged that the heavenly mandate to rule had passed to Emperor Shunzhi, Nanjing was peacefully occupied. Two other Southern Ming regimes then appeared in the far south, but again a failure to cooperate spelled their doom, and the last pretender was taken prisoner in 1662.

By this date Shunzhi had died of smallpox and the second Qing emperor, Kangxi, had been on the dragon throne for almost a year. The turncoat general Wu Sangui's attitude to the newly installed Qing dynasty underwent a change in the 1670s. Though honored with rank and an imperial princess as a bride, Wu Sangui decided to declare himself independent in Yunnan, where his campaigns against the rebels had ended. But Wu Sangui's bid for separate power failed, his army partly overcome by the powerful artillery made for the Manchus by the Jesuits.

A strongly religious temperament had caused Shunzhi to welcome the German Johann Adam Schall von Bell as the head of the Jesuit mission. One of the distinguished successors of Matteo Ricci, Schall had come to the Ming court in 1622 and remained in Beijing throughout the change of the dynasty. An expert in medicine and astronomy, the Jesuit came close to converting Shunzhi to Christianity, until in 1657 the emperor had a sudden conversion to Chan Buddhism. What most impressed the Qing emperor was Schall's knowledge of metallurgy, since at the request of Ming officials he had set up a bronze-cannon foundry in the imperial capital. Even though Chinese workshops were quite capable of designing and casting good cannon, the Qing emperors continued to use the services of the Jesuits in their manufacture. The Manchu artillery possessed some 150 cannons, but many were too heavy for a mountain campaign, so a decade after Schall's death in 1666 another Jesuit by the name of Ferdinand Verbeist cast over 300 field guns in a single year. To the annoyance of other missionaries, Verbiest did not hesitate to bless the guns and inscribe on each one a sacred name. By an extraordinary coincidence, two of his guns were captured by the British in 1860 and are now on display at the Tower of London. One field-gun is named "General of Holy Authority." It was cast, according to the inscription, in the twenty-eighth year of Kangxi's long reign.

Kangxi's attitude to theological differences among Christian missionaries illustrates his belief in the importance of traditional values. Jesuit tolerance of non-Christian practices, when of a moral purpose like ancestor worship, had been denounced by other religious orders and in 1705 the papal legate Maillard de Tournon arrived to settle the controversy. Though the legate was supposed to arbitrate impartially, he carried a secret document that already ruled against any accommodation of Confucian rites and his stay of five years in China comprised a bitter struggle against the Jesuits resident in Beijing. Having commissioned himself what was to become the standard dictionary of the Chinese language, something Manchu speakers urgently needed, Emperor Kangxi found it difficult to accept that he was in error over the usage of certain words. Yet Maillard de Tournon insisted that an incorrect term was being used for the supreme deity. Moreover, the legate's injunction against participation in Confucian ceremonies by Chinese Christians was an open act of defiance to the will of the dragon throne, which endorsed the liberal approach of Matteo Ricci. Edicts were issued to regulate the activities of the missionaries and discourage would-be converts. "Hereafter," the emperor informed the papal legate, "residence will be restricted to those who come to live in China for good. No one will be permitted to leave."

Whereas the first Qing ruler had struggled to learn Chinese, his son Kangxi quickly mastered the language, without which he would not have been seen as a model emperor. What the second Qing emperor appreciated was the necessity of governing China through a ruling class that somehow combined Manchu-controlled military power with Chinese political methods. Already imperial buildings carried inscriptions in Chinese and Manchu, and Qing emperors from Kangxi onwards were adept in both languages. They expected Manchu nobles and Chinese officials to be so as well. The poet Yuan Mei was a subject of mirth when struggling to learn the "tadpole script" used for writing the Manchu language. In 1742 Yuan Mei came bottom in the palace examinations in the Manchu paper, but he was still appointed to a provincial post. As his Manchu friend and patron Ortai remarked,

"I do not doubt that as a provincial official you will show yourself to be perfectly competent. Some people regard you as just a literary man and think you are unfit to be an official. But I know you better than that."

The confidence was well placed, although illness interrupted his official career to such an extent that Yuan Mei took early retirement at the age of forty. By then he was being paid for his literary compositions. In 1757 he acquired an overgrown garden in Nanjing that a thousand years earlier the Tang poet Li Bai had greatly admired. It was said that its layout was reminiscent of his rather intricate style of poetry. When completely restored and developed, Suiyuan garden comprised twenty-four pavilions, standing separately or around small courtyards, as well as a lake divided into two parts by a meandering causeway, with little humped bridges that enabled a boat to pass from one part of the lake to the other. The causeway was supposed to be an imitation of the one bisecting West Lake at Hangzhou. Here in his garden Yuan Mei wrote not only his greatly admired poems but also his famous cookery book, *The Menu*. He also taught a select group of pupils the art of poetical composition. An advocate and admirer of women's poetry, Yuan Mei took on female pupils and helped them secure publication. Before his death in 1798 Yuan Mei was recognized as China's greatest living poet, his fame spread by printed collections of his poems. Though he rarely gained financially from these publications, Yuan Mei was content to reach a larger audience through them.

Above and opposite: the grounds of the Summer Palace built in Qing Beijing

A view of the Summer Palace

Emperor Kangxi began laying out his own garden in the 1680s. This was to become the complex later known as the Summer Palace, northwest of Beijing. Kangxi's small pavilions there were enclosed in the middle of the eighteenth century by his grandson Qianlong. A major construction program followed: within a walled area of 346 hectares lakes were dug, pavilions and temples erected, and pathways built, some of them roofed as a protection from the elements. With the assistance of the Jesuits an unusual group of Western-style buildings was constructed and filled with contemporary European furniture. Qianlong also took over two adjacent hills and turned them into imperial parks, settling Banner troops nearby.

Inspired by his tours of south China, this emperor set about recreating its lakes and hills at the Summer Palace. In 1751 one hill was given the name of Longevity Mountain in honor of Qianlong's mother, whose sixtieth birthday was celebrated that year. Most of the buildings suffered damage at the hands of British and French troops in 1860; the Western-style complex was completely destroyed. In front of Longevity Mountain now is an array of palatial buildings, resplendent with red walls and yellow tiles. Named the Hall That Dispels Clouds, they were restored after the sacking of the Summer Palace. The most unusual pavilion at the Hall That Dispels Clouds is a one-story structure cast in bronze. Twice a month lamas recited Buddhist scriptures in it, and prayed for the good fortune of the imperial family. The pavilion survived the fires of 1860 but its contents were lost except for a bronze offering-table, which was seized by Japanese soldiers at the end of the Second World War. They were fortunately prevented from loading the table, along with other looted items, at the port of Tianjin by the suddenness of their country's surrender.

Even though in imperial times the Summer Palace, the Purple Forbidden City, and the lake gardens next to the imperial palace were closed to the public, they were used to receive special guests. Tributary ambassadors were sometimes received and entertained at the Summer Palace, since Qing emperors liked to work and relax in its spacious grounds. When a Dutch embassy came to Beijing in the winter of 1795, its members were invited to show off their skating skills on its lake, after a demonstration by Bannermen. The "swirling dragon," the most complicated skating exercise these soldiers performed for the amusement of the emperor, involved a series of very difficult turns at speed. The accommodating Dutch did their best to match the Manchu display, perhaps in an attempt to avoid the polite but indifferent reception just given to the British envoy Lord Macartney, who had contested Qing court ritual by insisting that he should show to the emperor the same respect that was due to his own sovereign.

Above and opposite: Inside the Purple Forbidden City.

Macartney was not prepared to kowtow when the court usher com-manded. A kowtow consisted of three separate kneelings, each one fol-lowed by a full prostration with the forehead knocking the ground three times. There had been intense negotiations over this prescribed court rit-ual before it was agreed that Macartney would be excused. The members of the Dutch embassy kowtowed readily on every occasion it was required of them, but to no advantage; its leader had made a fool of himself in the eyes of Qianlong when his wig fell off while kowtowing at a frozen road-side as the emperor passed. Naturally it was a blow to Manchu pride if an envoy did not kowtow, but Macartney's refusal was put down to barbarian ignorance. More to the point was the comment of Father Amiot, a French Jesuit then resident in Beijing. He told the British envoy that the imperial court regarded embassies as nothing more than ceremonies, the ritual reception of "men from afar." It had no wish to conclude treaties with European powers.

The frustration in London was palpable. If only the imperial frontiers could be forced, and a convenient island seized as a secure trading station.

This was of course to be Hong Kong, which was ceded to Britain in 1842. As Macartney had confided in his embassy diary, how could the imperial court

> possibly expect to feed us long on promises? Can they be ignorant that a couple of English frigates would be an overmatch for the whole naval force of their empire, that in half a summer they could totally destroy all the navigation of their coasts and reduce the inhabitants of the maritime provinces, which subsist chiefly on fish, to absolute famine?

The inability of Qianlong to see the danger of a seaborne attack was not as shortsighted as it appears to us now. In the 1760s his armies had completed the conquest of the Mongols. Ever since the formation of the Chinese empire the steppe peoples and the settled Chinese had lived in hostile proximity. The Chinese had never been free of invasion, the Great Wall massive testimony to this perennial problem. Qianlong and his commanders, however, devised a successful strategy against the

Inside the Purple Forbidden City

nomads when they used the agricultural resources of China to keep the Qing army permanently in the field, and then settled Chinese farmers to sustain garrisons on conquered lands. By 1800 there were at least 50,000 new households living in the far west. Having at last rid the Chinese empire of its traditional enemies, the land-oriented Manchus felt that they had no reason for further defensive measures, and certainly not at sea.

Well before Qianlong decided that China could safely ignore seaborne barbarians, voices were raised against internal corruption. There was even a suggestion that degrees could be purchased with discreet bribes. Tighter supervision of the examination compounds failed to solve the problem, for in 1858 it was discovered how the use of certain code words allowed examiners to identify favored candidates, whose poor papers could then be substituted with those deemed to have passed. Punishment was severe. Offending examiners were beheaded, dilatory examination officials banished to remote provinces, and the graduates who tried to cheat lost all the qualifications they had previously gained. Sensational as the purge was, it was only temporarily effective and the atmosphere in the examination compound grew more hopeless and corrupt as the Chinese empire visibly declined. The abolition of the whole system at the beginning of the twentieth century was a foregone conclusion after the failure of the Hundred Days of Reform in 1898. The final examinations held at Beijing in 1904 were an irrelevance in a world patently dominated by foreign knowledge and technology.

Beijing and its environs

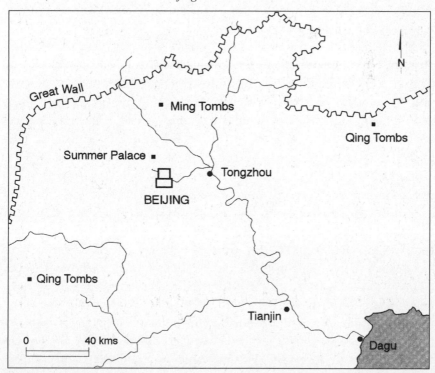

The stultification of the official outlook under Qing traditionalism cost China dearly, not least because its slowness to modernize was turned into a military disadvantage by the 1872 decision of the Meiji government to open Japan to European and American influences. The most telling image of the out-of-date Chinese scholar is the redundant student Kong Yuji, literally "Confucius himself." One of the startling characters created by Lu Xun, the first and perhaps the greatest of China's modern novelists, Kong Yuji is reduced to begging and stealing in order to satisfy his craving for wine. The narrowness of his literary studies had set the emaciated student's mind in a manner that kept him fascinated by the complexities of orthography.

It was the loss of the American colonies in the 1780s that turned Britain's imperial ambitions from North America to Asia, where India received most attention. Quite soon the Chinese empire was viewed as an adjunct of growing dominion in India through the trading activities of the East India Company, which drew its entire profit from the China trade. Like its oldest ally Portugal, Britain was keen to preserve a major commercial role in China, even if it involved the sale of opium. The transport of this drug from India, where the East India Company had deliberately stimulated production as an alternative to payment in silver for tea, caused such concern to Daoguang, the sixth Qing emperor, that in 1839 he dispatched a special commissioner by the name of Lin Zexu to Guangzhou in order to stamp out the whole business.

Canton, as Guangzhou was called by Europeans, was then the sole port of entry for foreign products. Opium had been used medicinally in the Chinese empire for centuries. In the early 1700s it became an addictive drug when mixed with tobacco: hence the notorious pipe favored in opium dens. Though the import of opium was banned, small quantities were still available via Portuguese Macao. In 1773, the East India Company decided to create an opium monopoly of its own in eastern India, but the imperial government was so upset about the drug that the company decided not to risk its tea trade by carrying opium directly to Guangzhou. It sold opium instead in Calcutta to English traders, who then acted as drug traffickers. Enterprising individuals like the Scot William Jardine, a former ship's surgeon, even dared to send his own heavily armed clippers north of Guangzhou to sell opium directly off their decks at small coves on the south China coast. By the time Lin Zexu arrived to deal with this sordid trade, opium had become the world's most valuable single commodity.

The abolition of the East India Company in 1833 had given men like Jardine unlimited scope for profit. When Lord Palmerston as foreign secretary named a Scottish lord, William Napier, for the post of British superintendent of trade at Guangzhou, there was nothing to curtail Jardine's activities. He made sure from the start that he had the inexperienced Napier's ear, lending him a house in Macao. When the Chinese governor refused to accept Napier as a British representative and ordered him to leave Guangzhou, the baffled superintendent on his own initiative ordered two warships to fight their way up to the city, and sent off to India for troops. These vessels were unable to reach Napier, who suffered the indignity of journey back to Macao in a Chinese boat, where he died shortly afterwards. Lady Napier returned to Britain along with James Matheson, Jardine's partner, who persuaded Palmerston to adopt a more forceful approach.

All that was required was a pretext for action, which Lin Zexu soon provided. First Lin Zexu broke up the network of Chinese importers and suppliers. Next he destroyed the opium stocks of European merchants without compensation, and obliged them to promise to end the odious traffic in the drug. As he found it impossible to believe that the opium trade was carried on with the assent of the British sovereign, Lin Zexu is supposed to have sent on a letter to Queen Victoria. In it he appealed to her sense of decency, when he wrote:

> I am told that in your country opium smoking is forbidden under severe penalties. This means you are aware how dangerous it is. But better than to forbid the smoking of opium would be to outlaw the production of the drug altogether. As long as you avoid opium yourselves, but continue to make it and tempt the people of China to purchase it, you will be seen to have compassion for your own lives, but none whatsoever for the lives of people who are ruined by your pursuit of gain. Who can say whether one day your own subjects will not only make opium, but also smoke it themselves.

Had the young queen received this communication she might have thought again about the justification for war. Dumping 2,000 tons of opium on the Chinese empire every year puts present-day excitement about police seizures of heroin in proper perspective. As it was, the British government disingenuously argued that the only way to end the opium traffic was the suppression of the drug's use in China, while the 1840 House of Commons debate revealed the worst attitudes of European imperialism when commercial profit carried the day.

News that Lin Zexu had excluded the British from Guangzhou was enough for war. Quite ignored was the reason for this action: a drunken brawl in which sailors had killed a Chinese man. As none of these men were handed over for justice, supplies were withheld from foreign shipping. Further fighting ensued, with casualties on both sides. In retaliation a British expeditionary force of twenty ships arrived off Macao with 4,000 troops on board. The Chinese empire was about to be humbled by a European power, for the British were overwhelmingly superior in arms. Their possessions in India provided ready troops and supplies, and their shallow-draught iron steamers could easily bombard upriver cities. After attacking Guangzhou, the expedition received further soldiers from India, and then sailed northwards inflicting heavy damage on coastal towns and cities.

Since Qing forces had little defense against the superior firepower of the invaders, the emperor was compelled to negotiate with the "outrageous and unreasonable" British. So protracted were the negotiations that the war was resumed in earnest, until the imperial government realized the impossibility of any military success. Bannermen fought bravely but were handicapped by fear of the Chinese siding with the invaders. On this occasion the British did not feel the need, as in 1860, to go all the way to Beijing, but they humiliated the Qing empire by making its representatives sign in 1842 a peace treaty on HMS *Cornwallis*, anchored off Nanjing. The Treaty of Nanjing awarded Britain a large indemnity, opened five ports to international commerce, and gave the island of Hong Kong to Britain as a sovereign base. Particularly obnoxious to Chinese sentiment was the "most-favored-nation" clause, which established the divisive principle of extra-territoriality. The total immunity this gave British residents from Chinese law was deeply resented, especially when they carved out for themselves privileged enclaves in the Treaty Ports.

Although the aim of the Qing emperor had been simply to stop the import of opium, the First Opium War shook the Chinese empire to its foundations. The demonstration of Manchu military weakness should have caused Beijing to reconsider its relations with the rest of the world. But with few Europeans yet resident in the imperial city and the new Treaty Ports all in the southern provinces, the Qing court remained almost completely isolated from current events. Indications of a growing Chinese disenchantment with the imperial government, and a degree of interest in foreign ways, ought to have alerted officials to the likelihood of disorder. Neither Manchu nor Chinese members of the imperial bureaucracy seem to have grasped the extent of the change then taking place within China, not to say the outside world. And they failed to appreciate that dynastic weakness made the Chinese empire vulnerable not only to foreign assault but internal rebellion as well.

Court extravagance, official corruption, and tax evasion among the wealthy landowners only added to the burden placed on the poor, many of whom were driven to banditry, if not outright rebellion. To deal with growing internal unrest the Qing emperors turned to regional militias formed by the local gentry, and they allowed some of these militias to develop into real armies. This step they were loath to take, but the shortcomings of the Bannermen left the embattled dynasty without any choice. The new armed forces, largely outside official control and under Chinese command, remained loyal to the Qing and put insurrection down, sometimes with foreign help. One of the powerful new army commanders was Li Hongzhang, who in 1865 patronized the establishment in Shanghai of a factory for making rifles, guns, and ammunition. He also lent his support to steamship navigation, mining, and textile mills. His advocacy of modern technology as a means of restoring the Chinese empire's strength was not without its problems. Apart from the nervousness of the dragon throne and the xenophobia of nearly all the ruling class, Li Hongzhang had to reconcile the adoption of modern ways with traditional learning. As he put it, combining "Western learning for practical purposes" and "Chinese learning for fundamentals."

The only previous borrowing from abroad the Chinese empire had made on any scale was from India, when it embraced Buddhism. As astute scholars saw, there were considerable dangers to the Confucian state in the wholesale import of Western-style manufacture. Liu Qihong, a member of the first permanent mission China sent to the West, described the dilemma succinctly. Noting how steamships, railway trains, mines, and roads were "mutually related," he commented: "One thing will lead to another, and we will not be able to refuse them." So profound was the transformation involved in imitating Europe that it would be impossible for China to accept only what it wanted and reject the rest.

Overlooked in this anxiety over modern technology was another foreign import, Protestant Christianity. It was to be the dynamic force behind the greatest rebellion faced by the Qing emperors, the Taiping uprising which lasted for fifteen years. A tragedy for the Taiping rebels, in spite of their professed Christian belief, was the coldness of the majority of the Europeans living in south China, especially those with commercial interests at stake or missionaries worried about doctrinal differences. They painfully learned that the Europeans were neither coreligionists nor allies against the Manchus.

Drawing on Protestant tracts and the visions he experienced after disappointment in the civil service examinations, Hong Xiuquan preached the overthrow of the Qing dynasty and the conversion of Chinese people to

Christianity. His Society for the Worship of God achieved astonishing successes against imperial troops and acted as a magnet for oppressed peasants, and by 1853 he had made Nanjing the capital of the Taiping Heavenly Kingdom. Taiping control of the populous southern provinces led to a long and bitter struggle, which was ended only by an alliance between the British and the Qing governments, as the British came to see the rebels as a threat to trade. An Anglo-French expeditionary force had in the meantime also taken Beijing and wrung more concessions from the imperial court.

Renewed conflict between Britain and China predictably began at Guangzhou. Bent on gaining the greatest advantages for British commercial interests, Lord Palmerston welcomed in 1856 the so-called *Arrow* incident as another opportunity for dressing down the Chinese. The *Arrow* was a lorcha, a schooner rigged with a junk's batten sails, and by registration in Hong Kong it was entitled to fly the British flag and claim British protection. A skirmish with Chinese pirates led to the intervention of Guangzhou's port authorities, who boarded the *Arrow* and took into custody both the crew and the pirates. The nominal Irish captain was not there when the police arrived. Yet this Chinese action over a Chinese-built boat, owned by a Chinese subject, manned by a Chinese crew, and sailing in Chinese waters was treated as "an insult of a very grave nature" by the British consul Harry Parkes. That on sailing into Guangzhou the *Arrow* would have lowered her flags in accordance with British nautical practice, and could therefore be mistaken as a Chinese vessel, was just brushed aside, even though the officer in charge of the marine police claimed on their arrival there were no flags displayed and no foreigners on board. Subsequently it was discovered that the *Arrow*'s registration had actually expired, but this technicality was not sufficient to stop armed action. In the heady days of the Great Exhibition, that triumphal celebration of industrial progress, this near-affront to the British flag was sufficient to start the Second Opium War. In concert with Britain over the Crimean War, France decided that the execution of a Catholic missionary in south China, where he had been stirring up rebellious feelings among the inhabitants, entitled it to any benefits that might be derived from another assault on the Chinese empire.

Lord Elgin was chosen to conduct the gunboat diplomacy on behalf of the Allies. Because the Indian Mutiny still tied up British and loyal Indian troops, Elgin was at first unable to negotiate from a position of strength. The necessary British firepower arrived in the form of 2,000 soldiers from Calcutta; they were supported by a powerful squadron of French ships. Negotiations with the local imperial officials got nowhere and, to the delight of British merchants resident in Hong Kong, the port of Guangzhou was seized. As Elgin noted in his diary,

> My difficulty has been to prevent the wretched Cantonese from being plundered and bullied. There is a word called "loot" which gives unfortunately a venial character to what would, in common English, be styled robbery. Add to this that there is no flogging in the French army, so that it is impossible to punish men for this class of offense.

Not that Elgin himself could resist loot, a Hindi word with which British soldiers were very familiar. The allied commander, however, restricted his own looting to silver and gold. Making no impression on the Qing court by the capture of Guangzhou, he directed the expedition northwards and anchored off Dagu, the fortress that guarded the estuary of the river leading to Beijing. An attack on the fortress was soon followed by the passage of eight gunboats up the river to the port of Tianjin, some forty kilometers from the imperial capital. A peace treaty named after the threatened port was quickly agreed in late 1858, which only just stopped short of legalizing the opium trade. Gunboat diplomacy seemed to have worked once more, until it was learned that the fortifications at Dagu were being strengthened and booms placed across the river. In 1859 a British attempt to force them was little short of a disaster, with six gunboats stranded and 500 men killed. Emperor Xianfeng only made matters worse. He was now a hopeless opium addict, dominated by his harem ladies. One of them in particular was influential, Cixi, the daughter of a Bannerman, who was also addicted to opium, despite keeping her dosage to a level that prevented physical damage. A fierce xenophobe, Cixi persuaded Xianfeng to defy all the foreigners threatening the Chinese empire.

The encouragement that Xianfeng gave to officials who flouted the terms of treaties already agreed with European powers was naturally unwise. Outraged by the reverse at Dagu, Lord Palmerston decided that Beijing itself should be attacked and occupied. It was only a question of time before Xianfeng's nemesis would arrive in the form of Elgin, who once more was sent to deal with China. British and French troops occupied Tianjin, where negotiations with senior officials representing the imperial government took place. As soon as Elgin became convinced that the Qing emperor was uninterested in reaching an agreement, he declared that in the future the negotiations would be conducted at Tongzhou, a city less than ten kilometers from Beijing. This proposal was rejected outright by the imperial government and Manchu cavalrymen were sent to block any further advance. The allied envoys sent ahead to Tongzhou included the over-zealous British consul Harry Parkes. When they and their escort fell into the hands of the Manchus, Parkes insisted that under a flag of truce he and his two colleagues should be able to move with freedom. An infuriated Manchu general told Parkes that he was personally responsible for China's woes. On the general's orders, Parkes was dragged from his horse and ordered to kowtow. When Parkes refused, Manchu soldiers banged his forehead three times on the ground.

After the envoys were imprisoned in Beijing, an all-out assault was launched on the imperial capital from which the emperor had already fled. Cixi had dissuaded Xianfeng from fighting a face-saving battle outside Beijing's wall, and leave instead his brother Prince Gong to treat with the invaders. As Elgin was reluctant to authorize any action that would bring about the downfall of the Qing dynasty, he simply requested the release of the envoys as a preliminary to serious negotiations. When Prince Gong demurred, Elgin felt he had no choice but commence hostilities and siege guns were readied to breach the ramparts of Beijing. The threat caused a negotiator to be lowered in a basket so that the city gates did not have to be opened. In return for keeping his troops out of the imperial capital, Elgin demanded the immediate release of Parkes and others captured on the way to Tongzhou. Of the thirty-nine French and British prisoners in Manchu custody, only nineteen were released alive. A timely surrender by Prince Gong saved Beijing from bombardment and Elgin was admitted with 500 soldiers. "In a matter of minutes," an eyewitness reported, "the English flag waved over the wall."

It is not a little ironic that Elgin, the son of the self-styled savior of the Parthenon friezes, should have chosen to avenge the murdered prisoners by ordering the destruction of the Summer Palace. Dense clouds of smoke drifted from the burning palace across the imperial city and deposited a heavy coating of ash. One senior British officer remarked that the sack was like "having the run of Buckingham Palace and being allowed to take away anything and everything you wanted. Things were plundered and pulled to pieces, floors were literally covered with fur robes, jade ornaments, porce-lain, and beautiful wood carvings." Afterwards Elgin insisted on being taken to the Purple Forbidden City in a litter carried by eight porters, the num-ber reserved for the highest officials. Thus was the absent Xianfeng doubly humiliated by a European conqueror who lined the great central avenue leading to the Meridian Gate with his own soldiers. No longer did the benign influence of a Son of Heaven flow down this axial way to sustain the Chinese empire.

Waiting to receive Elgin in the Purple Forbidden City was Prince Gong, who ratified the Treaty of Tianjin and leased to Britain the territory of Kowloon, opposite Hong Kong. A delighted Lord Palmerston later commented, "It was absolutely necessary to stamp by such a record our indignation at the treachery and brutality of these Tartars, for Chinese they are not." Quite unmentioned was the loss of the priceless collection of Chinese treasures housed at the Summer Palace.

After Xianfeng died in 1861, Cixi took dominated Qing court with the assistance of Prince Gong, who exercised considerable influence over imperial policy for several years. In 1865, though, the prince was accused at Cixi's insistence of disrespect for the emperor, obstructing the imperial will, and secretly fostering discord. Because foreign ambassadors now permanently resident in Beijing had a great respect for Prince Gong, the charges were dropped but the damage to the prince's prestige was done. He was never again the force he had been in political circles. It made little difference to the survival of the Qing dynasty. The Russians had taken advantage of its difficulties to appropriate vast territories along the Amur River, traditional Manchu possessions. The dismemberment of the imperial system then proceeded apace: Burma in 1885 passed into British hands, Vietnam the same year into French, and in a short campaign during 1894–5 Japan sought to dominate Korea, the Liaodong peninsula, and the island of Taiwan. European and American pressure denied the Japanese possession of the Liaodong peninsula, which the Russians occupied. But they were ejected by the Imperial Japanese Army in 1905 and Korea was annexed by Tokyo in 1910. By then the Taiwanese had been part of the Japanese empire for fifteen years and they were to remain a subject people till 1945.

Not that this dramatic shrinkage of imperial authority was necessary to convince the inhabitants of Beijing that all was not well with the Chinese empire. The presence of foreigners in the imperial capital, not submissively bearing tribute but making endless demands for concessions, was a token that the heavenly mandate to rule had largely been forfeited. Manchus like Cixi might cling to power there, obstinately blocking any attempt at modernization, but the end of Qing rule was rapidly approaching. Her first big mistake was to imprison the ninth Qing emperor Guangxu. When in 1895 the Treaty of Shimonoseki was signed with Japan after the Chinese defeat in Korea, Kang Youwei led a demonstration of students in Tiananmen Square against its humiliating terms.

The young emperor Guangxu had recently been freed from the constraint of his aunt Cixi's regency. In 1897, after the German seizure of Qingdao in Shandong province, the emperor asked all officials knowledgeable in military matters to suggest improvements. Later that year he asked for more general reform proposals, thus beginning the famous Hundred Days of Reform in 1898. One of the proposals came from Kang Youwei, who suggested abolishing the queue. In a lengthy account of the Meiji reforms entitled *A Study of the Governmental Reforms in Japan*, which he presented to the Qing court, he recommended that the Chinese empire should be brought up to date. He wrote that in Japan "the official dress had all been changed to the Western style and the Japanese emperor had personally cut short his hair." He implied Guangxu should follow suit. In daring to make such a radical proposal Kang Youwei knew that he was risking arrest for treason. It was already too much for Cixi, who staged a palace coup that restored reactionary forces to power. Instead of Kang Youwei, Emperor Guangxu was arrested and confined to Ocean Terrace, the island in the middle of the southern lake adjacent to the Purple Forbidden City. Twenty-three years earlier Cixi had placed him on the dragon throne at the age of four.

Buoyed up with the success of this intervention, Cixi made her second big mistake when in 1900 she supported the Boxers' attempt to expel foreigners from China by force. It was the height of folly, since the attack by Boxers and Bannermen on the Legation Quarter was bound to bring to its relief a punitive expedition of troops drawn from all the countries with diplomatic staff at Beijing. The previous year members of a secret society called the Righteous Harmonious Fist had enlarged their sacred boxing to include attacks on Christian missions and foreign importations such as telegraph poles. Seeking to use their xenophobia for her own purposes, Cixi backed their violent methods and the Legation Quarter, to the southwest of the Purple Forbidden City, was brought under siege shortly after the assassination of the German minister Baron Clemens von Ketteler. Six months later his murderer was executed by German troops on the spot where he had done the deed. Before his beheading, the Bannerman said that he was ordered to shoot the minister. "Otherwise," he pointedly asked, "why would a small person like myself venture to take the life of so exalted personage as the German ambassador?" As soon as news of Ketteler's death spread through the Legation Quarter, plans were drawn up for its defense. Outlying legations were evacuated as diplomats and residents fell back on more defensible legation compounds. In all there were 409 armed men to resist combined Chinese-Manchu attack.

Throughout June and July 1900 the defenders had to shift for themselves, while accounts of their massacre were sent back to Europe by excited newspaper correspondents living at a safe distance in Shanghai. In

London a memorial service for the victims of the massacre was actually arranged at St. Paul's Cathedral. In spite of being wholly imaginary, the newspaper reports of what had happened to the Legation Quarter were far more probable than what actually did happen. Few of the besieged held any real hope of survival. They were amazed to be still alive when the international relief force reached Beijing's city walls on the 13th of August. Field-Marshal Count Von Waldersee, its commander, had been told by the Kaiser "to give no quarter and take no prisoners" so that "no Chinese will ever again dare to look askance at a German." As anticipated, the Boxers made one last effort to overwhelm the Legation Quarter's defenses. They failed and the next day Russian and American soldiers, the first contingents of the relief force to break into the imperial capital, fought their way towards its exhausted defenders. They were just beaten to the Legation Quarter by Indian troops under the command of British officers. The Qing court had long since gone to Xi'an, the site of the Han, Sui, and Tang imperial capitals. Disguised as a Chinese peasant woman, Cixi had taken her captive emperor there as soon as the relief force arrived. "Who could have ever believed," the fugitive empress is reported to have said, "that it would come to this?"

The fall and the looting of an abandoned Beijing underscored the bankruptcy of Qing rule. The peace terms imposed on the Chinese empire were all that could be expected: huge reparations, punishment of war criminals, permanent garrisons of foreign soldiers in the imperial capital, and a 5 per cent import tariff. Had it not been for the declaration of an Open Door policy by the United States, whereby China was to remain an open market, there is every reason to believe that the spheres of influence belonging to the various colonial powers would have developed into sovereign possessions. Before her return to Beijing, a chastened Cixi had already begun to change her position on reform. In Guangxu's name she issued an imperial edict in which the inevitability of change was acknowledged. Cixi pardoned almost everyone who had been guilty of involvement in what she vaguely called "the 1898 Affair."

Notable exceptions to this blanket pardon were Kang Youwei and Sun Yatsen, whose shared belief in the urgent need to modernize China did not extend to personal friendship. Kang Youwei considered the revolutionary leader an "uneducated bandit," who in turn regarded the would-be reformer as a "corrupt Confucian." After participating in a failed uprising in Guangzhou, Sun Yatsen was a wanted man, so much so that Chinese diplomats had kidnapped him during a visit to London in 1896. For days the streets around the Chinese embassy were thronged with policemen, journalists, photographers, and spectators. On his dramatic release Sun Yatsen took advantage of the publicity to bring the revolutionary cause to the attention of the world. He wrote to the newspapers and gave press conferences, granted interviews, and won universal sympathy. That he spoke English clearly helped: unlike the traditionally educated Kang Youwei, Sun Yatsen had studied at colleges in Hong Kong and Hawaii. Thanks to the support of his elder brother, he had been able to begin training as a Western doctor.

No "uneducated bandit" then, Sun Yatsen regarded Kang Youwei's justification of reform by means of a reinterpretation of Confucianism as a waste of effort. To Kang Youwei the revolutionary leader's enthusiasm for foreign solutions to Chinese problems was no more than the seduction of Western materialistic ideas. Also a fugitive and the prey of assassins, Kang Youwei had to live as an exile in eleven different countries. The sudden death of Guangxu in 1908, immediately following that of Cixi, profoundly shocked Kang Youwei. Although it seems likely that the imprisoned emperor was poisoned on the old empress's orders, Kang Youwei believed the person responsible was Yuan Shikai, against whom he wrote venomous denunciations. Watching the disintegration of the imperial system from abroad, the frustrated Confucian scholar never ceased to argue for a constitutional monarchy as China's best hope for permanent reform. While he deplored the overthrow of the Qing dynasty, Kang Youwei never attacked the new republican government, even after his old enemy Yuan Shikai replaced Sun Yatsen as president.

The suppression of the Boxers was a turning point in Beijing's history. The rough handling of the city and the ruling house undermined the authority of the dragon throne, and the easy supremacy of the foreign occupiers encouraged better-off Chinese residents to look beyond the imperial system for an answer to modern difficulties. The Qing court's new emphasis on military and educational reform, and the lifting of the ban on Manchu-Chinese intermarriage, failed to satisfy enough people to secure any lasting respect for the dynasty. Prince Zaifeng, who in 1908 became regent for his young son Puyi, the last Qing emperor, found rising Chinese expectations impossible to meet. Cixi's last-minute decision to designate the young Puyi as the Son of Heaven was not at all unusual in the Qing dynasty. In order to avoid trouble with an heir apparent, each Qing ruler only announced a successor on his deathbed. According to Puyi's autobiography, Cixi chose him primarily because she expected his father to be pliable. "I do not believe," wrote Puyi, "that she thought herself fatally ill on the day she proclaimed me successor to the throne." But Cixi died the next day, and Zaifeng became regent for all but the last three months of Puyi's short reign.

What Zaifeng tried to do was return power to the central government and in particular to the imperial court. Too much authority had leaked out to provincial governors and army commanders during the period of Cixi's ascendancy. She had a weakness for powerful men and indulged her favorites, one of whom was Yuan Shikai. Zaifeng's efforts to impose his authority over the army, navy, and palace guard were largely successful. Where he made less headway was in his relations with the newly formed assemblies. The inaugural meeting of the National Assembly convened in 1910 at Beijing set the tone, as the assemblymen did not kneel in his presence but remained standing through Zaifeng's welcoming speech. During the three-month session the assembly clashed with the regent over a number of different issues, and especially over the formation of a "responsible cabinet."

As the National Assembly was only an advisory body with no right to make laws, the most important issue remained the summoning of a proper parliament. Zaifeng was compelled to agree to this in 1913 and to name a cabinet. Buying time by this compromise was not sufficient to save the Qing dynasty, because the queue was still there as a daily reminder of Chinese inferiority. The regent did himself no service by declaring that the Manchu-imposed custom was of long standing and ought not to be cast aside lightly. Nor did it help that Zaifeng appointed a majority of Manchus in the promised cabinet. But it was already too late for Zaifeng and Puyi anyway: the rebellion which would topple both father and son had broken out at Wuchang, one of the three cities which formed the Yangzi River port of Wuhan. News of the rising excited the Chinese residents in Beijing, not least because mixed as well as purely Chinese regiments were reported to have defected to the rebels. The slowness of the imperial counter-attack sealed the fate of the Qing dynasty and the Chinese empire. Later on it was alleged that officers loyal to the demoted Yuan Shikai had dragged their feet. Zaifeng had to swallow his pride and recall the general, offering him ministerial and military appointments. Gradually Yuan Shikai reasserted imperial authority north of the Yangzi River: his slowness was politically motivated, as he was secretly negotiating with the rebels.

In his autobiography Puyi is quite convinced that Yuan Shikai's reluctance to follow the wishes of his father was the result of foreign and revolutionary support. He wrote that:

within a month of his return to the imperial capital he was able to force the Prince Regent out of office. Immediately afterward, on the pretext of the need for money to meet military expenses, he took over the palace treasury. Thus political, military, and financial power were concentrated in his hands alone. Once this was accomplished, Yuan Shikai suggested to the Chinese minister to Russia as well as to other Chinese diplomats abroad that they cable the Qing court requesting my abdication.

With China's only really modern force, the New Army, at his disposal there was nothing the Qing imperial family could do to stop Yuan Shikai. On 12 February 1912 Puyi abdicated in Beijing and the general was declared president by unanimous vote of the provisional assembly in Nanjing, Sun Yatsen stepping aside in order to prevent a civil war. It was unfortunate for China that the European powers preferred the regime Yuan Shikai ran in Beijing, and floated enormous loans for its benefit, when Sun Yatsen's southern revolutionaries were such uncritical admirers of Western democratic institutions. Europe hardly batted an eyelid when, as his enemies predicted, Yuan Shikai tried to restore the Chinese empire with himself as ruler.

Yuan Shikai's attempt to turn the Purple Forbidden City back into an actual imperial palace occurred on 1 January 1916. Just before the announcement of Yuan Shikai's new dynasty was made, the general had celebrated the winter solstice at the Temple of Heaven. He was driven in an armored car down Beijing's great central avenue to the ninety-minute ceremony. The entire route was covered with yellow sand, as was customary for an imperial progress. At the Temple of Heaven Yuan Shikai changed his military uniform for a robe embroidered with dragons. The first emperor of the Great Constitution, as Yuan Shikai's dynasty was rather ambiguously called, did not enjoy a long reign. The outbreak of the First World War removed Europe's restraining influence on the Japanese, who occupied the German-leased territory of Qindao and adjoining parts of Shandong province. On 18 January Japan presented the notorious Twenty-One Demands, whose purpose was the reduction of China to a virtual protectorate. With no hope of assistance from the European powers, now locked in bloody conflict, Yuan Shikai was forced to accept the least offensive demands. To a large number of Chinese the agreement of the would-be dynast, however reluctant, was the final betrayal of a man who had successively betrayed the reforming emperor Guangxu, the child-emperor Puyi, and the Republic of China. Yuan Shikai's inability to stand up to Tokyo ended his dynastic plans, and he died on 6 June, following a collapse brought on by nervous exhaustion.

"The news of Yuan Shikai's death," Pu Yi tells us, "was received with great rejoicing in the Forbidden City." Beijing residents were heard to comment on Heaven's unwillingness to remove the mandate to rule from the Qing dynasty. The euphoria in Beijing soon led to the second attempt at restoration, and incidentally ushered in the warlord era, which was to last for over a decade. "The Forbidden City became lively again," recalls Puyi, "and with General Zhang Xun's audience in 1917 this second restoration movement reached a climax." As Beijing was the place where European powers with a financial stake in China recovered their loans through customs duties, the city represented a valuable prize for Zhang Xun. This is Puyi's account of his audience with the calculating general:

> After the general had kowtowed, I pointed to a chair and asked him to sit down. At this time the palace had abandoned the custom of having high officials report while in a kneeling position. He kowtowed once more to thank me, and then sat down. I followed my tutors' instructions in asking about the situation of the army under his command, but I did not pay much attention to his reply. I was somewhat disappointed in his looks. He wore a lightweight summer costume, his face was ruddy, he had very thick eyebrows and was fat. Had he not worn a moustache he could have passed for one of the eunuchs in charge of the imperial kitchens. I noticed, however, that he did in fact have a queue.

Two weeks after this audience Zhang Xun announced Puyi's restoration with a request that all the households in Beijing display "imperial dragon flags." According to Puyi, "the excitement was intense and citizens who did not have any flags handy made them out of paste and paper. Qing court attire that had disappeared for a few years appeared on the streets. It was as if the dead had stepped from their coffins in their burial robes. The press brought out extras about the restoration. Tailors made and sold dragon flags; secondhand clothing shops found that Qing court dress became their best-selling items since the newly appointed officials all wanted them, and theatrical supply shops were besieged with requests for artificial queues made out of horsehair.

But it all lasted little more than five days. Everything changed when an airplane from the forces stationed at Tianjin dropped some bombs on the palace. Then there were no longer people who came to kowtow to me and there were no more imperial edicts to read. Furthermore, most of the high officials who had a hand in government matters disappeared." Even though the air raid was no more than a warning, it worked. Puyi was aware that "the pilot did not really mean business," for the three small bombs he dropped caused little damage and only injured a single person. One bomb, however, "fell on a roof of a gateway and, even though it did not explode, it scared the living daylights out of some eunuchs who were gambling there."

Puyi was not expelled from the Purple Forbidden City until 1924. Then another warlord drove him to seek safety in the Legation Quarter, a remarkable refuge for an ex-Qing emperor after the 1900 siege. There Japanese diplomats welcomed Puyi with open arms. Later they persuaded him to head the puppet state of Manzhouguo, which covered most of the Manchu homeland. In 1934 he received the title of emperor once again, not from a Qing relative but Emperor Hirohito of Japan. Powerless though he was in his second empire, Puyi paid for collaborating with the Japanese after the establishment of the People's Republic. Branded a "war criminal," he had to undergo a thorough self-examination of his past actions prior to his rehabilitation as a gardener. Puyi's life after this was not entirely private, as he was consulted on issues affecting the Manchus, one of China's "minorities." He died in 1967 at the height of the Great Proletarian Cultural Revolution.

Though we remain ignorant as to the cause of his death, we are sure that his palace went largely unscathed during this upheaval. Its moveable treasures are now in the Palace Museum in Taipei, having first been shifted away from Beijing to forestall the Japanese. The palace buildings themselves are miraculously intact. Recent restoration makes the Purple Forbidden City the ultimate destination in the People's Republic, because it discloses to the attentive visitor something of the ordered magnificence of the late Chinese empire. It is also a testament to the two thousand years of urban splendor and sophistication that characterized China's great imperial capitals. As the young man with the boxed ears was so foolhardy enough to insist, the best of everything is still to be found in Beijing.

CHRONOLOGIES

The Imperial Dynasties

THE EARLY EMPIRE 221 BC–AD 589

Qin Dynasty 221–206 BC
Former Han Dynasty 202 BC–AD 9
Usurpation of Wang Mang AD 9–23
Later Han Dynasty 25–220
The Three Kingdoms 221–265
Western Jin Dynasty 265–316
Period of Division 316–588

THE MIDDLE EMPIRE 589–1368

Sui Dynasty 581–617
Tang Dynasty 618–907
Five Dynasties 907–960
Northern Song Dynasty 960–1127
Southern Song Dynasty 1127–1276
Yuan Dynasty 1276–1368

THE LATE EMPIRE 1368–1912

Ming Dynasty 1368–1644
Qing Dynasty 1644–1912

Emperors and Their Reigns

THE QIN DYNASTY

Personal name	Imperial title	Accession	Death
Ying Zheng	Qin Shi Huang Di	221 BC	210
Hu Hai	Erh Shi Huang Di	210	206

The titles of the two Qin emperors mean First Sovereign Qin Emperor and Second Sovereign Qin Emperor respectively. They were intended to signal the advent of an imperial house which was destined to last a thousand years. But this ambition overlooked the anger of the oppressed peasants whose first nationwide rebellion destroyed the Qin empire. Liu Bang took advantage of the subsequent turmoil to found the Han dynasty.

THE FORMER HAN DYNASTY

Personal name	Imperial title	Accession	Death
Liu Bang	Gaozu	202 BC	195
Liu Ying	Hui Di	195	188
Empress Lu's regency		188	180
Liu Heng	Wen Di	180	157
Li Qi	Jing Di	157	141
Liu Che	Wu Di	141	87
Liu Fuling	Zhao Di	87	74
Liu Ho	deposed after twenty-seven days	74	
Liu Xun	Xuan Di	74	49
Liu Shi	Yuan Di	49	33
Liu Ao	Cheng Di	33	7
Liu Xin	Ai Di	7	1
Liu Kan	Ping Di	1 BC	AD 5
Liu Ying	overshadowed by Wang Mang	6	9

During Empress Lu's regency, which lasted from 188 until her death from a dog bite in 180 BC, two children successively held the formal title of emperor: at least one was killed on her orders. But it was the usurpation of Wang Mang that really shook the dynasty. A complicated civil war only ended in AD 25 with its restoration as the Later Han.

THE LATER HAN DYNASTY

Personal name	Imperial title	Accession	Death
Liu Xiu	Guangwu Di	AD 25	57
Liu Zhuang	Ming Di	57	75
Liu Da	Zhang Di	75	88
Liu Zhao	He Di	88	106
Liu Long	Shang Di	106	106
Liu Hu	An Di	106	125
Liu Yi	Shao Di	125	125
Liu Bao	Shun Di	125	144
Liu Bing	Chong Di	144	145
Liu Zuan	Zhi Di	145	146
Liu Zhi	Huan Di	146	168
Liu Hong	Ling Di	168	189
Liu Bian	Shao Di	189	deposed 189
Liu Xie	Xian Di	189	deposed 220

The disintegration of the Han empire marked the start of a prolonged period of instability in China. Not until its reunification under the short-lived Sui dynasty in 588 would the Chinese empire recover enough strength to deter external enemies.

THE WEI DYNASTY

Personal name	Imperial title	Accession	Death
Cao Pi	Wen Di	220	226
Cao Rui	Ming Di	226	239
Cao Fang	Fei Di	239	254
Cao Mao	Shao Di	254	260
Cao Huan	Yuan Di	260	266

This was one of the dynasties which existed during the era of the Three Kingdoms (220-266). The other two, the Shu and the Wu, were not recognised as legitimate by Chinese historians, who always preferred to trace a single line of dynastic succession.

THE WESTERN JIN DYNASTY

Personal name	Imperial title	Accession	Death
Sima Yan	Wu Di	266	290
Sima Zhong	Hui Di	290	306
Sima Zhi	Huai Di	306	killed 313
Sima Ye	Min Di	313	killed 316

The great barbarian invasion of north China caused the Jin imperial house to flee southwards and at Nanjing refound the dynasty as the Eastern Jin. Because there were so many dynasties during the partition of China from 316 till 588 only their names and ethnic origins are indicated below.

A DIVIDED CHINA

North China	South China
Former Zhao (Hunnish) 304-329	Eastern Jin (Chinese) 317-419
Later Zhao (Hunnish) 328-350	
Former Qin (Tibetan) 351-383	
Later Qin (Tibetan) 384-417	
Western Qin (Hunnish) 385-431	
Former Yan (Turkish) 337-370	
Later Yan (Turkish) 384-409	
Western Yan(Turkish) 384-395	
Southern Yan (Turkish) 398-410	
Northern Yan (Turkish) 409-436	Liu Song (Chinese) 420-478
Former Liang (Chinese) 314-376	
Later Liang (Tibetan) 386-403	
Southern Liang (Turkish) 397-414	
Northern Liang (Hunnish) 398-439	
Western Liang (Chinese) 400-420	
Northern Wei (Turkish) 399-532	
Xia (Hunnish)407-431	
Eastern Wei (Turkish) 534-543	Southern Qi (Chinese) 479-501
Western Wei (Turkish) 535-550	Liang (Chinese) 501-556
Northern Qi (Chinese) 550-576	
Northern Zhou (Turkish) 557-579	Chen (Chinese) 557-588
Sui (Turko-Chinese) 580-618	and in the south from 588

THE SUI DYNASTY

Personal name	Imperial title	Accession	Death
Yang Jian	Wen Di	581	604
Yang Guang	Yang Di	604	617

This short-lived imperial house was almost a repeat of the Qin, the founder-dynasty of the Chinese empire. Under the Sui emperors a similar determination caused a nationwide peasant rebellion. And in 617 an attempt to replace Yang Di with a grandson also failed.

THE TANG DYNASTY

Personal name	Imperial title	Accession	Death
Li Yuan	Gaozu	618	abdicated 626
Li Shimin	Taizong	626	649
Li Zhi	Gaozong	649	683
Li Xian	Zhongzong three months	684	deposed 684
Li Dan	Ruizong	684	deposed 690
Wu Zhao	Empress Wu's usurpation	690	705
	Zhongzong restored	705	710
	Ruizong restored	710	abdicated 712
Li Longji	Xuanzong	712	abdicated 756
Li Heng	Suzong	756	762
Li Yu	Daizong	762	779
Li Shi	Dezong	779	805
Li Song	Shunzong	805	abdicated 805
Li Chun	Xianzong	805	killed 820
Li Heng	Muzong	820	824
Li Zhan	Jingzong	824	killed 826
Li Ang	Wenzong	826	840
Li Yan	Wuzong	840	846
Li Zhen	Xuanzong	846	859
Li Cui	Yizong	859	873
Li Yan	Xizong	873	888
Li Yi	Zhaozong	888	904
Li Zhu	Aizong	904	deposed 907

After the collapse of the Tang dynasty the Chinese empire split into the Ten Kingdoms. In north China the so-called Five Dynasties were believed to have preserved the legitimate succession of imperial houses. They were followed by the Northern Song dynasty, which swiftly reunited China.

THE FIVE DYNASTIES

Liang	907-923
Later Tang	923-937
Jin	937-947
Han	947-951
Zhou	951-960

THE NORTHERN SONG DYNASTY

Personal name	Imperial title	Accession	Death
Zhao Kuangyin	Taizu	960	976
Zhao Kuangyi	Taizong	976	997
Zhao Heng	Zhenzong	997	1022
Zhao Zhen	Renzong	1022	1063
Zhao Shu	Yingzong	1063	1067
Zhao Xu	Shenzong	1067	1085
Zhao Xu	Zhezong	1085	1100
Zhao Ji	Huizong	1100	abdicated 1125
Zhao Huan	Quizong	1125	captured 1127

The capture of Kaifeng by the Jin nomads in 1127 forced the Song imperial house to flee southwards and re-established itself at Hangzhou as the Southern Song dynasty.

THE SOUTHERN SONG DYNASTY

Personal name	Imperial title	Accession	Death
Zhao Gou	Gaozong	1127	abdicated 1162
Zhao Shen	Xiaozong	1162	abdicated 1189
Zhao Dun	Guangzong	1189	abdicated 1194
Zhao Kuo	Ningzong	1194	1224
Zhao Tian	Lizong	1224	1264
Zhao Qi	Duzong	1264	1274
Zhao Xian	Gong Di	1274	captured 1276

The last members of the Song imperial house, Zhao Xia and Zhao Bing, died as children in 1278–79. After this failed restoration the Mongols faced no rivals for the dragon throne.

THE YUAN DYNASTY

Personal name	Imperial title	Accession	Death
Kubilai Khan	Shi Zu	1260	1294
Timur Khan	Chengzong	1294	1307
Khaissan Khan	Wuzong	1307	1311
Ayutwarbadal Khan	Renzong	1311	1320
Shidebala Khan	Yingzong	1320	deposed 1323
Yesuntemur Khan	Tai Ding Di	1323	1328
Asugbal Khan	Tai Shun Di	1328	deposed 1328
Hooshal Khan	Mingzong	posthumous elevation	
Tugtemur Khan	Wenzong	1329	1332
Renqinbar Khan	Ningzong	one month 1332	1332
Togontemur Khan	Shun Di	1333	fled 1368

The flight of Togontemur Khan to Mongolia in 1368 was followed by a restoration of native rule. That Zhu Yuanzhang chose to call his dynasty "bright" indicates a desire to restore the Chinese empire to its former glory.

THE MING DYNASTY

Personal name	Imperial title	Accession	Death
Zhu Yuanzhang	Tai Zu	1368	1398
Zhu Yunwen	Hui Di	1398	1deposed 402
Zhu Di	Yongle	1402	1424
Zhu Gaozhi	Renzong	1424	1425
Zhu Zhanji	Xuanzong	1425	1435
Zhu Qizhen	Yingzong	1435	captured 1449
Zhu Qizu	Jing Di	1449	killed 1457
	Yingzong restored	1457	1464
Zhu Jianshen	Xianzong	1464	1487
Zhu Youtang	Xiaozong	1487	1505
Zhu Houzhao	Wuzong	1505	1521
Zhu Houzong	Shizong	1521	1567
Zhu Zaihou	Muzong	1567	1572
Zhu Yijun	Shenzong	1572	1620
Zhu Changluo	Guangzong two months	1620	1620
Zhu Youjiao	Xizong	1620	1627
Zhu Youjian	Sizong	1627	suicide 1644

The Ming dynasty fell during the complicated civil war which began in 1643. A year later the Manchus were admitted to China as allies of Wu Sangui, commander of the fortress in the Great Wall northeast of Beijing. They occupied the imperial capital and declared their king the first Qing emperor Shun Zhi.

THE QING DYNASTY

Personal name	Imperial title	Accession	Death
Aisin-Gioro Fulin	Shunzhi	1644	1661
Aisin-Gioro Yuanye	Kangxi	1661	1722
Aisin-Gioro Yinzhen	Yongzheng	1722	1735
Aisin-Gioro Hongli	Qianlong	1735	1796
Aisin-Gioro Yongyan	Renzong	1796	1820
Aaisin-Gioro Minning	Xuanzong	1820	1850
Aisin-Gioro Yining	Xianfeng	1850	1861
Aisin-Gioro Zaichun	Tongzhi	1861	1875
Aisin-Gioro Zaitian	Guangxu	1875	1908
Aisin-Gioro Puyi	Xuantong	1908	abdicated 1912

With the abdication of the last Manchu emperor, the Chinese empire came to an end. Pu Yi's attempted restoration in 1917, which lasted for only a few days, he continued to live in the imperial palace at Beijing until 1924.

NOTES AND REFERENCES

The following notes and references are intended to assist the reader in pursuing topics of special interest. They draw attention to publications that may provide greater detail themselves or suggest ways in which further investigation can take place. It has to be said, however, that coverage of imperial Chinese history is scant in English, although there are encouraging signs that this deficiency will soon be less serious. Two series of books in particular are doing much to round out our view of the imperial era. The first is Joseph Needham's *Science and Civilization in China*, begun in 1954. This monumental study is now almost complete. Another unfinished series is *The Cambridge History of China*, edited by D. Twitchett and J. K. Fairbank, several volumes of which have appeared since 1978.

PART ONE
ANCIENT ORIGINS c.1650 BC ONWARDS

Full treatment of the Shang, China's first historical dynasty, is to be found in *Shang Civilization*, Chang Kwang-chih, New Haven, 1980. Early cosmology is discussed in *The Pivot of the Four Quarters. A Preliminary Enquiry into the Origins and Character of the Ancient Chinese City*, P. Wheatley, Edinburgh, 1971. For the whole period down to the foundation of the Chinese empire, both the Shang and Zhou dynasties, there is *The Cambridge History of Ancient China. From the Origins of Civilization to 221 BC*, edited by M. Loewe and E. L. Shaughnessy, Cambridge, 1999. Books on individual thinkers prior to the unification of China by Qin Shi

Huangdi in 221 BC are *Confucius*, D. H. Smith, London, 1973; (Lao Zi) *The Way and Its Power: A Study of the Tao Teh Ching and Its Place in Chinese Thought*, A. Waley, London, 1934; (Shang Yang) *The Book of Lord Shang: A Classic of Chinese Law*, J. J. L. Duyvendak, London, 1928, reissued 1963.

PART TWO
THE EARLY EMPIRE 221 BC–AD 589

Two books deal exclusively with the Qin empire. The first is Derk Bodde's *China's First Unifier. A Study of the Ch'in Dynasty as Seen in the Life of Li Ssu, 280-208 BC*, Leiden, 1938, reissued Hong Kong, 1967. The second is the author's own *The First Emperor of China*, London and New York, 1981. Recently the Han empire has begun to receive more thorough attention in the West. There are *Han Social Structure*, Chu T'ung-tsu, edited by J. L. Dull, Seattle, 1972; *Han Agriculture. The Formation of Early Chinese Agrarian Economy, 206 BC – AD 220*, Cho-yun Hsu, edited by J. L. Dull, Seattle, 1980; *Han Civilization*, Wang Zhongshu, translated by K.C. Chang, New Haven, 1982; *Crisis and Conflict in Han China*, M. Loewe, London, 1974, plus his *Ways to Paradise: The Chinese Quest for Immortality*, London, 1979. For the period following the dissolution of the early empire there is T. J. Barfield's *The Perilous Frontier. Nomadic Empires and China, 221 BC to AD 1757*, Oxford, 1989, as well as W. F. J. Jenner's *Memories of Loyang. Yang Hsuan-chih and the Lost Capital (493-534)*, Oxford, 1987. As the imperial collapse undermined confidence in the ethical government which Confucius had advocated, it is hardly surprising that disenchantment informs the work of Tao Qian, the first of China's great poets, as can be seen in *The Poetry of T'ao Chien*, translated by J. F. Hightower, Oxford, 1970.

The arrival of Buddhism and its subsequent metamorphosis is chronicled in K. Chen's *Buddhism in China*, Princeton, 1964, and his *The Chinese Transformation of Buddhism*, Princeton, 1973, as well as E. Zurcher's *The Buddhist Conquest of China*, Leiden, 1959. Details of the later clampdown on the Buddhist faith under the Tang emperor Wu Zong are available in *Ennin's Diary. The Record of a Pilgrimage to China in Search of the Law*, translated by E. O. Reischauer, New York, 1955.

PART THREE
THE MIDDLE EMPIRE 589–1368

Studies of eminent figures include (Li Shimin, the second Tang emperor) *Son of Heaven*, C. P. Fitzgerald, Cambridge, 1933, reissued New York, 1971, as well as his *Empress Wu*, London, 1956. The interaction between Li Shimin and his outspoken minister Wei Zheng is examined in H. J. Wechsler's *Mirror to the Son of Heaven*, New Haven, 1974. For a general appeciation of Tang poetry S. Owen's translations and commentary are worth reading in *The Great Age of Chinese Poetry*, New Haven, 1981. Some of Bai Juyi's poems are translated in *The Life and Times of Po Chu-I*, A. Waley, London, 1949, while more appear in *Bai Juyi. 200 Selected Poems*, translated by Rewi Alley, Beijing, 1983.

It is fortunate that Robert Van Gulik's Judge Dee detective stories were reissued in the 1970s. A good story to start with is *The Chinese Gold Murders*, Chicago, 1977, because it recounts his very first posting. It opens with the newly appointed district magistrate being seen off at the Pavilion of Joy and Sadness, a restaurant just outside one of the imperial capital's gateways. Here colleagues were wont to bid farewell to metropolitan officials leaving for provincial posts, and welcome them back at the end of their assignments.

The half century of disunity between the Tang and Song empires is the subject of *Ouyang Xiu. Historical Records of the Five Dynasties*, translated by R. L. Davis, New York, 2004. It provides a fascinating account of the transitory imperial houses that tried to hold on to power in north China. Books that focus solely on the Song empire are rare, although F. W. Mote's *Imperial China, 900-1800,* Cambridge, Mass., 1999, offers an excellent approach to the Song, Yuan, Ming and early Qing dynasties.

Many books are now available on ceramics and painting, but a well-illustrated and reliable guide is W. Watson's *The Art of Dynastic China*, London, 1979. Two publications from the Metropolitan Museum of Art in New York offer a fresh view of Chinese painting: *Along the Riverbank*, M. K. Hearn and Wen C. Fong, 1999, and *Cultivated Landscapes*, M. K. Hearn, 2002. James Cahill's *Hills Beyond a River*, 1976, covers the Mongol period, while his *Parting at the Shore*, 1978, and *The Distant Mountains*, 1982, deal with most of the Ming dynasty: these books were also published in New York.

The Mongol conquest of China has attracted plenty of attention, possibly because of Marco Polo, whose *Travels* are well translated by R. Latham, Harmondsworth, 1958. Specific studies include *Mongol Imperialism. The Policies of the Grand Qan Mongke in China, Russia, and the Islamic Lands, 1251-1259*, T. A. Allsen, Los Angeles, 1987; *The Secret History of the*

Mongols, translated by A. Waley, London, 1963; *Genghiz Khan: His Life and Legacy*, P. Ratchnevsky, Oxford, 1991; and *Khubilai Khan: His Life and Times*, M. Rossabi, Los Angeles, 1988.

PART FOUR
THE LATE EMPIRE 1368–1912

There are a large number of books on the Ming and Qing dynasties. Especially recommended are *Perpetual Happiness: The Ming Emperor Yongle*, H. Tsai, Seattle, 2001; *An Embassy to China: Being the Journal Kept by Lord Macartney During His Embassy to Emperor Ch'ien-lung, 1793-1794*, edited by J. L. Cranmer-Bying, London, 1962; *The Opium War Through Chinese Eyes*, A Waley, London, 1958; *God's Chinese Son: The Taiping Heavenly Kingdom of Hong Qiuquan*, J Spence, New York, 1996; and *Rethinking the 1898 Reform Period: Political and Cultural Change in Late Qing China*, edited by R. E. Karl and P. Zarrow, Cambridge, Mass., 2002.

Off all the imperial capitals Beijing is the best served for detailed studies. Susan Naquin's *Peking: Temples and City Life, 1400-1900*, Los Angeles, 2000, has set a very high standard indeed for single-city studies. Still unmatched for its original photographs and plans, however, is Osvald Siren's *The Imperial Palaces of Peking*, Paris and Brussels, 1926, reissued New York, 1976. In his *Gardens of China*, New York, 1949, a subtle investigation of the Chinese garden's relationship with landscape painting, there is a discussion of Beijing's great gardens including those of the Summer Palace. An illustrated account of these, entitled *Summer Palace*, was published by the Summer Palace Administration Office and the Department of Architecture of Qinghua University in 1981.

The brief post-imperial period, from the abdication of the last Qing emperor in 1912 to his expulsion from the Purple Forbidden City in 1924, is described in *The Last Manchu: The Autobiography of Henry Pu Yi, Last Emperor of China*, translated by P. Tsai and edited by P. Kramer, London, 1967. For an account of the Boxers, whose assault on the Legation Quarter in 1900 set the scene for the final dethronement of the Qing dynasty, there is Peter Fleming's readable *The Siege of Peking*, London, 1960.

INDEX